Real Options SLS

User Manual

(Version 2014 & Later)

Johnathan Mun, Ph.D., MBA, MS, BS, CQRM, FRM, CFC, MIFC

Real Options Valuation, Inc.

Real Options SLS

PREFACE

Welcome to the Real Options Super Lattice Solver (SLS) software. This software has several modules including:

- Single Super Lattice Solver ("SLS")

- Multiple Super Lattice Solver ("MSLS")

- Multinomial Lattice Solver ("MNLS")

- Lattice Maker

- SLS Excel Solution

- SLS Functions

- ROV Strategy Tree

These modules embrace the financial concepts of options as applied to real or physical assets. For example, when you purchase a call option on an underlying stock, you are purchasing the right, but not the obligation, to buy a share of stock at a set cost or strike price. When the time comes to buy the stock, or exercise your option either at or before maturity, you exercise the option if the stock price is higher than the strike price of your option. Exercising the option means purchasing the stock at the strike price and selling it at the higher market price to make a profit (less any taxes, transaction costs, and premiums paid to obtain the option). However, if the price is less than the strike price, you don't buy the stock, and your only losses are the transaction costs and premiums. The future is difficult to predict and may be wrought with uncertainty and risk. You cannot know for certain whether a specific stock will increase or decrease in value. This is the beauty of options: You can maximize your gains (speculation with unlimited upside) while minimizing your losses (hedging against the downside by setting the maximum losses as the premium paid on the option). The same idea can be applied to assets. A firm's assets might include plants, patents, projects, research and development initiatives, and so forth. Each of these assets carries a level of uncertainty. For example, will a firm's multimillion-dollar research project develop into a revenue-generating product? Will investing in a successful start-up company help a firm expand into new markets? Management asks such questions every day. The Real Options Super Lattice Solver software (collectively, the SLS, MSLS, and MNLS) provide analysts and executives the ability to determine the value of investing in an uncertain future.

Who should use this software?

The SLS, MSLS, MNLS, Lattice Maker, Excel Solution, and Excel Functions are appropriate for analysts who are comfortable with spreadsheet modeling in Excel and with real options valuation. The software accompanies the books *Real Options Analysis: Tools and Techniques, 2nd Edition* (Wiley 2005), *Modeling Risk, 3rd Edition* (2015), and *Valuing Employee Stock Options* (Wiley 2004) all by Dr. Johnathan Mun, who designed the software.[1] There are several accompanying training courses: *Certified Quantitative Risk Management (CQRM), The Basics of Real Options* and *Advanced Real Options* also taught by Dr. Mun. While the software and its models are based on his books, the training courses cover the real options subject matter in more depth, including the solution to sample business cases and the framing of real options of actual cases. It is highly recommended that the user familiarizes him or herself with the fundamental concepts of real options as outlined in *Real Options Analysis: Tools and Techniques, 2nd Edition*, (Wiley, 2006).

---

[1] The Real Options SLS software's design and analytics were created by Dr. Johnathan Mun.

TABLE OF CONTENTS

SECTION I – GETTING STARTED

Single Asset Super Lattice Solver (SLS)

Multiple Asset Super Lattice Solver (MSLS)

Multinomial Lattice Solver (MNLS)

Lattice Audit Sheet

Lattice Maker

SLS Excel Solution

SLS Functions

Payoff Charts

Sensitivity Analysis

Scenario Tables

Convergence Analysis

Monte Carlo Risk Simulation

Strategy Trees

1.1 Introduction to the Super Lattice Software (SLS)

The Real Options Super Lattice Software (SLS) comprises several modules, including the: Single Super Lattice Solver (SLS), Multiple Super Lattice Solver (MSLS), Multinomial Lattice Solver (MNLS), Lattice Maker, Advanced Exotic Options Valuator, SLS Excel Solution, and SLS Functions. These modules are highly powerful and customizable binomial and multinomial lattice solvers and can be used to solve many types of options (including the three main families of options: real options which deals with physical and intangible assets; financial options, which deals with financial assets and the investments of such assets; and employee stock options, which deals with financial assets provided to employees within a corporation). This text illustrates some sample real options, financial options, and employee stock options applications that users will most frequently encounter.

- The **Single Asset Model** is used primarily for solving options with a *single underlying asset* using binomial lattices. Even highly complex options with a single underlying asset can be solved using the SLS.

- The **Multiple Asset Model** is used for solving options with *multiple underlying assets* and sequential compound options with *multiple phases* using binomial lattices. Highly complex options with multiple underlying assets and phases can be solved using the MSLS.

- The **Multinomial Model** uses *multinomial lattices* (trinomial, quadranomial, pentanomial) to solve specific options that cannot be solved using binomial lattices.

- The **Lattice Maker** is used to create lattices in Excel with visible and live equations, useful for running Monte Carlo simulations with the Risk Simulator software (an Excel add-in, risk-based simulation, forecasting, and optimization software also developed by Real Options Valuation, Inc.) or for linking to and from other spreadsheet models. The lattices generated also include decision lattices where the strategic decisions to execute certain options and the optimal timing to execute these options are shown.

- The **Advanced Exotic Financial Options Valuator** is a comprehensive calculator of more than 250 functions and models, from basic options to exotic options (e.g., from Black-Scholes to multinomial lattices to closed-form differential equations and analytical methods for valuing exotic options, as well as other options-related models such as bond options, volatility computations, delta-gamma hedging, and so forth). This valuator complements the ROV Risk Modeler and ROV Valuator software tools, with more than 800 functions and models, also developed by Real Options Valuation, Inc. (ROV), which are capable of running at extremely fast speeds, handling large datasets and linking into existing ODBC-compliant databases (e.g., Oracle, SAP, Access, Excel, CSV, and so forth).

- The **SLS Excel Solution** implements the SLS and MSLS computations within the Excel environment, allowing users to access the SLS and MSLS functions directly in Excel. This feature facilitates model building, formula and value linking and embedding, as well as running simulations, and provides the user sample templates to create such models.

- The **SLS Functions** are additional real options and financial options models accessible directly through Excel. This module facilitates model building, linking and embedding, and running simulations.

- The **Option Charts** are used to visually analyze the payoff structure of the options under analysis, the sensitivity and scenario tables of options to various inputs, convergence of the lattice results, and other valuable analyses.

The SLS software is created by Dr. Johnathan Mun, professor, consultant, and the author of numerous books including *Real Options Analysis: Tools and Techniques, 2nd Edition* (Wiley 2005), *Modeling Risk, Third Edition* (Wiley 2015), and *Valuing Employee Stock Options: Under 2004 FAS 123* (Wiley 2004). This software also accompanies the materials presented at different training courses on real options, simulation, and employee stock options valuation taught by Dr. Mun. While the software and its models are based on his books, the training courses cover the real options subject matter in more depth, including the solution of sample business cases and the framing of real options of actual cases. It is highly suggested that the user familiarizes him or herself with the fundamental concepts of real options in *Real Options Analysis: Tools and Techniques, 2nd Edition* (Wiley 2005) prior to attempting an in-depth real options analysis using this software. This manual will not cover some of the fundamental topics already discussed in the book.

Note: The 1st edition of *Real Options Analysis: Tools and Techniques* published in 2002 shows the *Real Options Analysis Toolkit* software, an older precursor to the *Super Lattice Solver*, also created by Dr. Johnathan Mun. The *Real Options Super Lattice Solver* supersedes the *Real Options Analysis Toolkit* by providing the following enhancements, and is introduced in *Real Options Analysis, 2nd edition* (2005):

- Runs 100X faster and is completely customizable and flexible

- All inconsistencies, computation errors, and bugs have been fixed and verified

- Allows for changing input parameters over time (customized options)

- Allows for changing volatilities over time

- Incorporates Bermudan (vesting and blackout periods) and Customized Options

- Has flexible modeling capabilities in creating or engineering your own customized options

- Includes general enhancements to accuracy, precision, and analytical prowess

- Includes more than 250 exotic options models (closed-form, exotic, multinomial lattice)

As the creator of both the Super Lattice Solver and Real Options Analysis Toolkit (ROAT) software, the author suggests that the reader focuses on using the Super Lattice Solver as it provides many powerful enhancements and analytical flexibility over its predecessor, ROAT. The SLS software requires the following minimum requirements:

- Windows 7, Windows 8, Windows 10, and beyond

- Excel 2007, Excel 2010, Excel 2013

- .NET Framework 2.0 or later

- Administrative rights (for software installation)

- Minimum 2GB of RAM (4GB recommended)

- 200MB of free hard drive space

The software will work on most foreign operating systems such as foreign language Windows or Excel, and the SLS software has been tested to work on most international Windows operating systems with just a quick change in settings by clicking on *Start | Control Panel | Regional and Language Options*. Select *English (United States)*. This change is required because the numbering convention is different in foreign countries (e.g., one thousand dollars and fifty cents is written as 1,000.50 in the United States versus 1.000,50 in certain European countries).

To install the software, make sure that your system has all the prerequisites described above. If you require .NET Framework 2.0, please browse the software installation CD and install the file named *dotnetfx20.exe* or if you do not have the installation CD, you can download the file from the following web location:

www.realoptionsvaluation.com/attachments/dotnetfx20.exe.

You need to first install this software before proceeding with the SLS software installation. Note that .NET 2.0 works in parallel with .NET 1.1 and you do not and should not uninstall one version in preference to the other. You should have both versions running concurrently on your computer for best performance.

Next, install the SLS software by either using the installation CD or going to the following web location: www.realoptionsvaluation.com, clicking on Downloads, and selecting Real Options SLS. You can either select to download the FULL version (assuming you have already purchased the software and have received the permanent license keys and the instructions to permanently license the software) or a TRIAL version. The trial version is exactly the same as the full version except that it expires after 10 days, during which you would need to obtain the full license to extend the use of the software. Install the software by following the onscreen prompts.

If you have the trial version and wish to obtain the permanent license, visit www.realoptionsvaluation.com and click on the Purchase link (left panel of the web site) and complete the purchase order. You will then receive the pertinent instructions on installing the permanent license. See Appendix D and E for additional installation details and Appendix F for licensing instructions. Please visit www.realoptionsvaluation.com and click on FAQ and DOWNLOADS for any updates on installation instructions and troubleshooting issues.

1.2 Single Asset Super Lattice Solver

Figure 1 illustrates the SLS software's Main Screen. After installing the software, the user can access the SLS Main Screen by clicking on *Start | Programs | Real Options Valuation | Real Options SLS | Real Options SLS*. From this Main Screen, you can run the Single Asset model, Multiple Asset model, Multinomial model, Lattice Maker, and Advanced Exotic Financial Options Valuator, open example models, and open an existing model. You can move your mouse over any one of the items to obtain a short description of what that module does. You may also purchase or install a newly obtained permanent license from this main screen by clicking on each of the two license links at the bottom. Finally, Real Options SLS supports 7 languages, including English, Chinese, Spanish, Japanese, Italian, German and Portuguese and you can change the language using the droplist on the main screen. To access the SLS Functions, SLS Excel Solutions, or a sample Volatility computation file, go to *Start | Programs | Real Options Valuation | Real Options SLS* and select the relevant module.

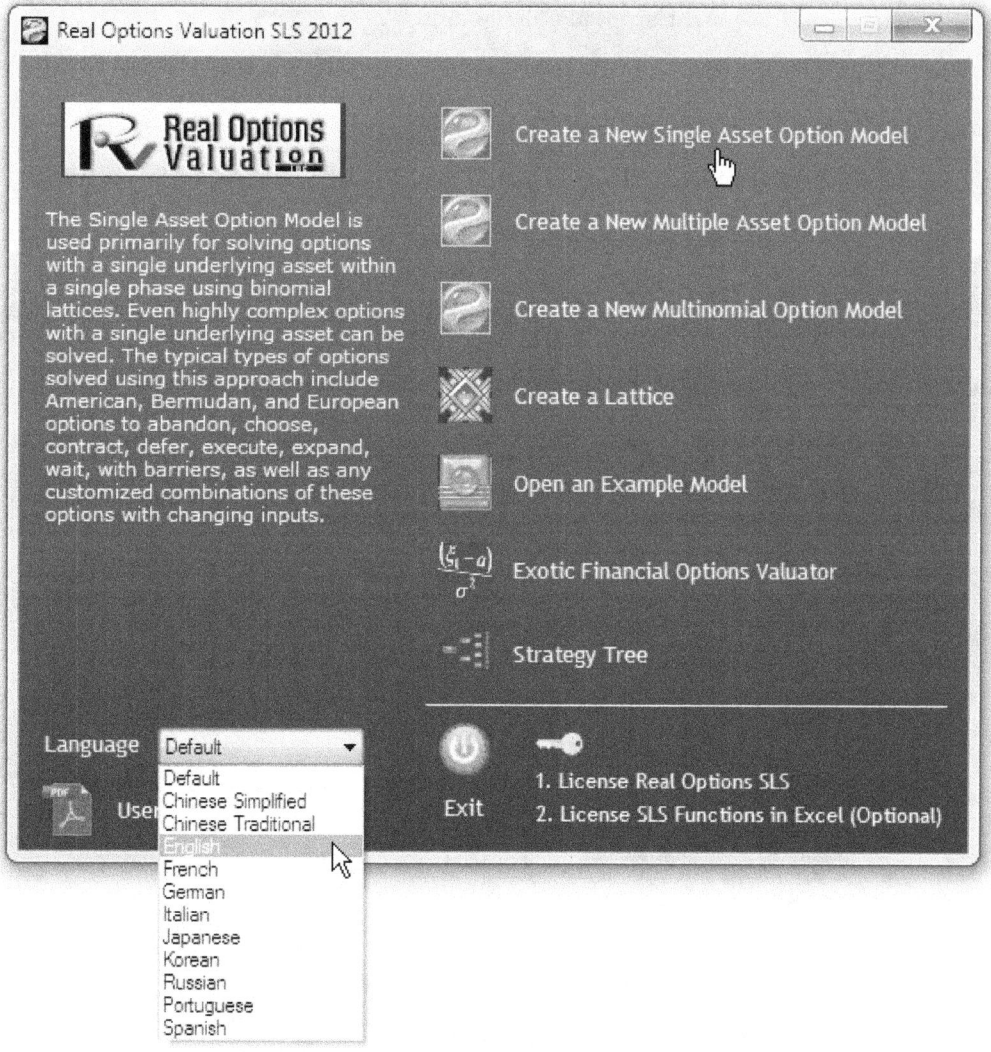

Figure 1 – Single Super Lattice Solver (SLS)

1.3 Single Asset SLS Examples

To help you get started, several simple examples are in order. A simple European call option is computed in this example using SLS. To follow along, in the Main Screen, click on New Single Asset Model, and then click on *File | Examples | Plain Vanilla Call Option I*. This example file will be loaded into the SLS software as seen in Figure 2. The starting PV Underlying Asset or starting stock price is $100, and the Implementation Cost or strike price is $100 with a 5-year maturity. The annualized risk-free rate of return is 5%, and the historical, comparable, or future expected annualized volatility is 10%. Click on *RUN* (or Alt-R) and a 100-step binomial lattice is computed with the results indicating a value of $23.3975 for both the European and American call options. Benchmark values using Black-Scholes and partial differential Closed-Form American approximation models as well as standard plain-vanilla Binomial American and Binomial European Call and Put Options with 1,000-step binomial lattices are also computed. Notice that only the American and European Options are selected and the computed results are for these simple plain-vanilla American and European Call Options.

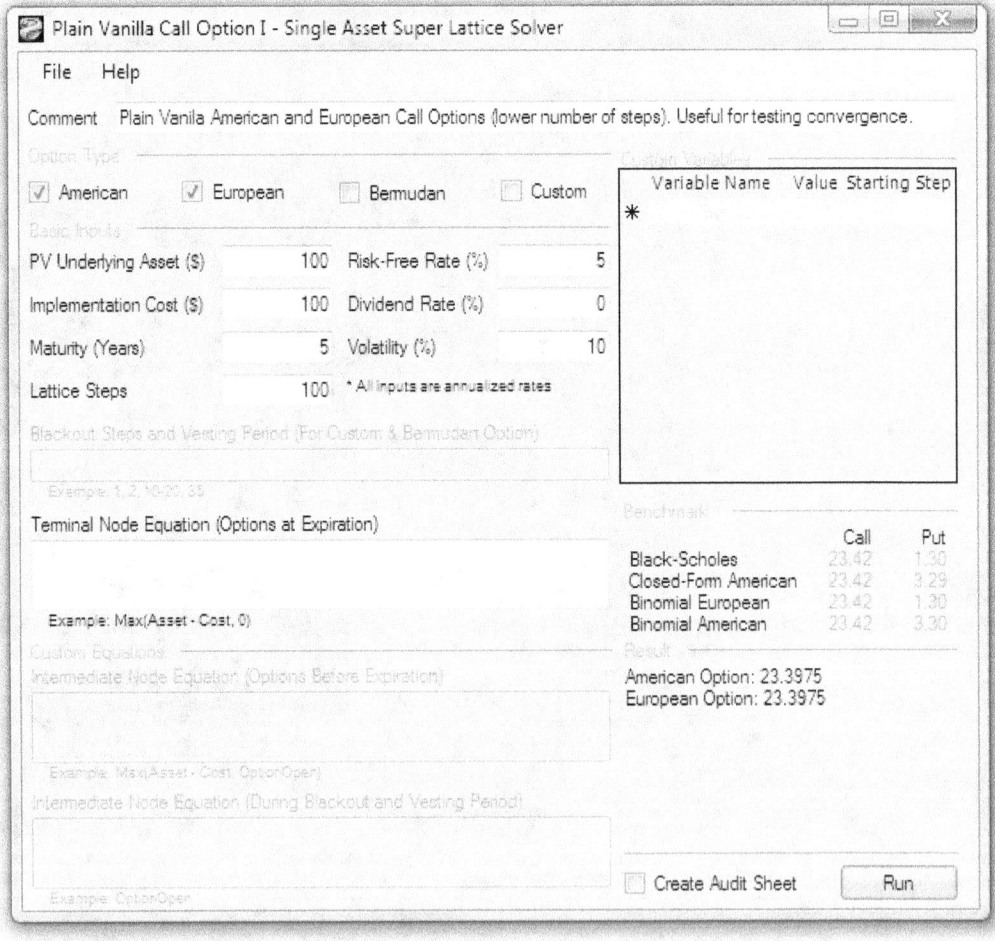

Figure 2 – SLS Results of a Simple European and American Call Option

The benchmark results use both closed-form models (Black-Scholes and Closed-Form Approximation models) and 1,000-step binomial lattices on plain vanilla options. You can change the steps to *1000* in the basic inputs section to verify that the answers computed are equivalent to the benchmarks as seen in Figure 3. Notice that, of course, the values computed for the American and European options are identical to each other and identical to the benchmark values of $23.4187, as it is never optimal to exercise a standard plain-vanilla call option early if there are no dividends. Be aware that the higher the lattice step, the longer it takes, of course, to compute the results. It is advisable to start with lower lattice steps to make sure the analysis is robust and then progressively increase lattice steps to check for results convergence. See Appendix A on convergence criteria on lattices for more details about binomial lattice convergence as to how many lattice steps are required for a robust option valuation.

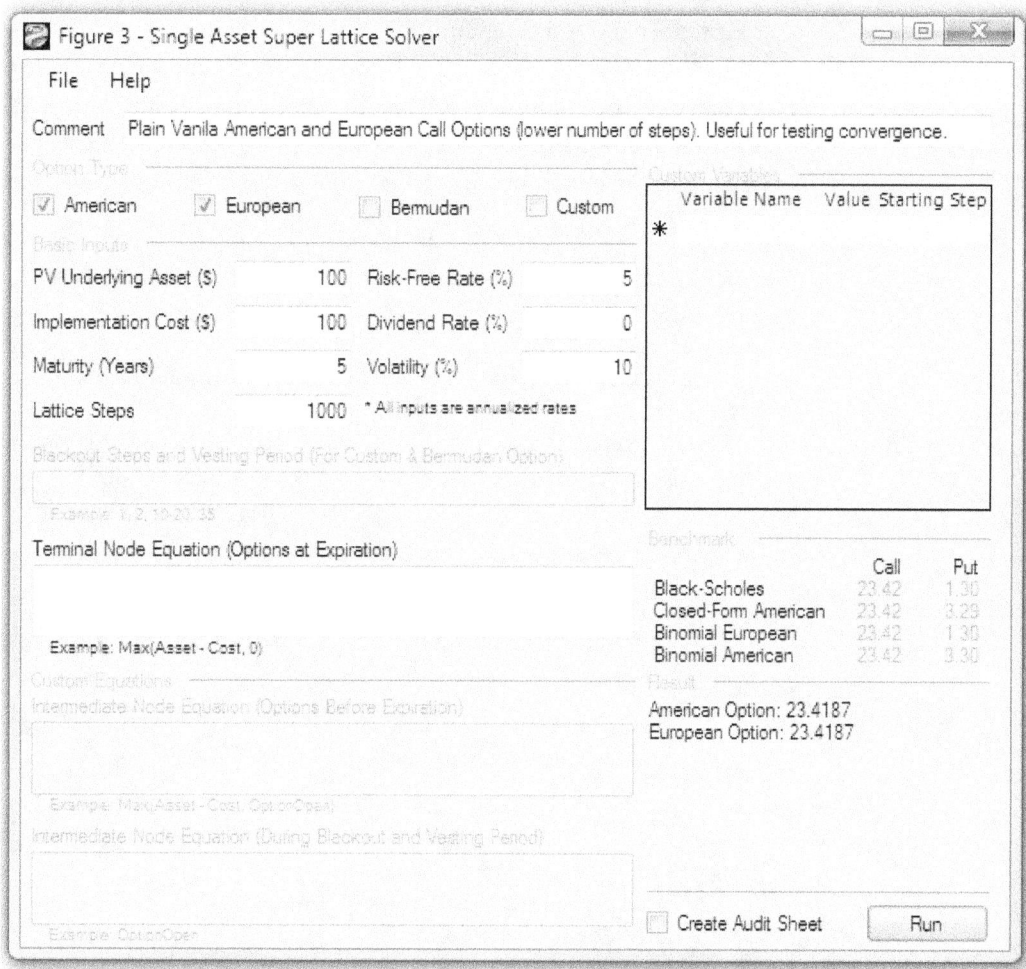

Figure 3 – SLS Comparing Results with Benchmarks

Alternatively, you can enter Terminal and Intermediate Node Equations for a call option to obtain the same results. Notice that using 100 steps and creating your own Terminal Node Equation of *Max(Asset-Cost,0)* and Intermediate Node Equation of *Max(Asset-*

Cost,OptionOpen) will yield the same answer. When entering your own equations, make sure that Custom Option is first checked.

When entering your own equations, make sure that Custom Option is first checked.

Figure 4 illustrates how this analysis is done. Notice that the value $23.3975 in Figure 4 agrees with the value in Figure 2. The Terminal Node Equation is the computation that occurs at maturity, while the Intermediate Node Equation is the computation that occurs at all periods prior to maturity, and is computed using backward induction. The term "*OptionOpen*" represents "keeping the option open," and is often used in the Intermediate Node Equation when analytically representing the fact that the option is not executed but kept open for possible future execution. Therefore, in Figure 4, the Intermediate Node Equation *Max(Asset-Cost,OptionOpen)* represents the profit maximization decision of either executing the option or leaving it open for possible future execution. In contrast, the Terminal Node Equation of *Max(Asset-Cost,0)* represents the profit maximization decision at maturity of either executing the option if it is in-the-money, or allowing it to expire worthless if it is at-the-money or out-of-the-money.

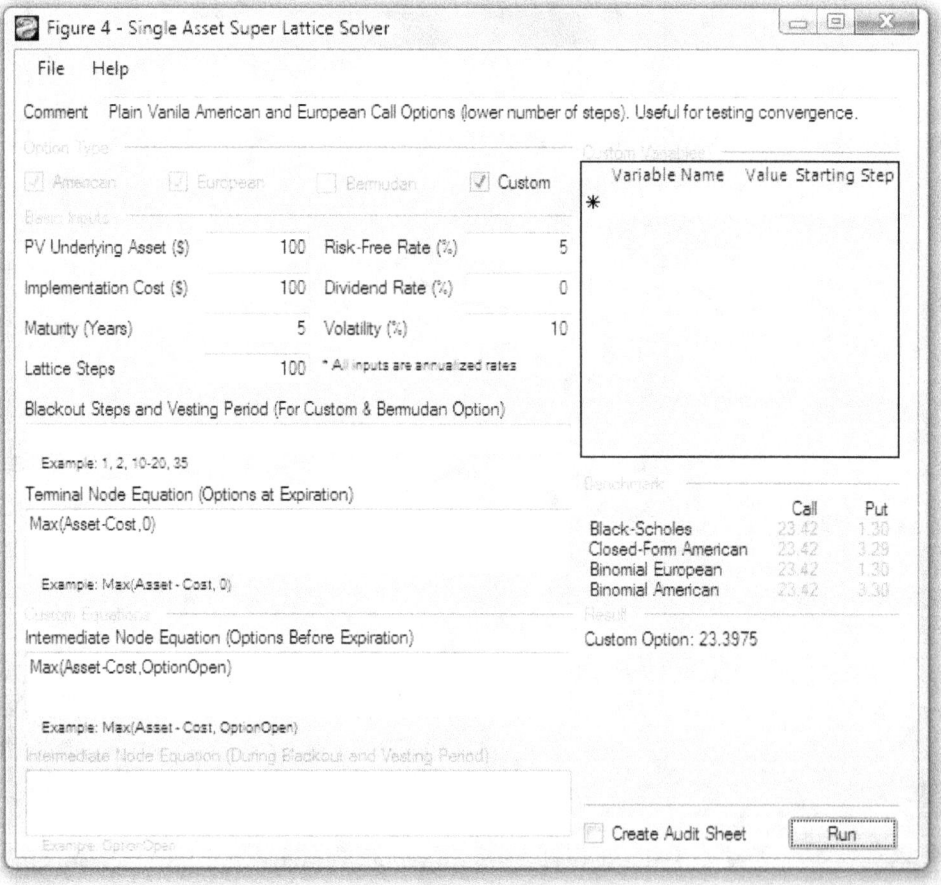

Figure 4 – Custom Equation Inputs

In addition, you can create an Audit Worksheet in Excel to view a sample 10-step binomial lattice by checking the box *Generate Audit Worksheet*. For instance, loading the example file *Plain Vanilla Call Option I* and selecting the box creates a worksheet as seen in Figure 5. There are several items that should be noted about this audit worksheet:

- The audit worksheet generated will show the first 10 steps of the lattice, regardless of how many you enter. That is, if you enter 1,000 steps, the first 10 steps will be generated. If a complete lattice is required, simply enter 10 steps in the SLS and the full 10-step lattice will be generated instead. The Intermediate Computations and Results are for the Super Lattice, based on the number of lattice steps entered, and not based on the 10-step lattice generated. To obtain the Intermediate Computations for 10-step lattices, simply re-run the analysis inputting *10* as the lattice steps. This way, the Audit Worksheet generated will be for a 10-step lattice, and the results from SLS will now be comparable (Figure 6).

- The worksheet only provides values as it is assumed that the user was the one who entered the terminal and Intermediate Node Equations, hence there is really no need to recreate these equations in Excel again. The user can always reload the SLS file and view the equations or print out the form if required (by clicking on *File | Print*).

The software also allows you to save or open analysis files. That is, all the inputs in the software will be saved and can be retrieved for future use. The results will not be saved because you may accidentally delete or change an input and the results will no longer be valid. In addition, re-running the super lattice computations will only take a few seconds, and it is always advisable for you to re-run the model when opening an old analysis file.

You may also enter Blackout Steps. These are the steps on the super lattice that will have different behaviors than the terminal or intermediate steps. For instance, you can enter *1000* as the lattice steps, *0-400* as the blackout steps, and some Blackout Equation (e.g., *OptionOpen*). This means that for the first 400 steps, the option holder can only keep the option open. Other examples include entering *1, 3, 5, 10* if these are the lattice steps where blackout periods occur. You will have to calculate the relevant steps within the lattice where the blackout exists. For instance, if the blackout exists in years 1 and 3 on a 10-year, 10-step lattice, then steps 1, 3 will be the blackout dates. This blackout step feature comes in handy when analyzing options with holding periods, vesting periods, or periods where the option cannot be executed. Employee stock options have blackout and vesting periods, and certain contractual real options have periods during which the option cannot be executed (e.g., cooling-off periods, or proof of concept periods).

If equations are entered into the Terminal Node Equation box and American, European, or Bermudan Options are chosen, the Terminal Node Equation you entered will be the one used in the super lattice for the terminal nodes. However, for the intermediate nodes, the American option will assume the same Terminal Node Equation plus the ability to keep the option open; the European option will assume that the option can only be kept open and not executed; while the Bermudan option will assume that during the blackout lattice steps, the option will be kept open and cannot be executed. If you also wish to enter the Intermediate Node Equation, the Custom Option should be first chosen (otherwise you cannot use the Intermediate Node Equation box). The Custom Option result will use all the equations you have entered in the Terminal, Intermediate, and Intermediate with Blackout sections.

The Custom Variables list is where you can add, modify, or delete custom variables, the variables that are required beyond the basic inputs. For instance, when running an abandonment option, you will require the salvage value. You can add this in the Custom Variables list, provide it a name (a variable's name must be a single word without spaces), the appropriate value, and the starting step when this value becomes effective. For example, if you have multiple salvage values (i.e., if salvage values change over time), you can enter the same variable name (e.g., *salvage*) several times, but each time, its value changes and you can specify when the appropriate salvage value becomes effective. For instance, in a 10-year, 100-step super lattice problem where there are two salvage values—$100 occurring within the first 5 years and increases to $150 at the beginning of Year 6—you can enter two salvage variables with the same name; $100 with a starting step of 0, and $150 with a starting step of 51. Be careful here as Year 6 starts at step 51 and not 61. That is, for a 10-year option with a 100-step lattice, we have: Steps 1–10 = Year 1; Steps 11–20 = Year 2; Steps 21–30 = Year 3; Steps 31–40 = Year 4; Steps 41–50 = Year 5; Steps 51–60 = Year 6; Steps 61–70 = Year 7; Steps 71–80 = Year 8; Steps 81–90 = Year 9; and Steps 91–100 = Year 10. Finally, incorporating 0 as a blackout step indicates that the option cannot be executed immediately.

A Custom Variable's name must be a single continuous word

Option Valuation Audit Sheet

Assumptions

PV Asset Value ($)	$100.00
Implementation Cost ($)	$100.00
Maturity (Years)	5.00
Risk-free Rate (%)	5.00%
Dividends (%)	0.00%
Volatility (%)	10.00%
Lattice Steps	100
Option Type	European

Terminal Equation
Intermediate Equation
Intermediate Equation (Blackouts)

Intermediate Computations

Stepping Time (dt)	0.0500
Up Step Size (up)	1.0226
Down Step Size (down)	0.9779
Risk-neutral Probability	0.5504

Results

Auditing Lattice Result (10 steps)	23.19
Super Lattice Results)	23.40

Underlying Asset Lattice

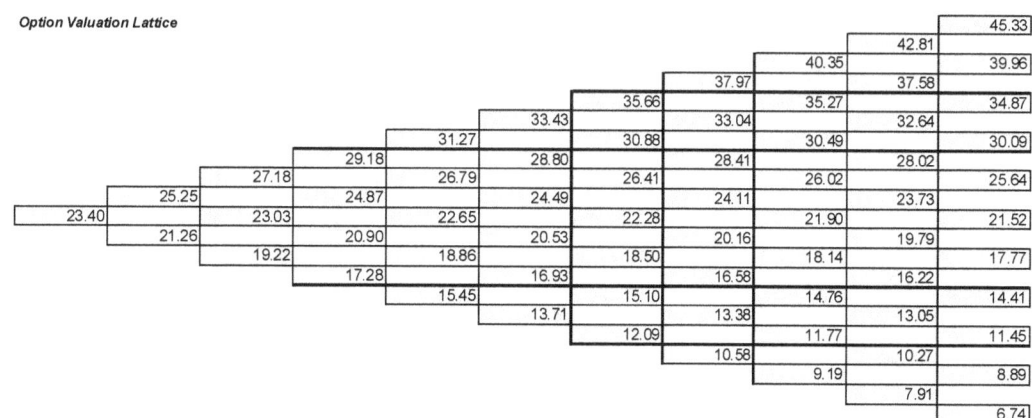

Option Valuation Lattice

Figure 5 – SLS Generated Audit Worksheet

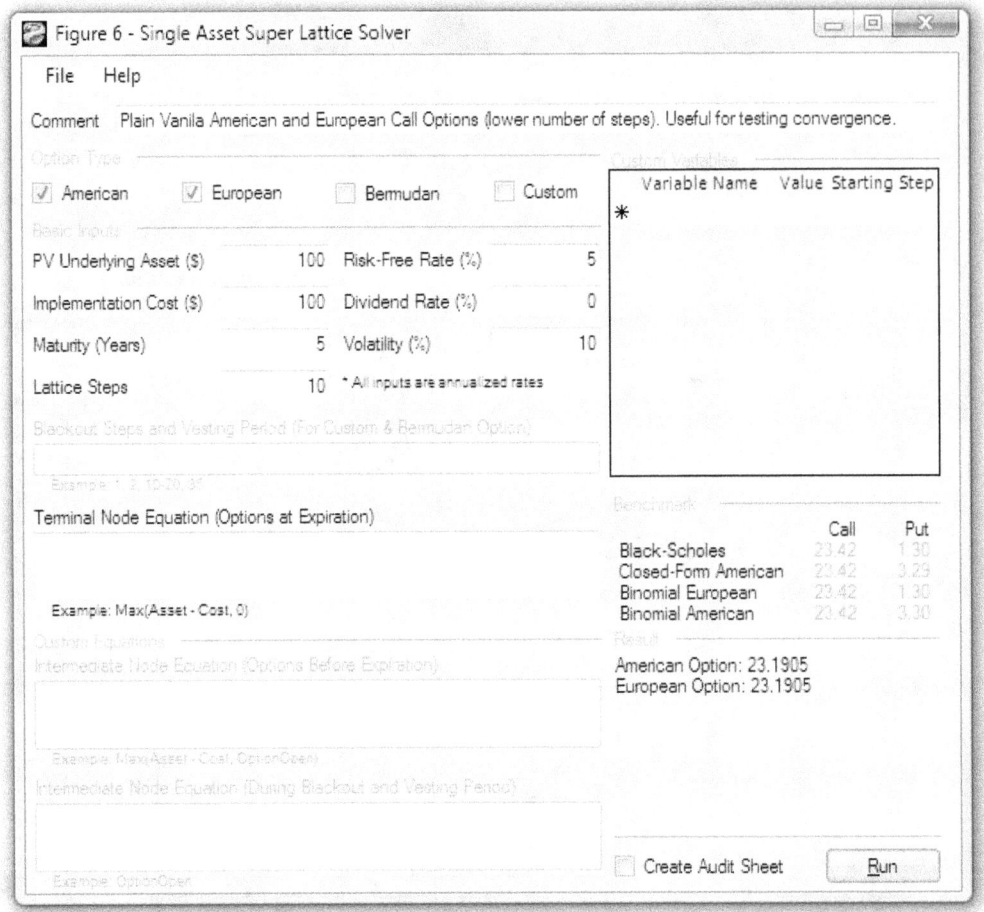

Figure 6 – SLS Results with a 10-Step Lattice

1.4 Multiple Asset Super Lattice Solver (MSLS)

The MSLS is an extension of the SLS in that the MSLS can be used to solve options with multiple underlying assets and multiple phases. The MSLS allows the user to enter multiple underlying assets as well as multiple valuation lattices. These valuation lattices can call to user-defined custom variables. Some examples of the types of options that the MSLS can be used to solve include:

- Sequential Compound Options (two-, three-, and multiple-phased sequential options)

- Simultaneous Compound Options (multiple assets with multiple simultaneous options)

- Chooser and Switching Options (choosing among several options and underlying assets)

- Floating Options (choosing between calls and puts)

- Multiple Asset Options (3D binomial option models)

The MSLS software has several areas including a *Maturity* and *Comment* area. The Maturity value is a global value for the entire option, regardless of how many underlying or valuation lattices exist. The Comment field is for your personal notes describing the model you are building. There is also a *Blackout and Vesting Period Steps* section and a *Custom Variables* list similar to the SLS. The MSLS also allows you to create Audit Worksheets. Notice, too, that the user interface is resizable (e.g., you can click and drag the right side of the form to make it wider).

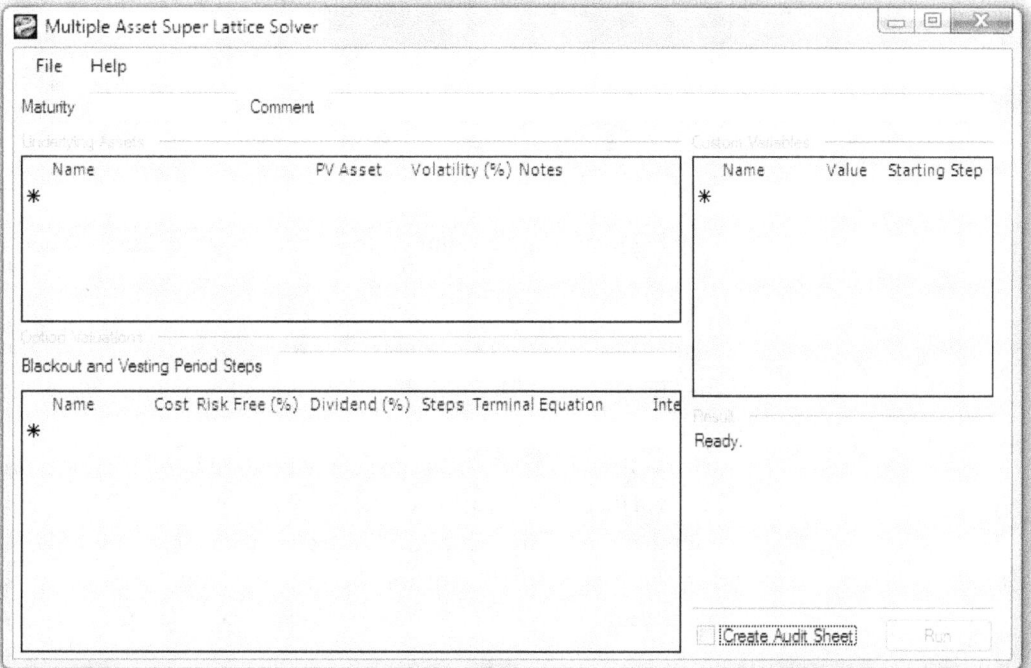

Figure 8 – Multiple Super Lattice Solver

To illustrate the power of the MSLS, a simple illustration is in order. Click on Start | Programs | Real Options Valuation | Real Options SLS | Real Options SLS. In the Main Screen, click on New Multiple Asset Option Model, and then select File | Examples | Simple Two Phased Sequential Compound Option. Figure 9 shows the MSLS example loaded. In this simple example, a single underlying asset is created with two valuation phases.

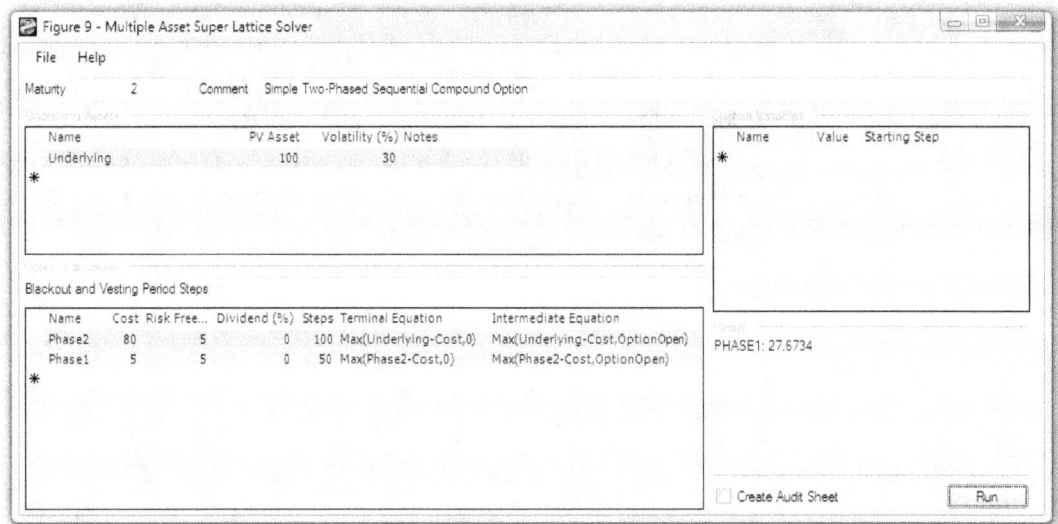

Figure 9 – MSLS Solution to a Simple Two-Phased Sequential Compound Option

The strategy tree for this option is seen in Figure 10. The project is executed in two phases——the first phase within the first year costs $5 million, while the second phase within two years but only after the first phase is executed, and costs $80 million, both in present value dollars. The PV Asset of the project is $100 million (NPV is therefore $15 million) and faces 30% volatility in its cash flows (see the Appendix on Volatility for the relevant volatility computations). The computed strategic value using the MSLS is $27.67 million, indicating that there is a $12.67 million in option value. That is, spreading out and staging the investment into two phases has significant value (an expected value of $12.67 million to be exact).

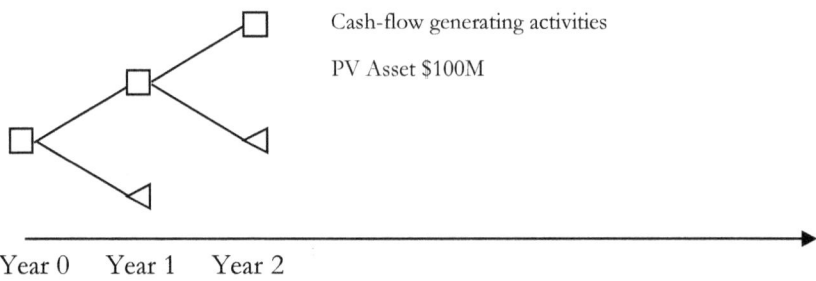

Figure 10 – Strategy tree for two-phased sequential compound option

1.5 Multinomial Lattice Solver

The *Multinomial Lattice Solver* (MNLS) is another module of the Real Options Super Lattice Solver software. The MNLS applies multinomial lattices—where multiple branches stem from each node—such as trinomials (three branches), quadranomials (four branches), and pentanomials (five branches). Figure 11 illustrates the MNLS module. The module has a Basic Inputs section, where all of the common inputs for the multinomials are listed. Then, there are four sections with four different multinomial applications complete with the additional required inputs and results for both American and European call and put options. To follow along with this simple example, in the *Main Screen*, click on *New Multinomial Option Model*, and then select *File | Examples | Trinomial American Call Option*, and set dividend to 0% and then hit run.

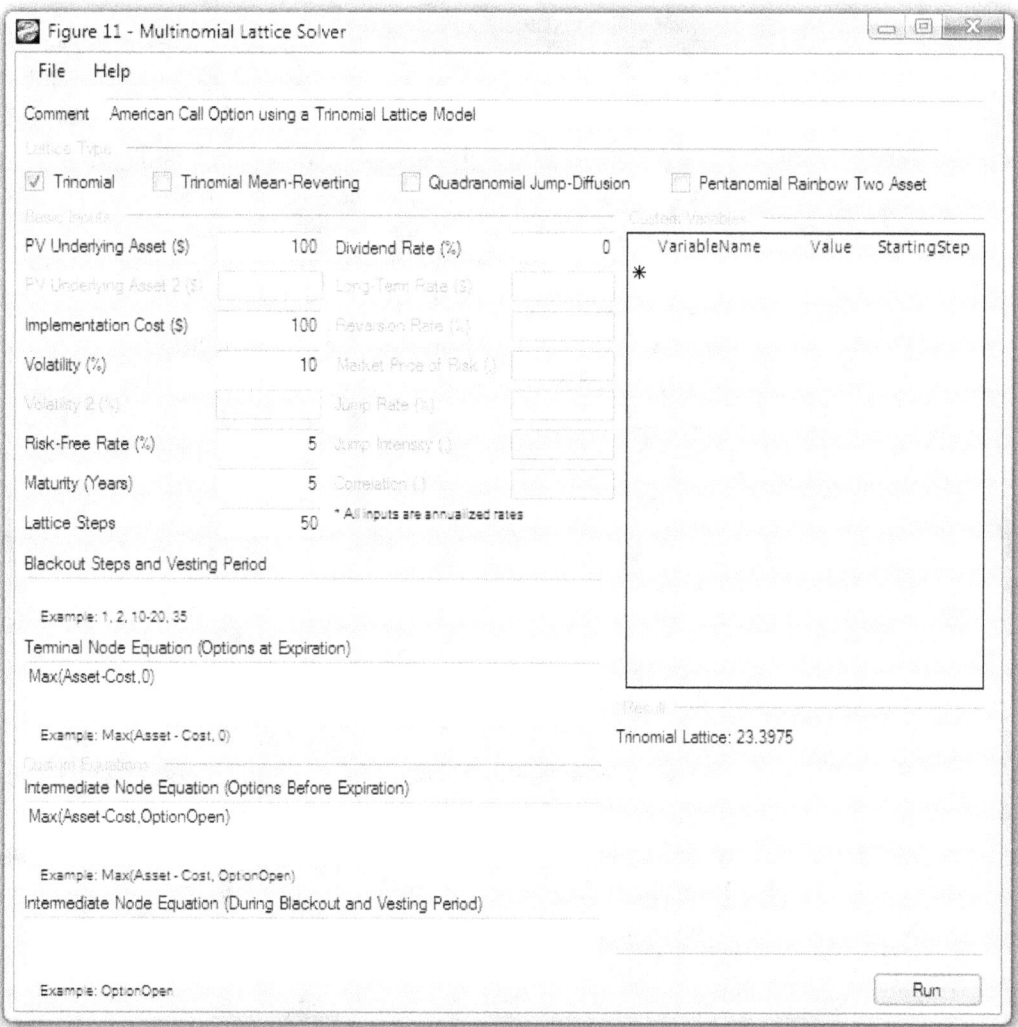

Figure 11 – Multinomial Lattice Solver

Figure 11 shows a sample call and put option computation using trinomial lattices. Note that the results shown in Figure 11 using a 50-step lattice are equivalent to the results shown in Figure 2 using a 100-step binomial lattice. In fact, a trinomial lattice or any other multinomial lattice provides identical answers to the binomial lattice at the limit, but convergence is achieved faster at lower steps. Because both yield identical results at the limit but trinomials are much more difficult to calculate and take a longer computation time, in practice, the binomial lattice is usually used instead. Nonetheless, using the SLS software, the computation times are only seconds, making this traditionally difficult to run model computable almost instantly. However, a trinomial is required only under one special circumstance: when the underlying asset follows a mean-reverting process.

With the same logic, quadranomials and pentanomials yield identical results as the binomial lattice with the exception that these multinomial lattices can be used to solve the following different special limiting conditions:

- Trinomials: Results are identical to binomials and are most appropriate when used to solve mean-reverting underlying assets.

- Quadranomials: Results are identical to binomials and are most appropriate when used to solve options whose underlying assets follow jump-diffusion processes.

- Pentanomials: Results are identical to binomials and are most appropriate when used to solve two underlying assets that are combined, called rainbow options (e.g., price and quantity are multiplied to obtain total revenues, but price and quantity each follows a different underlying lattice with its own volatility, but both underlying parameters could be correlated to one another).

See the sections on Mean-Reverting, Jump-Diffusion, and Rainbow Options for more details, examples, and results interpretation. In addition, just like in the single asset and multiple asset lattice modules, you can customize these multinomial lattices using your own custom equations and custom variables.

1.6 SLS Lattice Maker

The Lattice Maker module is capable of generating binomial lattices and decision lattices with visible formulas in an Excel spreadsheet (it is compatible with Excel 2007, 2010, and 2013). Figure 12 illustrates an example option generated using this module. The illustration shows the module inputs (you can obtain this module by clicking on *Create A Lattice* from the *Main Screen*) and the resulting output lattice. Notice that the visible equations are linked to the existing spreadsheet, which means this module will come in handy when running Monte Carlo simulations or when used to link to and from other spreadsheet models. The results can also be used as a presentation and learning tool to peep inside the analytical black box of binomial lattices. Last but not least, a decision lattice is also available with specific decision nodes indicating expected optimal times of execution of certain options in this module. The results generated from this module are identical to those generated using the SLS and Excel functions, but has the added advantage of a visible lattice (lattices of up to 200 steps can be generated using this module).

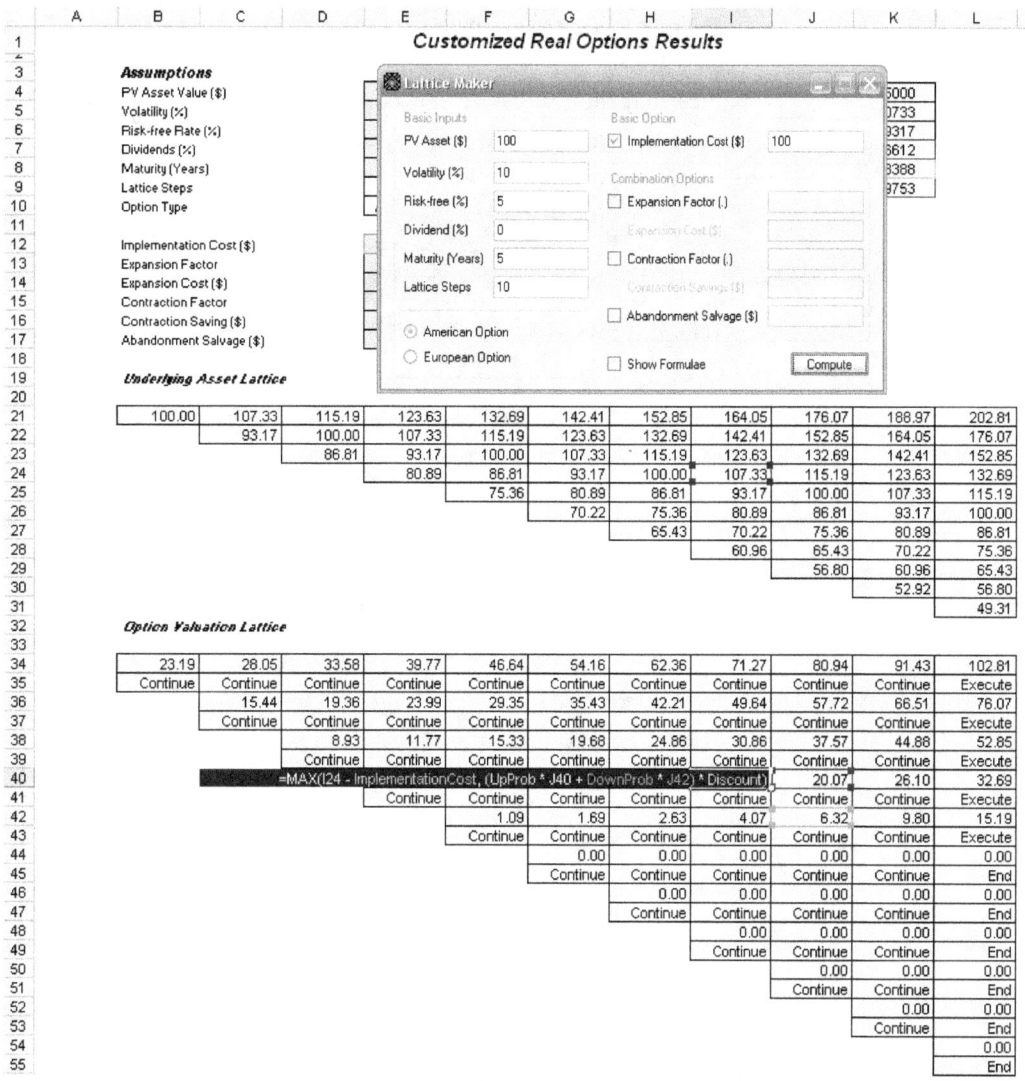

Figure 12 – Lattice Maker Module and Worksheet Results with Visible Equations

1.7 SLS Excel Solution (SLS, MSLS, and Changing Volatility Models in Excel)

The SLS software also allows you to create your own models in Excel using customized functions. This is an important functionality because certain models may require linking from other spreadsheets or databases, run certain Excel macros and functions, or certain inputs need to be simulated, or inputs may change over the course of modeling your options. This Excel compatibility allows you the flexibility to innovate within the Excel spreadsheet environment. Specifically, the sample worksheet solves the SLS, MSLS, and Changing Volatility model.

To illustrate, Figure 13 shows a Customized Abandonment Option solved using SLS (from the *Single Asset Module*, click on *File* | *Examples* | *Abandonment Customized Option*). The same problem can be solved using the *SLS Excel Solution* by clicking on *Start | Programs | Real Options Valuation | Real Options SLS | Excel Solution.* The sample solution is seen in Figure 14. Notice that the results are the same using the SLS versus the SLS Excel Solution file. You can use the template provided by simply clicking on *File | Save As* in Excel and use the new file for your own modeling needs.

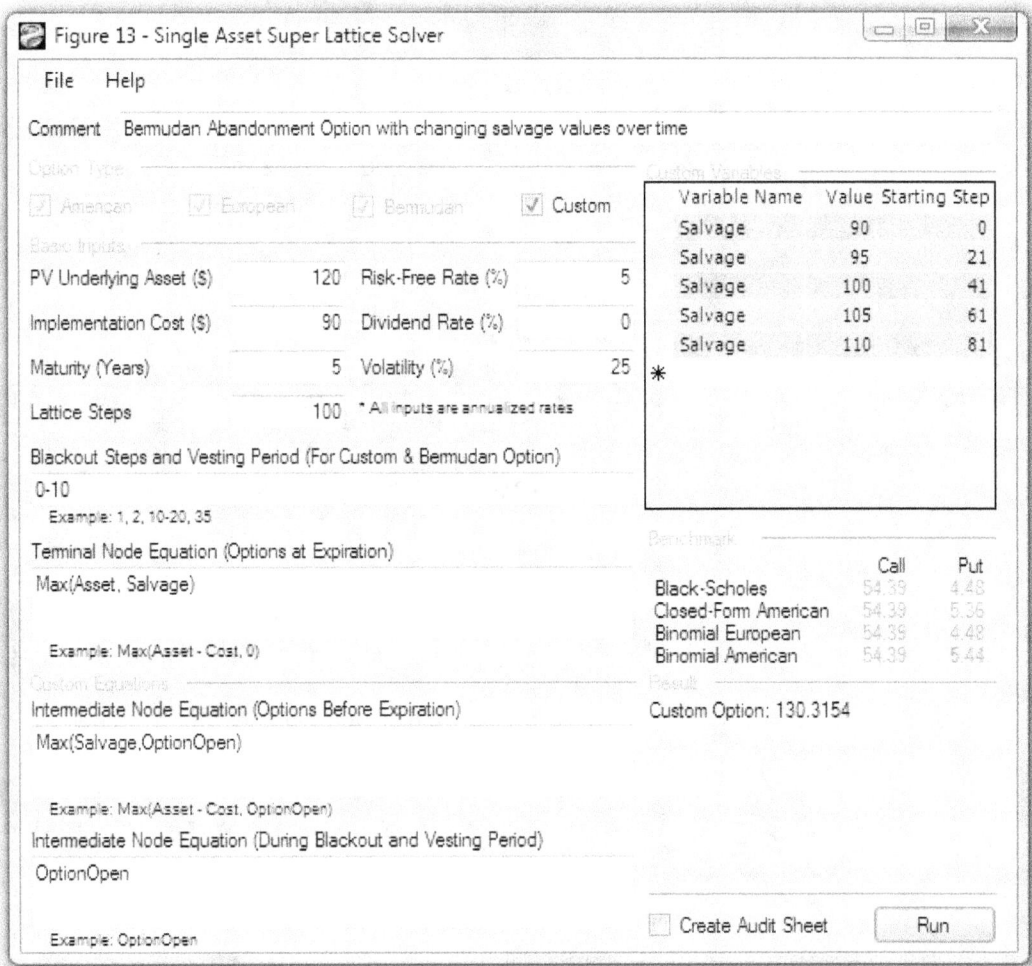

Figure 13 – Customized Abandonment Option using SLS

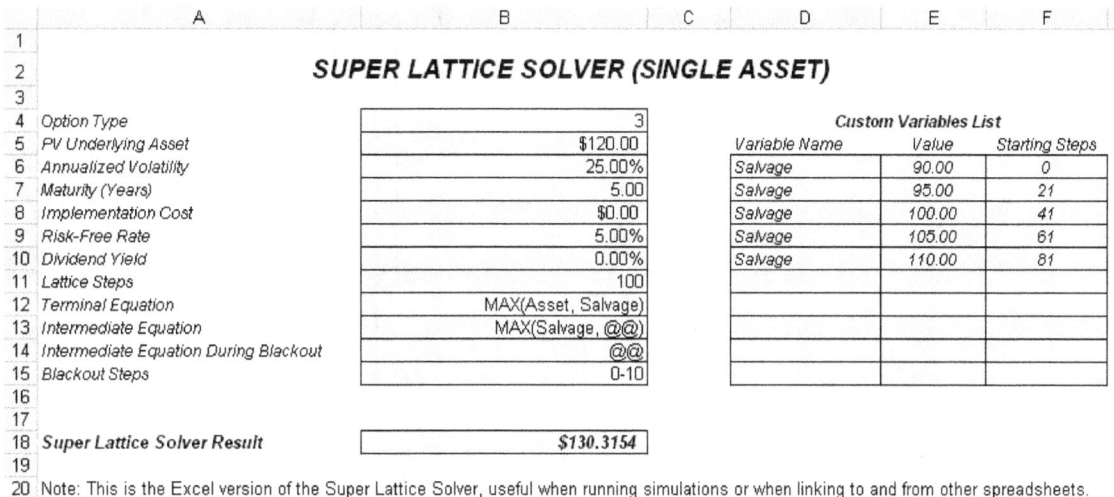

Figure 14 – Customized Abandonment Option using SLS Excel Solution

The only difference is that in the Excel Solution, the function (cell B18 in Figure 14) has an added input, specifically, the *Option Type*. If the option type value is set to 0, you get an American option; 1 for European option; 2 for Bermudan option; and 3 for customized options.

Similarly, the MSLS can also be solved using the SLS Excel Solver. Figure 15 shows a complex multiple-phased sequential compound option solved using the SLS Excel Solver. The results shown are identical to the results generated from the MSLS module (example file: *Multiple Phased Complex Sequential Compound Option*). One small note of caution here is that if you add or reduce the number of option valuation lattices, make sure you change the function's link for the MSLS Result to incorporate the right number of rows, otherwise the analysis will not compute properly. For example, the default shows 3 option valuation lattices, and by selecting the MSLS Results cell in the spreadsheet and clicking on *Insert | Function*, you will see that the function links to cells A24:H26 for these three rows for the OVLattices input in the function. If you add another option valuation lattice, change the link to A24:H27, and so forth. You can also leave the list of custom variables as is. The results will not be affected if these variables are not used in the custom equations.

Finally, Figure 16 shows a Changing Volatility and Changing Risk-free Rate Option. In this model, the volatility and risk-free yields are allowed to change over time and a non-recombining lattice is required to solve the option. In most cases, it is recommended that you create option models without the changing volatility term structure because getting a single volatility is difficult enough let alone a series of changing volatilities over time. If different volatilities that are uncertain need to be modeled, run a Monte Carlo simulation on volatilities instead. This model should only be used when the volatilities are modeled robustly, are rather certain, and change over time. The same advice applies to a changing risk-free rate term structure.

MULTIPLE SUPER LATTICE SOLVER (MULTIPLE ASSET & MULTIPLE PHASES)

Maturity (Years)	5.00
Blackout Steps	0-20
Correlation*	

MSLS Result $134.0802

Underlying Asset Lattices

Lattice Name	PV Asset	Volatility
Underlying	100.00	25.00

Custom Variables

Name	Value	Starting Steps
Salvage	100.00	31
Salvage	90.00	11
Salvage	80.00	0
Contract	0.90	0
Expansion	1.50	0
Savings	20.00	0

Option Valuation Lattices

Lattice Name	Cost	Riskfree	Dividend	Steps	Terminal Equation	Intermediate Equation	Intermediate Equation for Blackout
Phase3	50.00	5.00	0.00	50	Max(Underlying*Expansion-Cost,Underlying,Salvage)	Max(Underlying*Expansion-Cost,Salvage,@@)	@@
Phase2	0.00	5.00	0.00	30	Max(Phase3,Phase3*Contract+Savings,Salvage,0)	Max(Phase3*Contract+Savings,Salvage,@@)	@@
Phase1	0.00	5.00	0.00	10	Max(Phase2,Salvage,0)	Max(Salvage,@@)	@@

Note: This is the Excel version of the Multiple Super Lattice Solver, useful when running simulations or when linking to and from other spreadsheets. Use this sample spreadsheet for your models. You can simply click on File, Save As to save as a different file and start using the model.
*Because this is an Excel solution, the correlation function is not supported and is linked to an empty cell.

Figure 15 – Complex Sequential Compound Option using SLS Excel Solver

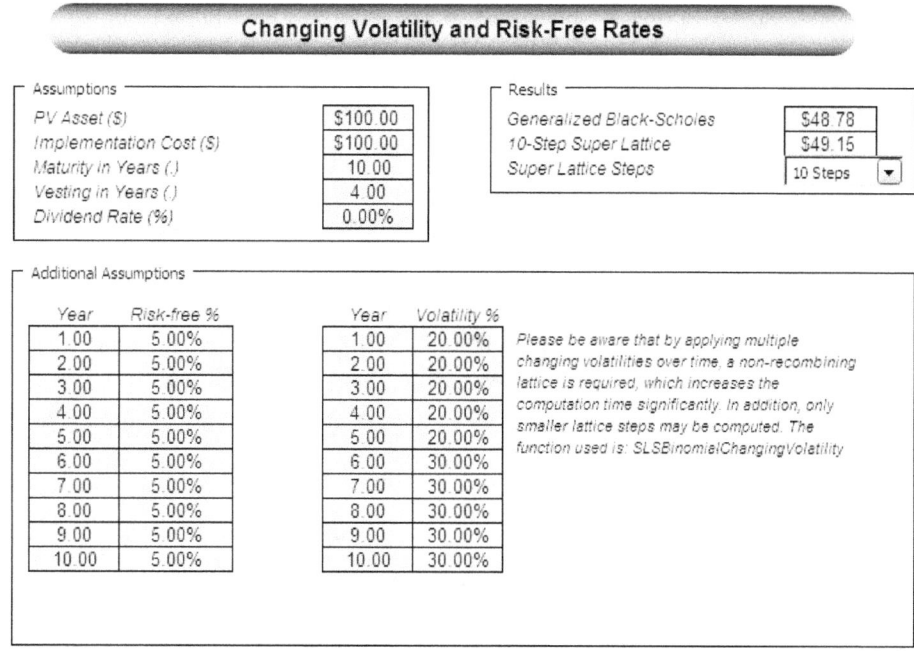

Figure 16 – Changing Volatility and Risk-Free Rate Option

1.8 SLS Functions

The software also provides a series of SLS functions that are directly accessible in Excel. To illustrate its use, start the SLS Functions by clicking on *Start | Programs | Real Options Valuation | Real Options SLS | SLS Functions*, and Excel will start. When in Excel, you can click on the function wizard icon or simply select an empty cell and click on *Insert | Function*. While in Excel's equation wizard, select the *ALL* category and scroll down to the functions starting with the SLS prefixes. Here you will see a list of SLS functions that are ready for use in Excel. Figure 17 shows the Excel equation wizard.

Start the Excel Functions module and select the ALL category when in Excel's function wizard, then scroll down to access the SLS functions.

You may have to check your macro security settings before starting in Excel 2003 (click on Tools, Macro, Security, and make sure it is set to Medium or below) as well as in Excel 2007/2010/2013 (click on the File or large Office Button on the top left corner of Excel, click on Excel Options, Trust Center, Trust Center Settings, Add-Ins, uncheck all 3 options, then click on Macro Settings and select Enable All Macros and check Trust Access to the VBA project, click OK).

Suppose you select the first function, *SLSBinomialAmericanCall* and hit OK. Figure 17 shows how the function can be linked to an existing Excel model. The values in cells B1 to B7 can be linked from other models or spreadsheets, can be created using VBA macros, or can be dynamic and changing as in when running a simulation.

Note: Be aware that certain functions require many input variables, and Excel's equation wizard can only show 5 variables at a time. Therefore, remember to scroll down the list of variables by clicking on the vertical scroll bar to access the rest of the variables.

If you are a new user of Real Options SLS or have upgraded from an older version, do spend some time reviewing the Key SLS Notes and Tips starting on the next few pages to familiarize yourself with the modeling intricacies of the software.

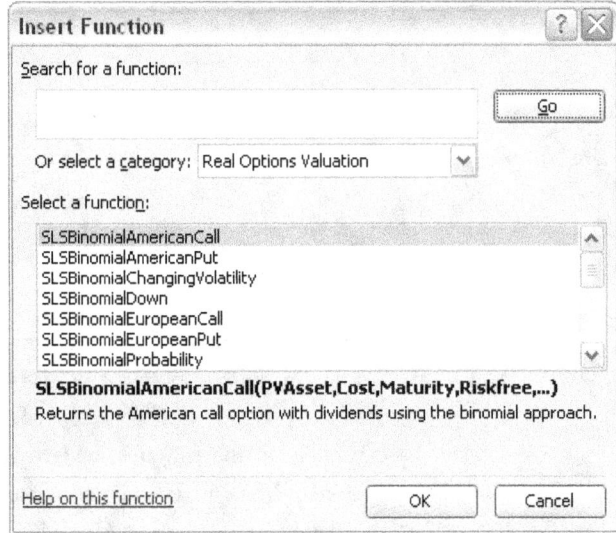

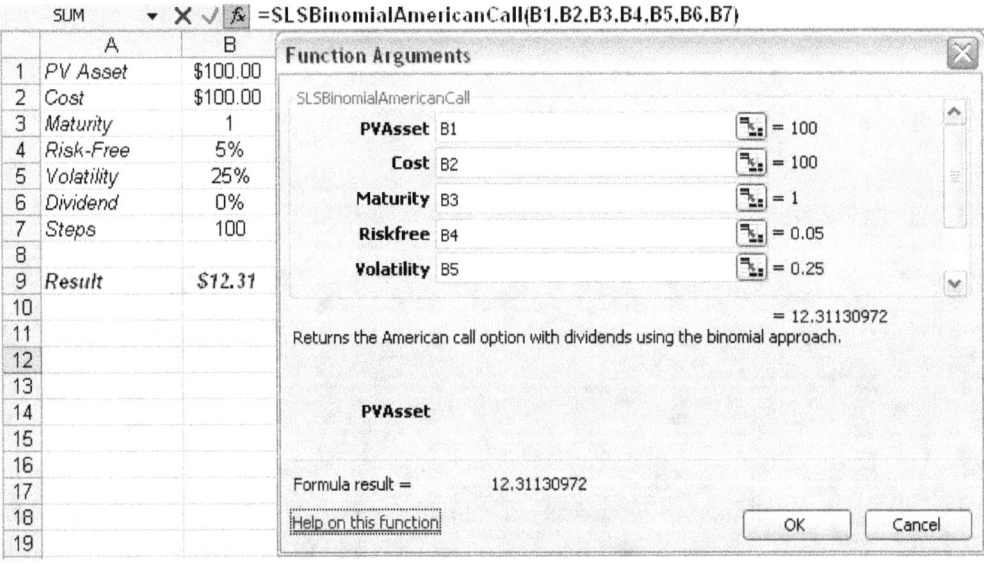

Figure 17 – Excel's Equation Wizard

1.9 Exotic Financial Options Valuator

The Exotic Financial Options Valuator is a comprehensive calculator of more than 250 functions and models, from basic options to exotic options (e.g., from Black-Scholes to multinomial lattices to closed-form differential equations and analytical methods for valuing exotic options, as well as other options-related models such as bond options, volatility computations, delta-gamma hedging, and so forth). Figure 18 illustrates the valuator. You can click on the *Load Sample Values* button to load some samples to get started. Then, select the *Model Category* (left panel) as desired and select the *Model* (right panel) you wish to run. Click *COMPUTE* to obtain the result. Note that this valuator complements the ROV Risk Modeler and ROV Valuator software tools, with more than 800 functions and models, also developed by Real Options Valuation, Inc. (ROV), which are capable of running at extremely fast speeds and handling large datasets and linking into existing ODBC-compliant databases (e.g., Oracle, SAP, Access, Excel, CSV, and so forth). Finally, if you wish to access these 800 functions (including the ones in this Exotic Financial Options Valuator tool), use the ROV Modeling Toolkit software instead, where, in addition to having access to these functions and more, you can run Monte Carlo simulation on your models using ROV's Risk Simulator software.

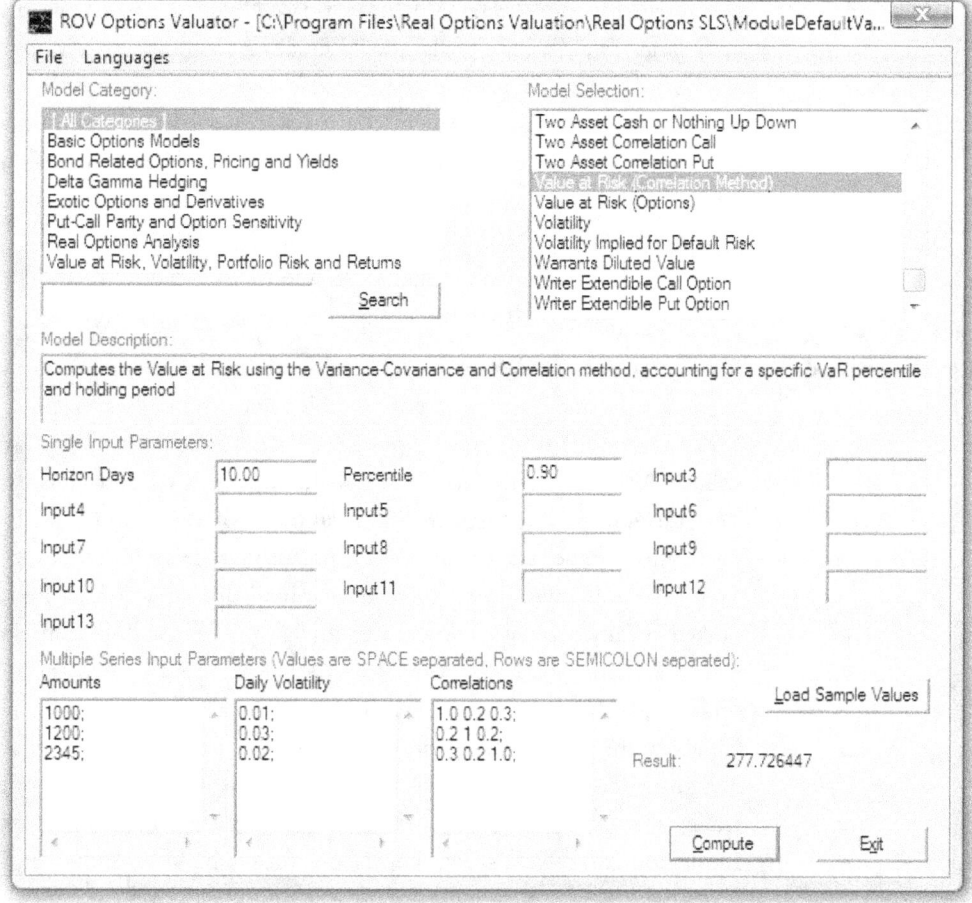

Figure 18 – Exotic Financial Options Valuator

*1.10 Payoff Charts, Tornado,
Convergence, Scenario, Sensitivity
Analysis, Monte Carlo Risk Simulation*

The main Single Asset SLS module also comes with payoff charts, sensitivity tables, scenario analysis and convergence analysis (Figure 18A). To run these analyses, first create a new model or open and run an existing model (e.g., from the first tab *Options SLS*, click on *File*, *Examples*, and select *Plain Vanilla Call Option I* then hit *Run* to compute the option value, and click on any one of the tabs). To use these tools, you need to first have a model specified in the main *Options SLS* tab. Here are brief explanations of these tabs and how to use their corresponding controls as shown in Figure 18A:

Payoff Chart

The *Payoff Chart* tab *(A)* allows you to generate a typical option payoff chart where you have the ability to choose the input variable to chart *(B)* by entering some minimum and maximum values *(C)* to chart as well as its step size (e.g., setting minimum as 20 and maximum as 200 with a step of 10 means to run the analysis for the values 20, 30, 40, ..., 180, 190, 200) and lattice steps (the lower the lattice step number, the faster the analysis runs but the less precise the results—see the following discussion of *Lattice Step Convergence* for more details). Click Update Chart *(D)* to obtain a new payoff chart *(E)* each time. The default is to show a line chart *(F)* but you can opt to choose area or bar charts, and the generated chart and table can be copied and pasted into other applications or printed out as is *(G)*. If you do not enter in any minimum and maximum values, the software automatically picks some default test values for you, the PV Underlying Asset is chosen by default, and the typical hockey-stick payoff chart will be displayed. Finally, there will be a warning message if any of the original input is zero, requiring you to manually insert these minimum, maximum, and step size values in order to generate the payoff chart.

Tornado Sensitivity Analysis

The *Sensitivity* tab *(H)* runs a quick static sensitivity of each input variable of the model one at a time and lists the input variables with the highest impact to the lowest impact. You can control the option type, lattice steps, and sensitivity % to test *(I)*. The results will be returned in the form of a tornado chart *(J)* and sensitivity analysis table *(K)*. Tornado analysis captures the static impacts of each input variable on the outcome of the option value by automatically perturbing each input some preset ±% amount, captures the fluctuation on the option value's result, and lists the resulting perturbations ranked from the most significant to the least. The results are shown as a sensitivity table with the starting base case value, the perturbed input upside and downside, the resulting option value's upside and downside, and the absolute swing or impact. The precedent variables are ranked from the highest impact to the lowest impact. The tornado chart illustrates this data in graphic form. Green bars in the chart indicate a positive effect while red bars indicate a negative effect on the option value. For example, Implementation Cost's red bar is on the right side, indicating a negative effect of investment cost—in other words, for a simple call option, implementation cost (option strike price) and option value are negatively correlated. The opposite is true for PV

Underlying Asset (stock price) where the green bar is on the right side of the chart, indicating a positive correlation between the input and output.

Scenario Analysis

The *Scenario* tab runs a two-dimensional scenario of two input variables *(L)* based on the selected option type and lattice steps *(M)* and returns a scenario analysis table *(N)* of the resulting option values based on the various combinations of inputs.

Lattice Step Convergence Analysis

The *Convergence* tab shows the option results from 5 to 5000 steps, where the higher the number of steps, the higher the level of precision (granularity in lattices increases), where at some point the results of the lattice converge and once convergence is achieved no additional lattice steps are required. The number of steps is set by default, from 5 to 5000, but you can select the option type and number of decimals to show *(O)*, and the convergence chart is displayed *(Q)* depending on your selection. You can also copy or print the table with the chart as required *(P)*.

Monte Carlo Simulation

The *Simulation* tab allows you to run Monte Carlo risk simulations on the real options lattice model. The input variables are listed in the bottom grid. To set an assumption, click on the *ADD* or *EDIT* button specific to the input variable row in the grid. An *Assumption Properties* window will appear for you to select the relevant probability distribution and to set the required distributional parameters. Click *RUN* when ready, and the simulation will execute and once completed, you can select the one- or two-tail confidence interval, and either enter the relevant X-values to recover their respective probability confidence interval or enter in the certainty percentage and obtain the options value confidence interval (remember to hit *TAB* on the keyboard after entering the desired values in order to activate the computations). The number of simulation trials, seed values, decimals, and corresponding simulation statistics are also available on the page. For more technical details on running simulations or to better understand probability distributions and simulation statistics, please refer to Modeling Risk, Third Edition (2015) by Dr. Johnathan Mun or review the Risk Simulator software (see the software's user manuals, hands-on examples, and getting started guides).

1.11 ROV Strategy Tree

The **ROV Strategy Trees** module (Figure 18B) is available from the main SLS user interface and is used to create visually appealing representations of strategic real options. This module is used to simplify the drawing and creation of strategy trees but is not used for the actual real options valuation modeling (use the Real Options SLS software modules for actual modeling purposes). The following are some main quick getting started tips and procedures in using this intuitive tool:

- There are 11 localized languages available in this module and the current language can be changed through the Language menu.

- Insert Option nodes or insert Terminal nodes by first selecting any existing node and then clicking on the option node icon (square box) or terminal node icon (triangle box) or use the Insert menu.

- Modify Individual Option and Terminal Node properties by double-clicking on a node. Sometimes when you click on a node, all subsequent child nodes are also selected (this allows you to move the entire tree starting from that selected node) or if you wish to select only that node, you may have to click on the empty background and click back on that node to select it individually. Also, you can move individual nodes or the entire tree started from the selected node depending on the current setting (right-click or in the Edit menu, you can select to move nodes individually or together). The following are some quick descriptions of the things that can be customized and configured in the node properties user interface. It is simplest to try different settings for each of the following to see its effects in the Strategy Tree:

  o Name

  o Value

  o Excel Link

  o Notes (Insert Above or Below a Node)

  o Show in Model (Name, Value, Notes)

  o Local Color versus Global Color

  o Label Inside Shape

  o Branch Event Name

  o Select Real Options

- Global Elements are all customizable, including elements of the Strategy Tree's Background, Connection Lines, Option Nodes, Terminal Nodes, and Text Boxes. For instance, the following settings can be changed for each of the elements:

  o Font settings on Name, Value, Notes, Label, Event names

  o Node Size (minimum and maximum height and width)

  o Borders (line styles, width, color)

  o Shadow (colors and whether to apply a shadow or not)

  o Global Color

  o Global Shape

- The Edit menu's View Data Requirements Window command opens a docked window on the right of the Strategy Tree such that when an option node or terminal node is selected, the properties of that node will be displayed and can be updated directly. This provides an alternative to double-clicking on a node each time.

- Example Files are available in the File menu to help you get started on building Strategy Trees.

- Protect File from the File menu allows the Strategy Tree to be encrypted with up to a 256-bit password encryption. Be careful when a file is being encrypted because if the password is lost, the file can no longer be opened.

- Capturing the Screen or printing the existing model can be done through the File menu. The captured screen can then be pasted into other software applications.

- Add, Duplicate, Rename, Delete a Strategy Tree can be performed through right-clicking the Strategy Tree tab or the Edit menu.

- You can also Insert a File Link and Insert a Comment on any option or terminal node, or Insert Text or Picture anywhere in the background or canvas area.

- You can Change Existing Styles, or Manage and Create Custom Styles of your Strategy Tree (this includes size, shape, color schemes, and font size/color specifications of the entire Strategy Tree).

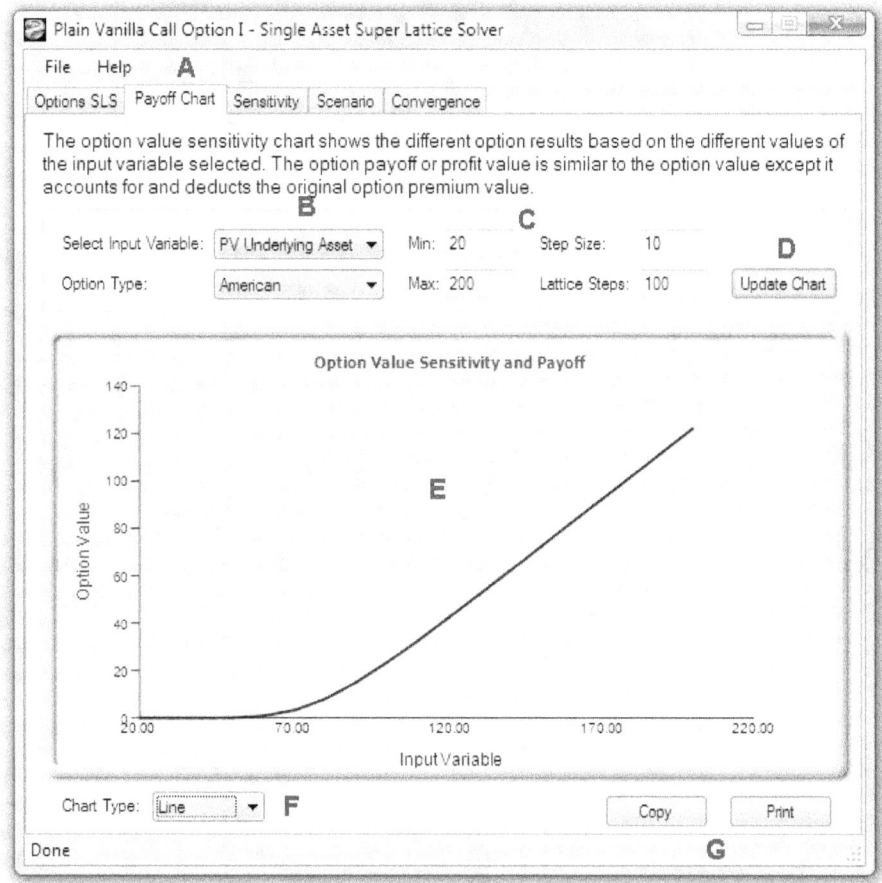

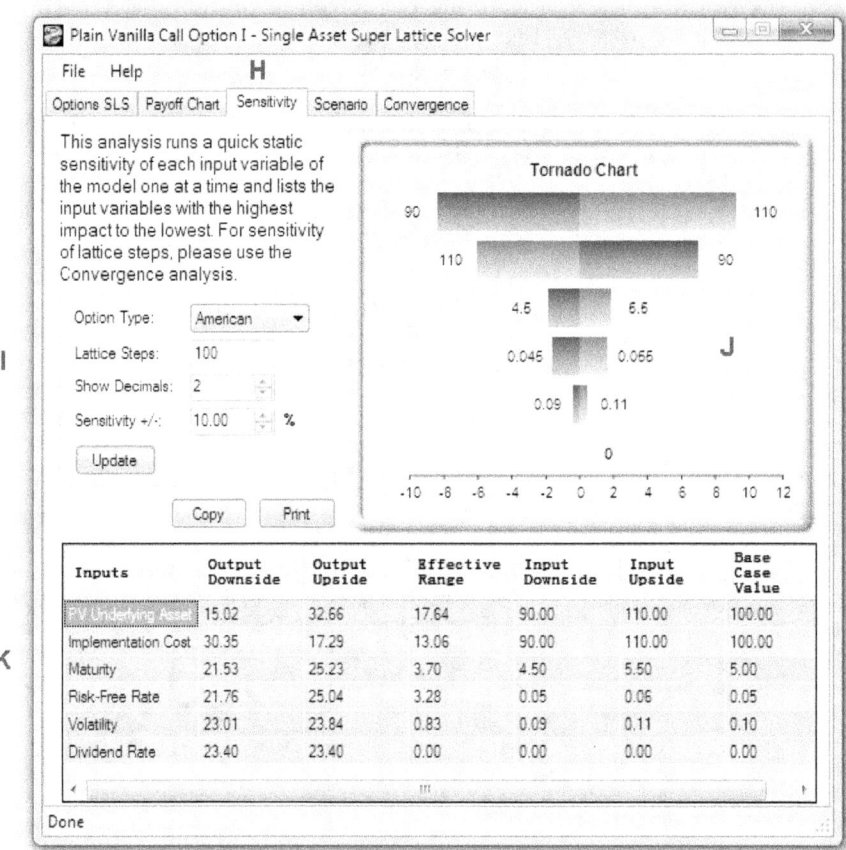

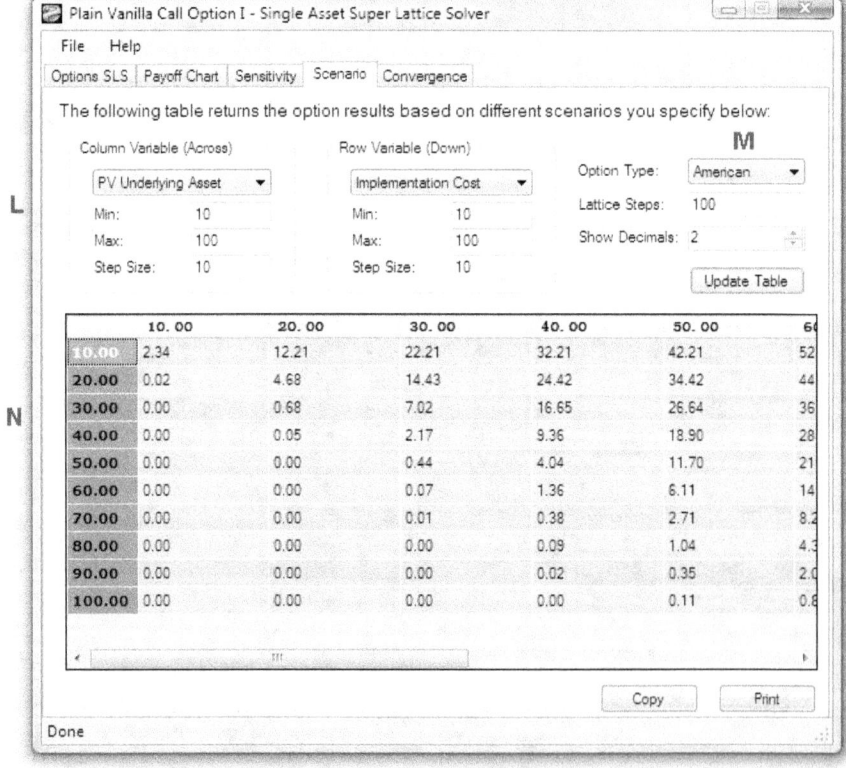

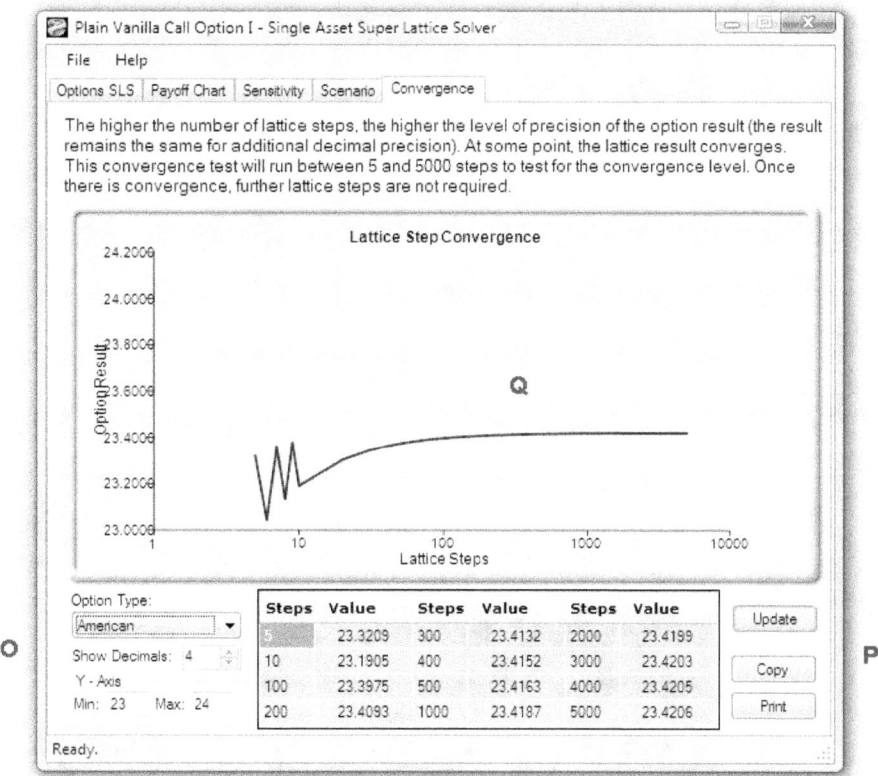

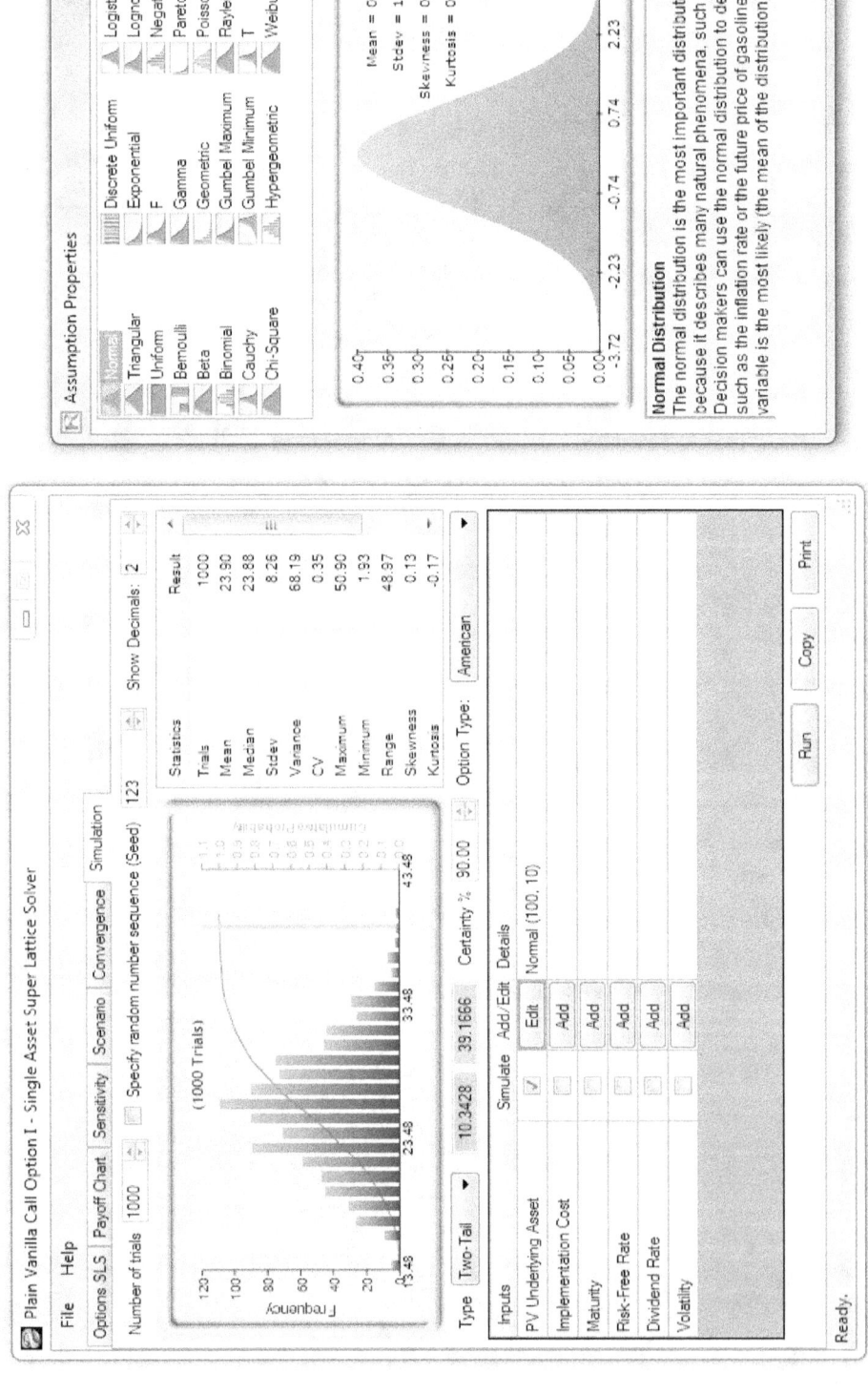

Figure 18A – Payoff Charts, Sensitivity Analysis, Scenario Tables, Convergence Analysis, Monte Carlo Risk Simulation

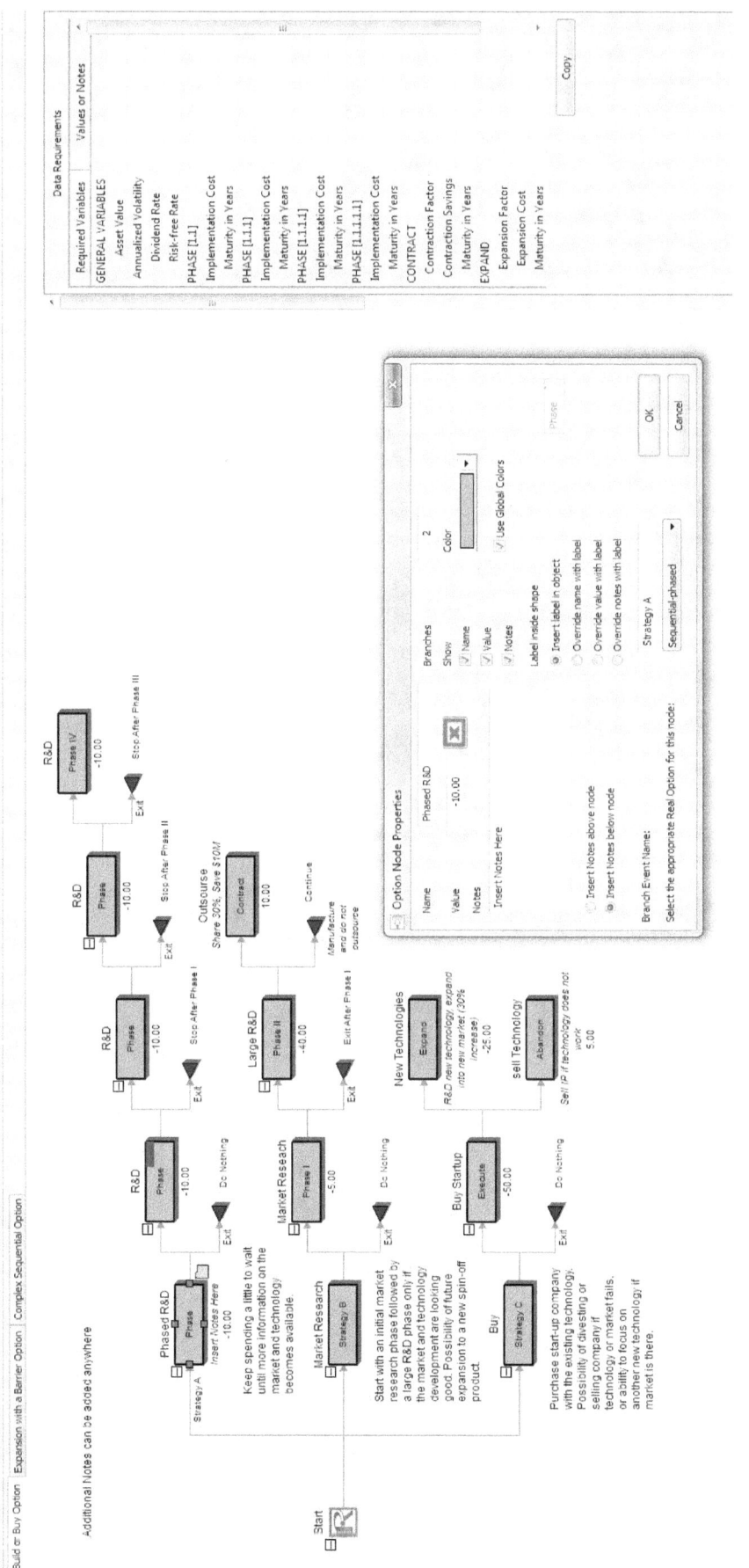

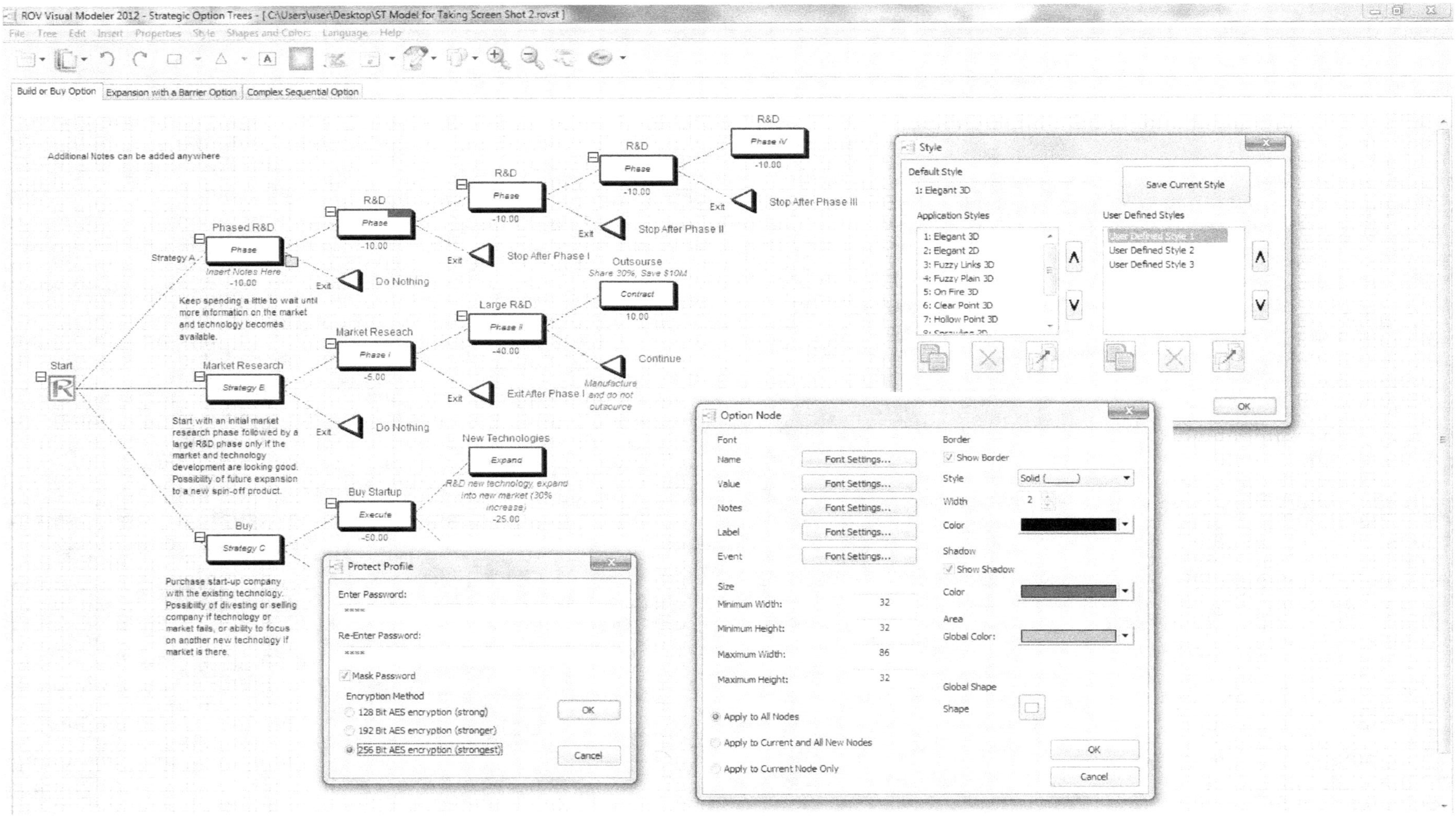

Figure 18B – Strategy Trees

1.12 Key SLS Notes and Tips

Here are some noteworthy changes from the previous version and interesting tips on using Real Options SLS:

- The **User Manual** is accessible within SLS, MSLS or MNLS. For instance, simply start the Real Options SLS software and create a new model or open an existing SLS, MSLS, or MNLS model. Then, click on *Help* | *User Manual.*

- **Example Files** are accessible directly in the SLS Main Screen; when in the SLS, MSLS or MNLS models, you can access the example files at *File* | *Examples.*

- Current **License** information can be obtained in SLS, MSLS or MNLS at *Help* | *About.*

- A **Variable List** is available in SLS, MSLS and MNLS by going to *Help* | *Variable List.* Specifically, the following are allowed variables and operators in the *custom equations* boxes:

  o Asset   – The value of the underlying asset at the current step (in currency)

  o Cost   – The implementation cost (in currency)

  o Dividend   – The value of dividend (in percent)

  o Maturity   – The years to maturity (in years)

  o OptionOpen   – The value of keeping the option open (formerly @@ in version 1.0)

  o RiskFree   – The annualized risk-free rate (in percent)

  o Step   – The integer representing the current step in the lattice

  o Volatility   – The annualized volatility (in percent)

  o -   – Subtract

  o !   – Not

  o !=, <>   – Not equal

  o &   – And

  o *   – Multiply

  o /   – Divide

  o ^   – Power

  o | – Or

  o +   – Add

  o <, >, <=, >=   – Comparisons

  o =   – Equal

- **OptionOpen at Terminal Nodes** in SLS or MSLS. If *OptionOpen* is specified as the Terminal Node equation, the value will always evaluate to *Not a Number* error (NaN). This is clearly a user error as *OptionOpen* cannot apply at the terminal nodes.

- **Unspecified interval of custom variables**. If a specified interval with a custom variable has no value, the value is assumed zero. For example, suppose a model exists with 10 steps where a custom variable *"myVar"* of value 5 starts at step 6 exists. This specification means *myVar* will be substituted with the value 5 from step 6 onwards. However, the model did not specify the value of *myVar* from steps 0 to 5. In this situation, the value of *myVar* is assumed to be 0 for steps 0 to 5.

- **Compatibility with SLS 1.0.** Super Lattice Solver 2014 has a user interface similar to the previous version with the exception that SLS, MSLS, MNLS, and Lattice Maker are all integrated into one Main Screen. The data files created in SLS 1.0 can be loaded in SLS. However, because SLS includes advanced features that do not exist in the previous version, the models created in SLS 1.0 may not run in SLS without some minor modifications. The following lists the differences between SLS 1.0 and SLS:

    o The "@@" variable in SLS 1.0 has been replaced by *"OptionOpen"* in SLS. Therefore, SLS still recognizes "@@" as a special variable and will automatically convert it to *"OptionOpen"* before it runs. Consequently, a potential problem exists because a model that defines "OptionOpen" as a custom variable will have errors as OptionOpen is now a special variable.

    o A model that uses advanced worksheet function in the custom equations will not work. Functions supported include:

        ▪ ABS, ACOS, ASIN, ATAN2, ATAN, CEILING, COS, COSH, EXP, FLOOR, LOG, MAX, MIN, REMAINDER, ROUND, SIN, SINH, SQRT, TAN, TANH, TRUNCATE, and IF

    o Variables in SLS are case sensitive except for function names. Models that mix and match cases will not work in SLS. Therefore, it is suggested that when using custom variables in SLS and MSLS, you are consistent with the use of case for the custom variable names.

- **AND() and OR() functions** are missing and are replaced with special characters in SLS. The "&" and " | " symbols represent the AND and OR operators. For example: "Asset > 0 | Cost < 0" means "OR(Asset > 0, Cost < 0)" while "Asset > 0 & Cost < 0" is "AND(Asset > 0, Cost < 0)."

- **Blackout Step Specifications**. To define the blackout steps, use the following examples as a guide:

    - 3   Step 3 is a blackout step.

    - 3, 5   Steps 3 and 5 are blackout steps.

- 3, 5-7   Steps 3, 5, 6, 7 are blackout steps.

- 1, 3, 5-6   Steps 1, 3, 5, 6 are blackout steps.

- 5-7   Steps 5, 6, 7 are blackout steps.

- 5-10|2   Steps 5, 7, 9 are blackout steps (the | symbol means skip size).

- 5-14|3   Steps 5, 8, 11, 14 are blackout steps.

- 5-6|3   Step 5 is a blackout step.

- 5 - 6 | 3   Step 5 is a blackout step (white spaces are ignored).

- **Identifiers**. An identifier is a sequence of characters that begins with a-z, A-Z, _ or $. After the first character, a-z, A-Z, 0-9, _, $ are valid characters in the sequence. Note that space is not a valid character. However, it can be used if the variable is enclosed in a pair of curly braces { }. Identifiers are case sensitive, except for function names. The following are some examples of valid identifiers: myVariable, MYVARIABLE, _myVariable, _____myVariable, $myVariable, {This is a single variable}.

- **Numbers**. A number can be an integer, defined as one or more characters between 0 and 9. The following are some examples of integers: 0, 1, 00000, 12345. Another type of number is a *real* number. The following are some examples of real numbers: 0., 3., 0.0, 0.1, 3.9, .5, .934, .3E3, 3.5E-5, 0.2E-4, 3.2E+2, 3.5e-5,

- **Operator Precedence**. The operator precedence when evaluating the equations is shown below. However, if there are two terms with two identical precedence operators, the expression is evaluated from left to right.

  - ( )   – Parenthesized expression has highest precedence
  - !, -   – Not, and unary minus, e.g., -3
  - ^
  - *, /
  - +, -
  - =, <>, !=, <, <=, >, >=
  - &, |

- **Mathematical Expression**. The following shows some examples of valid equations usable in the *custom equations* boxes. Review the rest of the user manual, recommended texts, and example files for more illustrations of actual options equations and functions used in SLS.

  - Max(Asset-Cost,0)
  - Max(Asset-Cost,OptionOpen)
  - 135
  - 12 + 24 * 12 + 24 * 36 / 48

- o   3 + ABS(-3)

- o   3*MAX(1,2,3,4) - MIN(1,2,3,4)

- o   SQRT(3) + ROUND(3) * LOG(12)

- o   IF(a > 0, 3, 4)   – returns 3 if a > 0, else 4

- o   ABS+3

- o   MAX(a + b, c, MIN(d,e), a > b)

- o   IF(a > 0 | b < 0, 3, 4)

- o   IF(c <> 0, 3, 4)

- o   IF(IF(a <= 3, 4, 5) <> 4, a, a-b)

- o   MAX({My Cost 1} - {My Cost 2}, {Asset 2} + {Asset 3})

This concludes a quick overview and tour of the software. You are now equipped to start using the SLS software in building and solving real options, financial options, and employee stock options problems. These applications are introduced starting the next section. However, it is highly recommended that you first review Dr. Johnathan Mun's *"Real Options Analysis: Tools and Techniques, Second Edition,"* (Wiley, 2006) for details on the theory and application of real options.

2

SECTION II: REAL OPTIONS ANALYSIS

2.1 American, European, Bermudan, and Customized Abandonment Options

The *Abandonment Option* looks at the value of a project's or asset's flexibility in being abandoned over the life of the option. As an example, suppose that a firm owns a project or asset and that based on traditional discounted cash flow (DCF) models, it estimates the present value of the asset (*PV Underlying Asset*) to be $120M (for the abandonment option this is the net present value of the project or asset). Monte Carlo simulation indicates that the *Volatility* of this asset value is significant, estimated at 25%. Under these conditions, there is a lot of uncertainty as to the success or failure of this project (the volatility calculated models the different sources of uncertainty and computes the risks in the discounted cash flow (DCF) model including price uncertainty, probability of success, competition, cannibalization, and so forth), and the value of the project might be significantly higher or significantly lower than the expected value of $120M. Suppose an abandonment option is created whereby a counterparty is found and a contract is signed that lasts 5 years (*Maturity*) such that for some monetary consideration now, the firm has the ability to sell the asset or project to the counterparty at any time within these 5 years (indicative of an American option) for a specified *Salvage* of $90M. The counterparty agrees to this $30M discount and signs the contract.

What has just occurred is that the firm bought itself a $90M insurance policy. That is, if the asset or project value increases above its current value, the firm may decide to continue funding the project, or sell it off in the market at the prevailing fair market value. Alternatively, if the value of the asset or project falls below the $90M threshold, the firm has the right to execute the option and sell off the asset to the counterparty at $90M. In other words, a safety net of sorts has been erected to prevent the value of the asset from falling below this salvage level. Thus, how much is this safety net or insurance policy worth? One can create competitive advantage in negotiation if the counterparty does not have the answer and you do. Further assume that the 5-year Treasury Note *Risk-Free Rate* (zero coupon) is 5% from the U.S. Department of Treasury[2]. The *American Abandonment Option* results in Figure 19 show a value of $125.48M, indicating that the option value is $5.48M as the present value of the asset is $120M. Hence, the **maximum** value one should be willing to pay for the contract on **average** is $5.48M. This resulting expected value weights the continuous probabilities that the asset value exceeds $90M versus when it does not (where the abandonment option is valuable). Also, it weights when the timing of executing the abandonment is optimal such that the expected value is $5.48M.

In addition, some experimentation can be conducted. Changing the salvage value to $30M (this means a $90M discount from the starting asset value) yields a result of $120M, or $0M for the option. This result means that the option or contract is worthless because the safety net is set so low that it will never be utilized. Conversely, setting the

---

[2] http://www.treas.gov/offices/domestic-finance/debt-management/interest-rate/yield-hist.html

salvage level to thrice the prevailing asset value or $360M would yield a result of $360M, and the results indicate $360M, which means that there is no option value, there is no value in waiting and having this option, or simply, execute the option immediately and sell the asset if someone is willing to pay three times the value of the project right now. Thus, you can keep changing the salvage value until the option value disappears, indicating the *optimal trigger value* has been reached. For instance, if you enter $166.80 as the salvage value, the abandonment option analysis yields a result of $166.80, indicating that at this price and above, the optimal decision is to sell the asset immediately. At any lower salvage value, there is option value, and at any higher salvage value, there will be no option value. This breakeven salvage point is the optimal trigger value. Once the market price of this asset exceeds this value, it is optimal to abandon. Finally, adding a *Dividend Rate*, the **cost of waiting before abandoning the asset** (e.g., the annualized taxes and maintenance fees that have to be paid if you keep the asset and not sell it off, measured as a percentage of the present value of the asset) will decrease the option value. Hence, the breakeven trigger point, where the option becomes worthless, can be calculated by successively choosing higher dividend levels. This breakeven point again illustrates the trigger value at which the option should be optimally executed immediately, but this time with respect to a dividend yield. That is, if the **cost of carry** or holding on to the option, or the option's **leakage value** is high, that is, if the **cost of waiting** is too high, don't wait and execute the option immediately.

Other applications of the abandonment option include buy-back lease provisions in a contract (guaranteeing a specified asset value); asset preservation flexibility; insurance policies; walking away from a project and selling off its intellectual property; purchase price of an acquisition; and so forth. To illustrate, here are some additional quick examples of the abandonment option (and sample exercises for the rest of us):

- An aircraft manufacturer sells its planes of a particular model in the *primary* market for say $30M each to various airline companies. Airlines are usually risk-adverse and may find it hard to justify buying an additional plane with all the uncertainties in the economy, demand, price competition, and fuel costs. When uncertainties become resolved over time, airline carriers may have to reallocate and reroute their existing portfolio of planes globally, and an excess plane on the tarmac is very costly. The airline can sell the excess plane in the *secondary* market where smaller regional carriers buy used planes, but the price uncertainty is very high and is subject to significant volatility, of say, 45%, and may fluctuate wildly between $10M and $25M for this class of aircraft. The aircraft manufacturer can reduce the airline's risk by providing a *buy-back provision* or abandonment option, where at anytime within the next five years, the manufacturer agrees to buy back the plane at a guaranteed residual salvage price of $20M, at the request of the airline. The corresponding risk-free rate for the next five years is 5%. **This reduces the downside risk of the airline, and hence reduces its risk, chopping off the left tail of the price fluctuation distribution, and shifting the expected value to the right. This abandonment option provides risk reduction and value enhancement to the airline.** *Applying the abandonment option in SLS using a 100-step binomial lattice, this option is worth $3.52M. If the airline is the smarter counterparty and calculates this* *value and gets this buy-back provision for free as part of the deal, the aircraft manufacturer has just lost over 10% of its aircraft value that it left on the negotiation table. Information and knowledge is highly valuable in this case.*

- A high-tech disk-drive manufacturer is thinking of acquiring a small startup firm with a new micro drive technology (a super-fast and high-capacity pocket hard drive) that may revolutionize the industry. The startup is for sale and its asking price is $50M based on an NPV fair market value analysis some third-party valuation consultants have performed. The manufacturer can either develop the technology themselves or acquire this technology through the purchase of the firm. The question is, how much is this firm worth to the manufacturer, and is $50M a good price? Based on internal analysis by the manufacturer, the NPV of this micro drive is expected to be $45M, with a cash flow volatility of 40%, and it would take another 3 years before the micro drive technology is successful and goes to market. Assume that the 3-year risk-free rate is 5%. In addition, it would cost the manufacturer $45M in present value to develop this drive internally. If using an NPV analysis, the manufacturer should build it themselves. However, if you include an abandonment option analysis whereby if this specific micro drive does not work, the startup still has an abundance of intellectual property (patents and proprietary technologies) as well as physical assets (buildings and manufacturing facilities) that can be sold in the market at up to $40M. *The abandonment option together with the NPV yields $51.83, making buying the startup worth more than developing the technology internally, and making the purchase price of $50M worth it.*[3]

Figure 19 shows the results of a simple abandonment option with a 10-step lattice as discussed previously, while Figure 20 shows the audit sheet that is generated from this analysis.

Figure 21 shows the same abandonment option but with a 100-step lattice. To follow along, open the Single Asset SLS example file *Abandonment American Option*. Notice that the 10-step lattice yields $125.48 while the 100-step lattice yields $125.45, indicating that the lattice results have achieved convergence. The Terminal Node Equation is *Max(Asset,Salvage)* which means the decision at maturity is to decide if the option should be executed, selling the asset and receiving the salvage value, or not to execute, holding on to the asset. The Intermediate Node Equation used is *Max(Salvage,OptionOpen)* indicating that before maturity, the decision is either to execute early in this American option to abandon and receive the salvage value, or to hold on to the asset, and hence, hold on to and keeping the option open for potential future execution, denoted simply as *OptionOpen*. Figure 22 shows the European version of the abandonment option, where the Intermediate Node Equation is simply *OptionOpen*, as early execution is prohibited before maturity. Of course being only able to execute the option at maturity is worth less ($124.5054 compared to $125.4582) than being able to exercise earlier. The example files used are: *Abandonment American Option* and *Abandonment European Option*.

---

[3] See the section on Expansion Option for more examples on how this startup's technology can be used as a platform to further develop newer technologies that can be worth a lot more than just the abandonment option.

For example, the airline manufacturer in the previous case example can agree to a buy-back provision that can be exercised at any time by the airline customer versus only at a specific date at the end of five years—the former American option will clearly be worth more than the latter European option.

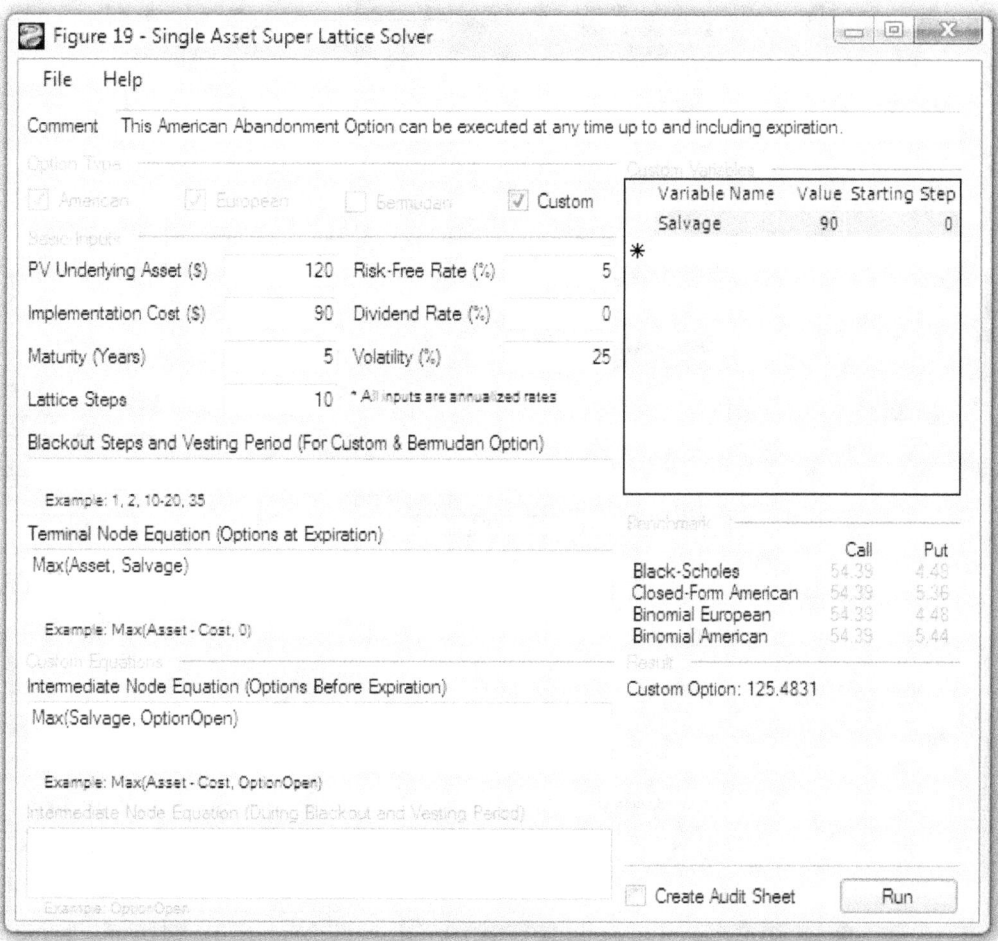

Figure 19 – Simple American Abandonment Option

Option Valuation Audit Sheet

Assumptions

PV Asset Value ($)	$120.00
Implementation Cost ($)	$90.00
Maturity (Years)	5.00
Risk-free Rate (%)	5.00%
Dividends (%)	0.00%
Volatility (%)	25.00%
Lattice Steps	10
Option Type	Custom

Intermediate Computations

Stepping Time (dt)	0.5000
Up Step Size (up)	1.1934
Down Step Size (down)	0.8380
Risk-neutral Probability	0.5272

Results

Auditing Lattice Result (10 steps)	$125.48
Super Lattice Result (10 steps)	$125.48

User-Defined Inputs

Terminal: Max(Asset, Salvage)
Intermediate: Max(Salvage, @@)

Name	salvage									
Value	90.00									
Starting Step	0									

Underlying Asset Lattice

										702.93
									589.03	
								493.59		493.59
							413.61		413.61	
						346.59		346.59		346.59
					290.43		290.43		290.43	
				243.37		243.37		243.37		243.37
			203.94		203.94		203.94		203.94	
		170.89		170.89		170.89		170.89		170.89
	143.20		143.20		143.20		143.20		143.20	
120.00		120.00		120.00		120.00		120.00		120.00
	100.56		100.56		100.56		100.56		100.56	
		84.26		84.26		84.26		84.26		84.26
			70.61		70.61		70.61		70.61	
				59.17		59.17		59.17		59.17
					49.58		49.58		49.58	
						41.55		41.55		41.55
							34.82		34.82	
								29.17		29.17
									24.45	
										20.49

Option Valuation Lattice

										702.93
									589.03	
								493.59		493.59
							413.61		413.61	
						346.59		346.59		346.59
					290.43		290.43		290.43	
				243.43		243.37		243.37		243.37
			204.30		204.06		203.94		203.94	
		172.07		171.61		171.15		170.89		170.89
	146.01		145.36		144.61		143.77		143.20	
125.48		124.77		123.88		122.77		121.22		120.00
	109.32		108.49		107.41		105.93		103.20	
		97.95		97.13		96.03		94.57		90.00
			91.44		90.88		90.13		90.00	
				90.00		90.00		90.00		90.00
					90.00		90.00		90.00	
						90.00		90.00		90.00
							90.00		90.00	
								90.00		90.00
									90.00	
										90.00

Figure 20 – Audit Sheet for the Abandonment Option

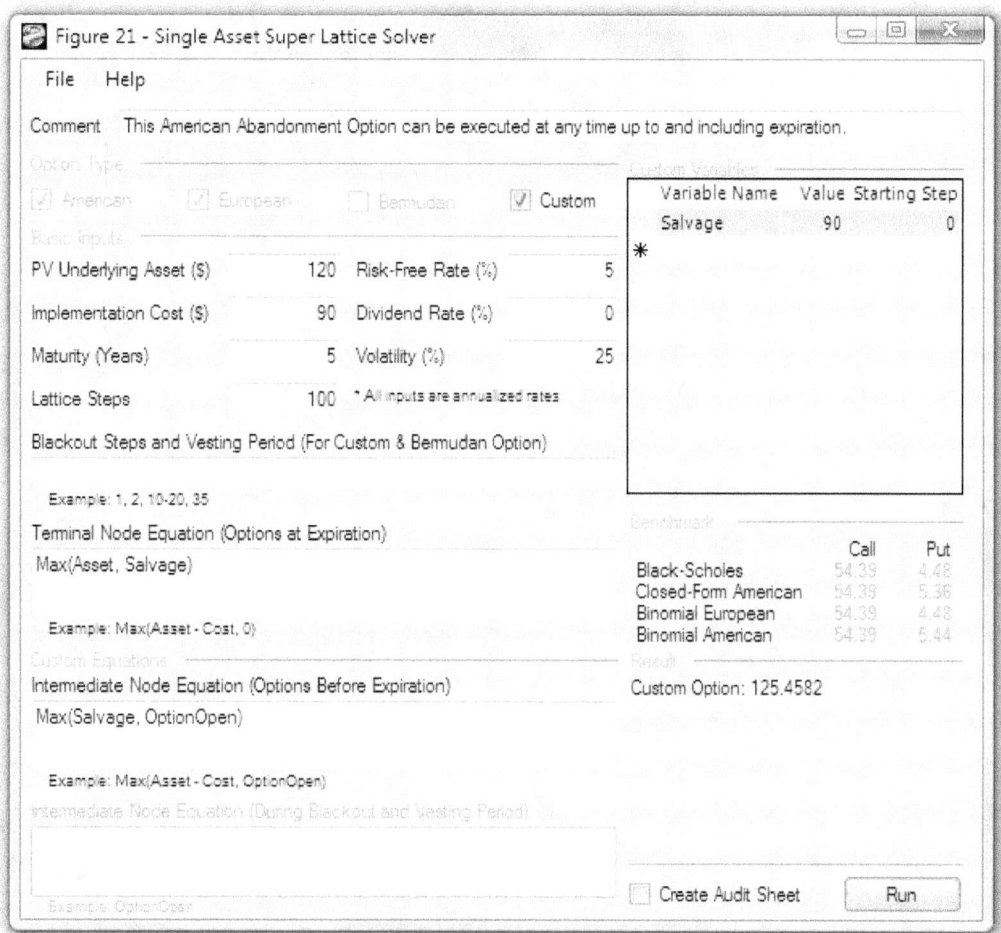

Figure 21 – American Abandonment Option with 100-Step Lattice

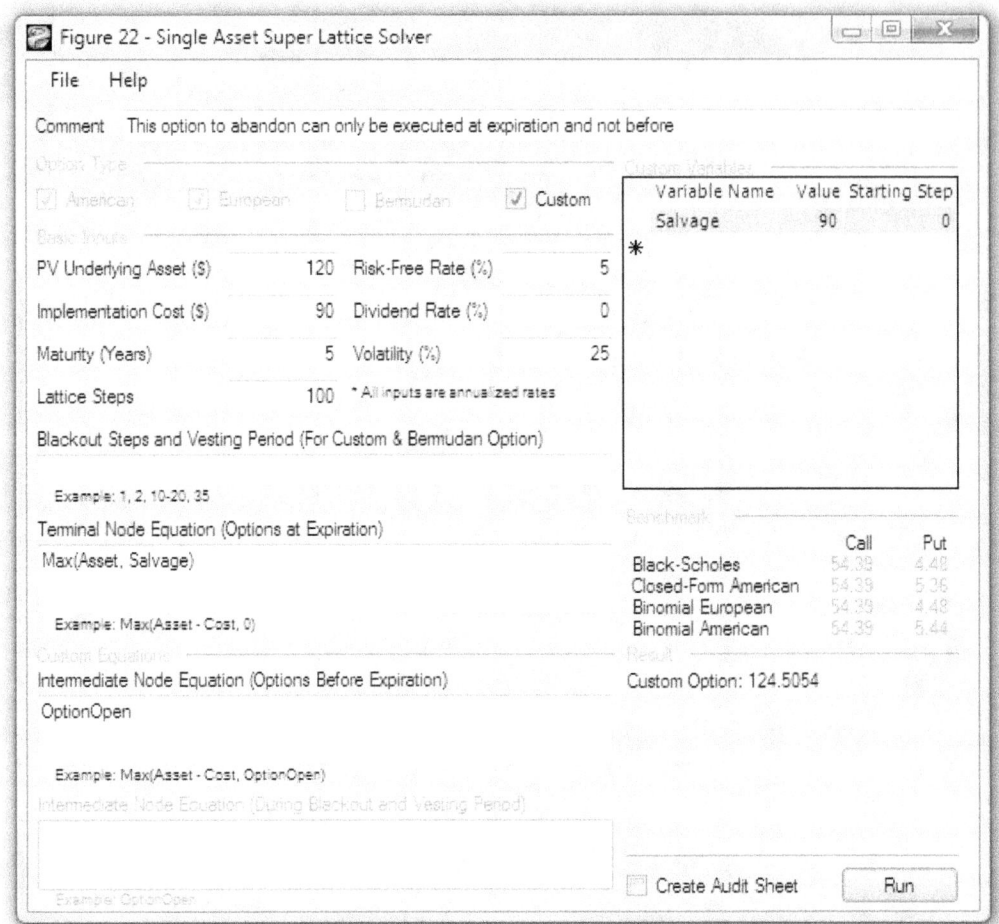

Figure 22 – European Abandonment Option with 100-Step Lattice

Sometimes, a Bermudan option is appropriate, where there might be a vesting period or blackout period when the option cannot be executed. For instance, if the contract stipulates that for the 5-year abandonment buy-back contract, the airline customer cannot execute the abandonment option within the first 2.5 years. This is shown in Figure 23 using a Bermudan option with a 100-step lattice on 5 years, where the blackout steps are from 0-50. This means that during the first 50 steps (as well as right now or step 0), the option cannot be executed. This is modeled by inserting *OptionOpen* into the Intermediate Node Equation During Blackout and Vesting Periods. This forces the option holder to only keep the option open during the vesting period, preventing execution during this blackout period.

You can see that the American option is worth more than the Bermudan option, which is worth more than the European option in Figure 23, by virtue of each option type's ability to execute early and the frequency of execution possibilities.

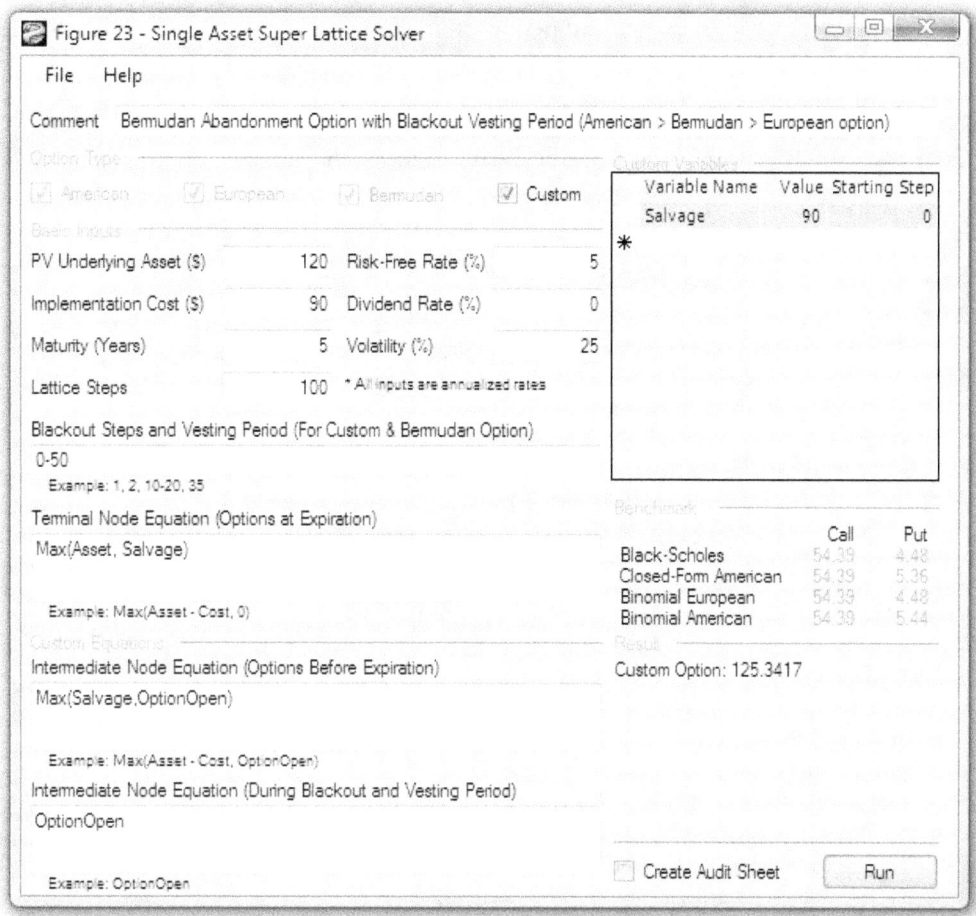

Figure 23 – Bermudan Abandonment Option with 100-Step Lattice

Sometimes, the salvage value of the abandonment option may change over time. To illustrate, in the previous example of an acquisition of a startup firm, the intellectual property will most probably increase over time because of continued research and development activities, thereby changing the salvage values over time. An example is seen in Figure 24, where there are five salvage values over the 5-year abandonment option. This can be modeled by using the Custom Variables. Type in the *Variable Name*, *Value*, and *Starting Step* and hit *ENTER* to input the variables one at a time as seen in Figure 24's Custom Variables list. Notice that the same variable name (*Salvage*) is used but the values change over time, and the starting steps represent when these different values become effective. For instance, the salvage value $90 applies at step 0 until the next salvage value of $95 takes over at step 21. This means that for a 5-year option with a 100-step lattice, the first year including the current period (steps 0 to 20) will have a salvage value of $90, which then increases to $95 in the second year (steps 21 to 40), and so forth. Notice that as the value of the firm's intellectual property increases over time, the option valuation results also increase, which makes logical sense. You can also model in blackout vesting periods for the first 6 months (steps 0-10 in the blackout area). The blackout period is very typical of contractual obligations of abandonment options where during specified periods, the option cannot be executed (a cooling-off period).

Note that you may use *TAB* on the keyboard to move from the variable name column to the value column, and on to the starting step column. However, remember to hit *ENTER* on the keyboard to insert the variable and to create a new row so that you may enter a new variable.

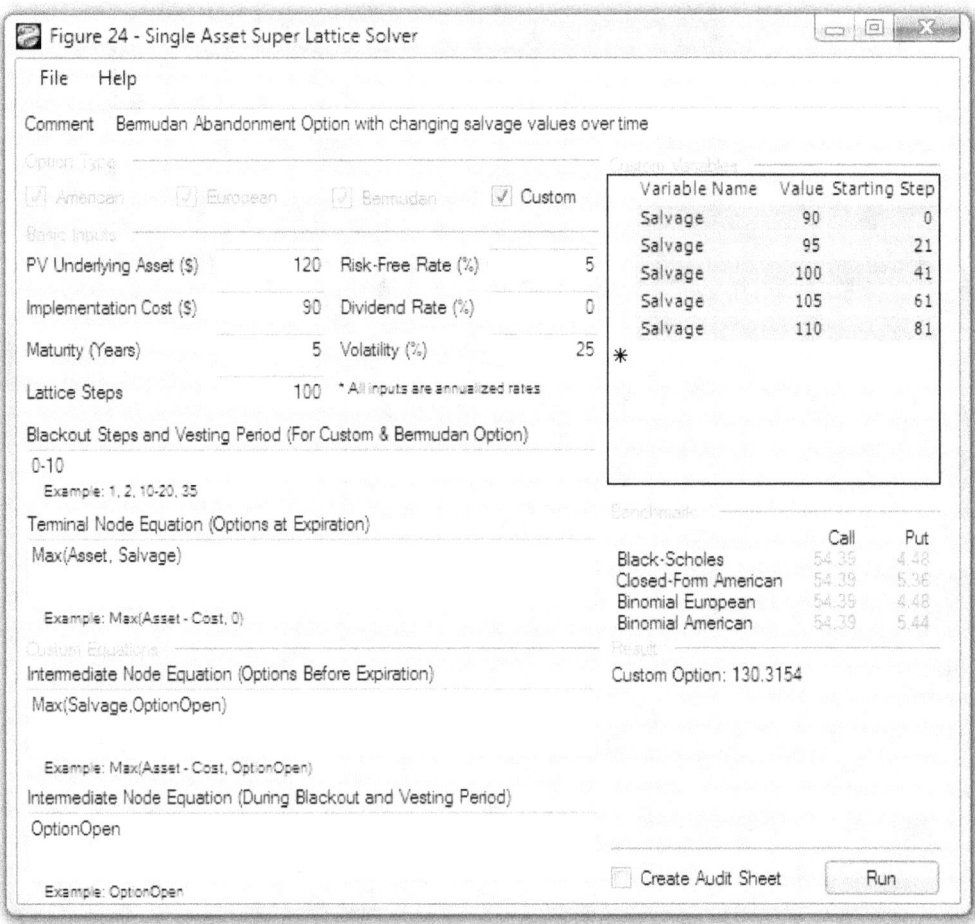

Figure 24 – Customized Abandonment Option

2.2 American, European, Bermudan, and Customized Contraction Options

A *Contraction Option* evaluates the flexibility value of being able to reduce production output or to contract the scale and scope of a project when conditions are not as amenable, thereby reducing the value of the asset or project by a *Contraction Factor*, but at the same time creating some cost *Savings*. As an example, suppose you work for a large aeronautical manufacturing firm that is unsure of the technological efficacy and market demand for its new fleet of long-range supersonic jets. The firm decides to hedge itself through the use of strategic options, specifically an option to contract 10% of its manufacturing facilities at any time within the next 5 years (i.e., the *Contraction Factor* is 0.9).

Suppose that the firm has a current operating structure whose static valuation of future profitability using a discounted cash flow model (in other words, the present value of the expected future cash flows discounted at an appropriate market risk-adjusted discount rate) is found to be $1,000M (*PV Asset*). Using Monte Carlo simulation, you calculate the implied volatility of the logarithmic returns of the asset value of the projected future cash flows to be 30%. The risk-free rate on a riskless asset (5-year U.S. Treasury Note with zero coupons) is found to be yielding 5%.

Further, suppose the firm has the option to contract 10% of its current operations at any time over the next 5 years, thereby creating an additional $50 million in savings after this contraction. These terms are arranged through a legal contractual agreement with one of its vendors, who had agreed to take up the excess capacity and space of the firm. At the same time, the firm can scale back and lay off part of its existing workforce to obtain this level of savings (in present values).

The results indicate that the strategic value of the project is $1,001.71M (using a 10-step lattice as seen in Figure 25), which means that the NPV currently is $1,000M and the additional $1.71M comes from this contraction option. This result is obtained because contracting now yields 90% of $1,000M + $50M, or $950M, which is less than staying in business and not contracting and obtaining $1,000M. Therefore, the optimal decision is to not contract immediately but keep the ability to do so open for the future. Hence, in comparing this optimal decision of $1,000M to $1,001.71M of being able to contract, the option to contract is worth $1.71M. This should be the maximum amount the firm is willing to spend to obtain this option (contractual fees and payments to the vendor counterparty).

In contrast, if *Savings* were $200M instead, then the strategic project value becomes $1,100M, which means that starting at $1,000M and contracting 10% to $900M and keeping the $200 in savings, yields $1,100M in total value. Hence, the additional option value is $0M which means that it is optimal to execute the contraction option immediately as there is no option value and no value to wait to contract. So, the value of executing now is $1,100M as compared to the strategic project value of $1,100M; there is no additional option value, and the contraction should be executed immediately. That is, instead of asking the vendor to wait, the firm is better off executing the contraction option now and capturing the savings.

Other applications include shelving an R&D project by spending a little to keep it going but reserving the right to come back to it should conditions improve; the value of synergy in a merger and acquisition where some management personnel are let go to create the additional savings; reducing the scope and size of a production facility; reducing production rates; a joint venture or alliance, and so forth. To illustrate, here are some additional quick examples of the contraction option (as before, providing some additional sample exercises for the rest of us):

- A large oil and gas company is embarking on a deep-sea drilling platform that will cost the company billions to implement. A DCF analysis is run and the NPV is found to be $500M over the next 10 years of economic life of the offshore rig. The 10-year risk-free rate is 5%, and the volatility of the project is found to be at an annualized 45% using historical oil prices as a proxy. If the expedition is highly successful (oil prices are high and production rates are soaring), then the company will continue its operations. However, if things are not looking too good (oil prices are low or moderate and production is only decent), it is very difficult for the company to abandon operations (why lose everything when net income is still positive although not as high as anticipated and not to mention the environmental and legal ramifications of simply abandoning an oil rig in the middle of the ocean). Hence, the oil company decides to hedge its downside risk through an American Contraction Option. The oil company was able to find a smaller oil and gas company (a former partner on other explorations) to be interested in a joint venture. The joint venture is structured such that the oil company pays this smaller counterparty a lump sum right now for a 10-year contract whereby at any time and at the oil company's request, the smaller counterparty will have to take over all operations of the offshore oil rig (i.e., taking over all operations and hence all relevant expenses) and keep 30% of the net revenues generated. The counterparty is in agreement because it does not have to partake in the billions of dollars required to implement the rig in the first place, and it actually obtains some cash up front for this contract to assume the downside risk. The oil company is also in agreement because it reduces its own risks if oil prices are low and production is not up to par, and it ends up saving over $75M in present value of total overhead expenses, which can then be reallocated and invested somewhere else. *In this example, the contraction option using a 100-step lattice is valued to be $14.24M using SLS. This means that the maximum amount that the counterparty should be paid should not exceed this amount. Of course the option analysis can be further complicated by analyzing the actual savings on a present value basis. For instance, if the option is exercised within the first 5 years, the savings is $75M but if exercised during the last 5 years then the savings is only $50M. The revised option value is now $10.57M.*

- A manufacturing firm is interested in outsourcing its manufacturing of children's toys to a small province in China. By doing so, it will produce overhead savings of over $20M in present value over the economic life of the toys. However, outsourcing this internationally will mean lower quality control, delayed shipping problems, added importing costs, and assuming the added risks of unfamiliarity with the local business practices. In addition, the firm will only consider outsourcing only if the quality of the workmanship in this Chinese firm is up to the stringent quality standards it requires. The NPV of this particular line of toys is $100M with a 25% volatility. The firm's executives decide to purchase a contraction option by locating a small manufacturing firm in China, spending some resources to try out a *small-scale proof of concept* (thereby reducing the uncertainties of quality, knowledge, import-export issues, and so forth). If successful, the firm will agree to give this small Chinese manufacturer 20% of its net income as remuneration for their services, plus some startup fees. The question is, how much is this option to contract worth, that is, how much should the firm be willing to pay, on average, to cover the initial startup fees plus the costs of this proof of concept stage? *A contraction option valuation result using SLS shows that the option is worth $1.59M, assuming a 5% risk-free rate for the 1-year test period. So, as long as the total costs for a pilot test costs less than $1.59, it is optimal to obtain this option, especially if it means potentially being able to save over $20M.*

Figure 25 illustrates a simple 10-step Contraction Option while Figure 26 shows the same option using 100 lattice steps (example file used is *Contraction American and European Option*). Figure 27 illustrates a 5-year Bermudan Contraction Option with a 4-year vesting period (blackout steps of 0 to 80 out of a 5-year, 100-step lattice) where for the first 4 years, the option holder can only keep the option open and not execute the option (example file used is *Contraction Bermudan Option*). Figure 28 shows a customized option where there is a blackout period and the savings from contracting change over time (example file used is *Contraction Customized Option*). These results are for the aeronautical manufacturing example.

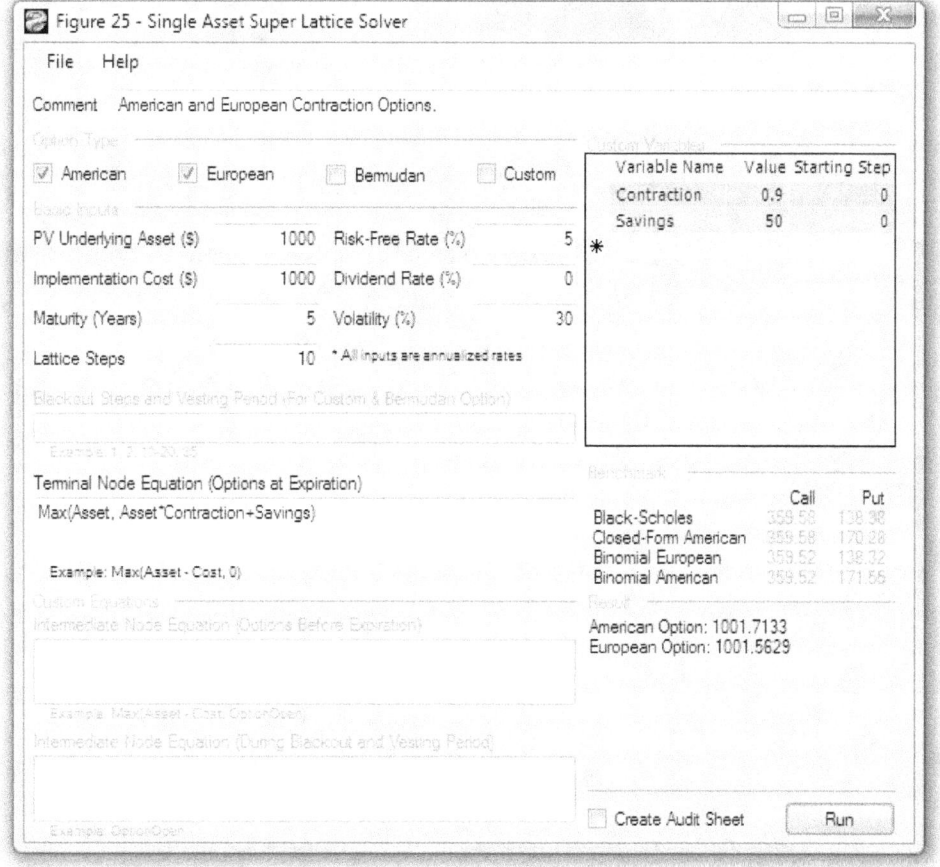

Figure 25 – A Simple American and European Options to Contract with 10-Step Lattice

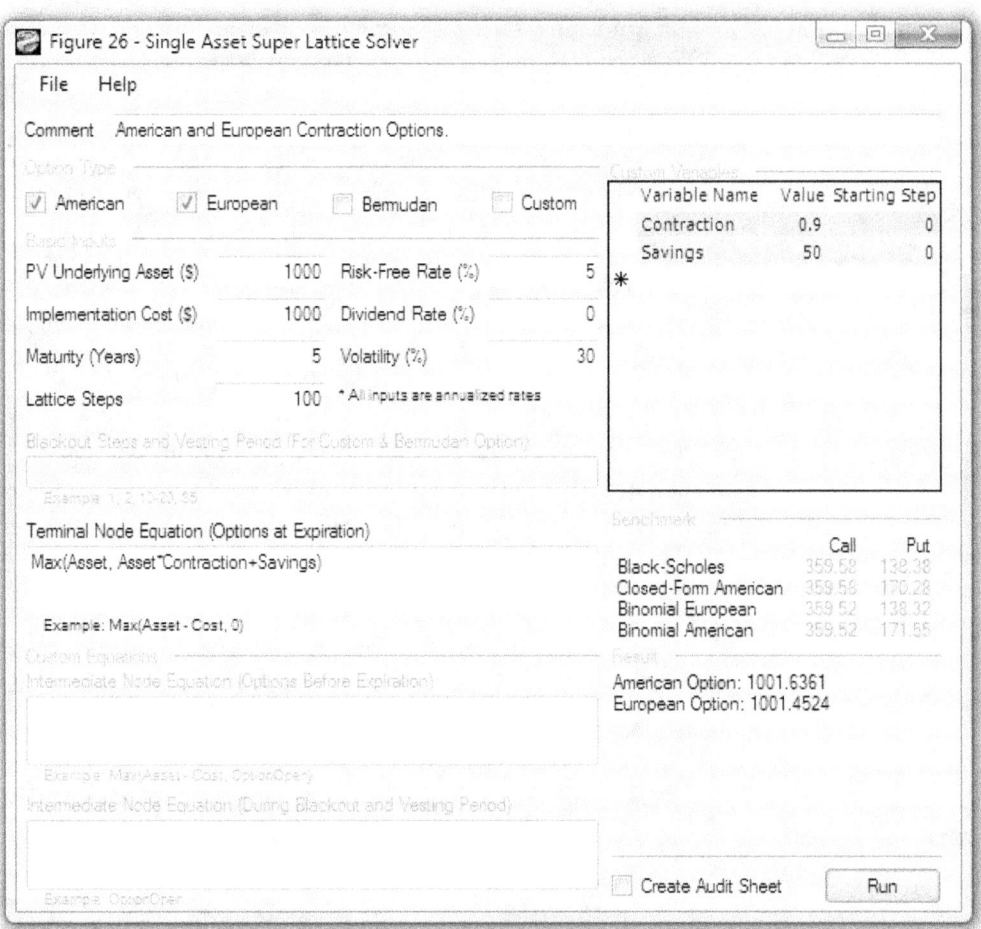

Figure 26 – American and European Options to Contract with a 100-Step Lattice

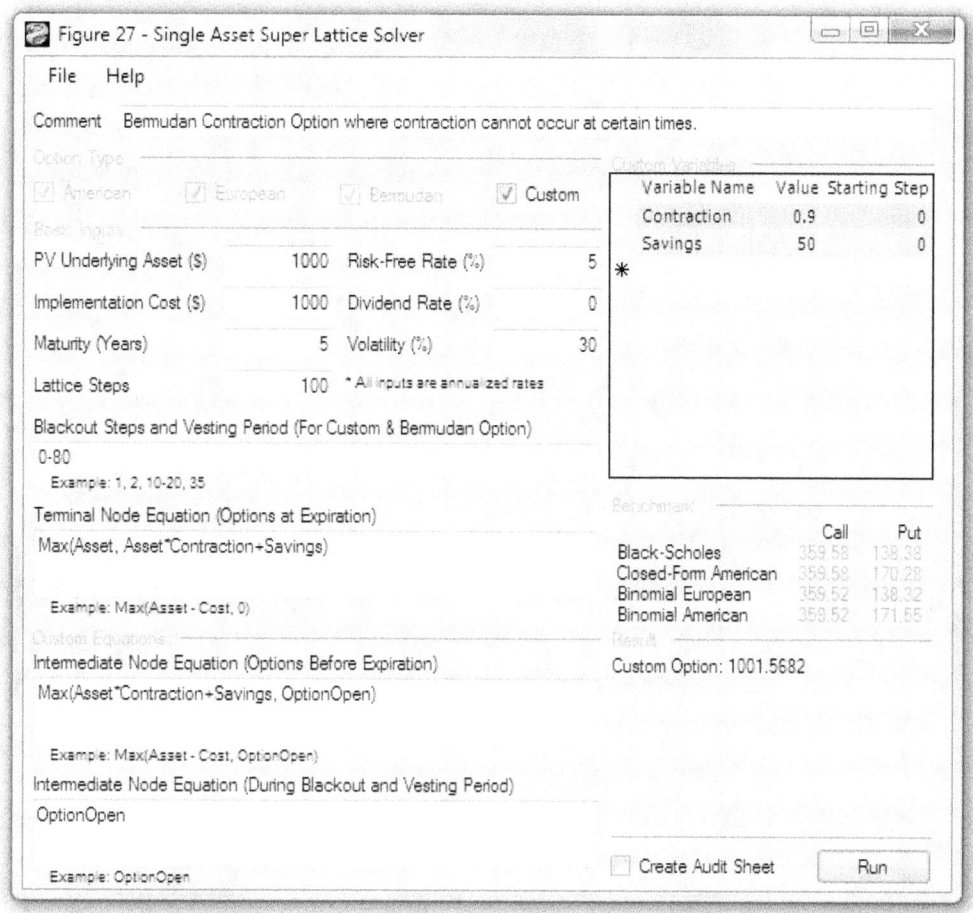

Figure 27 – A Bermudan Option to Contract with Blackout Vesting Periods

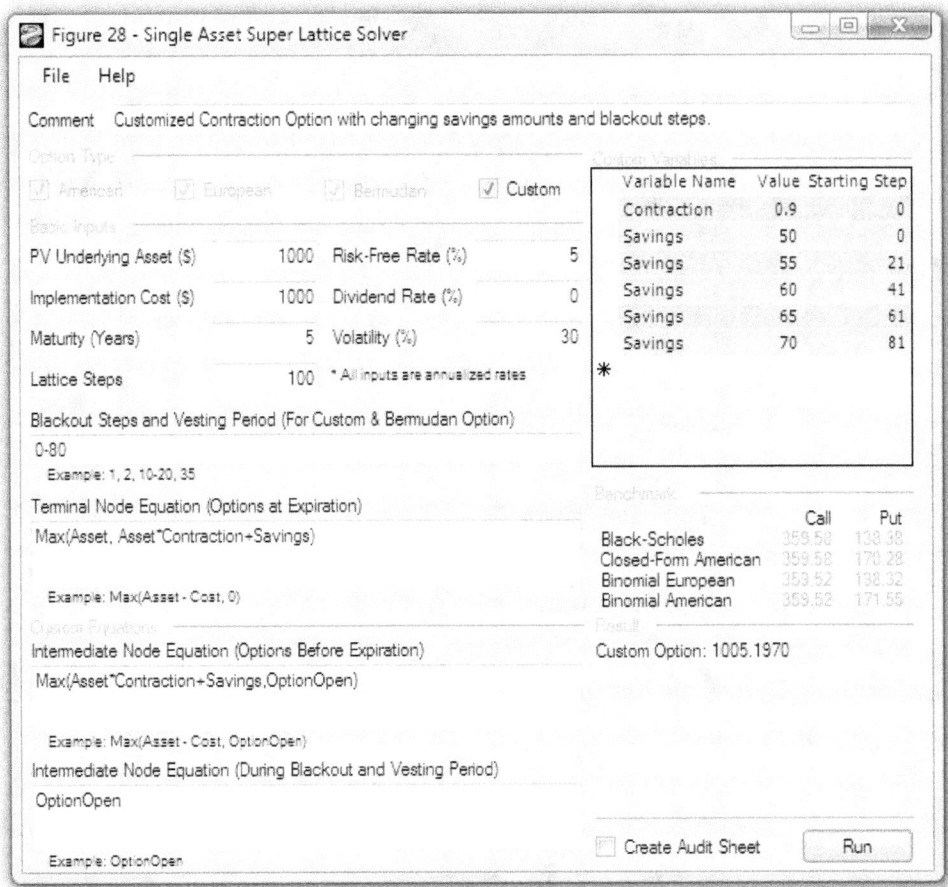

Figure 28 – A Customized Option to Contract with Changing Savings

2.3 American, European, Bermudan, and Customized Expansion Options

The *Expansion Option* values the flexibility to expand from a current existing state to a larger or expanded state. Therefore, an existing state or condition must first be present in order to use the expansion option. That is, there must be a base case to expand upon. If there is no base case state, then the simple *Execution Option* (calculated using the simple *Call Option*) is more appropriate, where the issue at hand is whether or not to execute a project immediately or to defer execution.

As an example, suppose a growth firm has a static valuation of future profitability using a discounted cash flow model (in other words, the present value of the expected future cash flows discounted at an appropriate market risk-adjusted discount rate) that is found to be $400 million (*PV Asset*). Using Monte Carlo simulation, you calculate the implied *Volatility* of the logarithmic returns on the assets based on the projected future cash flows to be 35%. The *Risk-Free Rate* on a riskless asset (5-year U.S. Treasury Note with zero coupons) for the next 5 years is found to be 7%.

Further suppose that the firm has the option to expand and double its operations by acquiring its competitor for a sum of $250 million (*Implementation Cost*) at any time over the next 5 years (*Maturity*). What is the total value of this firm, assuming that you account for this expansion option? The results in Figure 29 indicate that the strategic project value is $638.73 M (using a 10-step lattice), which means that the expansion option value is $88.73M. This result is obtained because the net present value of executing immediately is $400M x 2 – $250M, or $550M. Thus, $638.73 M less $550M is $88.73M, the value of the ability to *defer* and to wait and see before executing the expansion option. The example file used is *Expansion American and European Option*.

Increase the dividend rate to say 2% and notice that both the American and European Expansion Options are now worth less, and that the American Expansion Option is worth more than the European Expansion Option by virtue of the American Option's ability for early execution (Figure 30). The dividend rate implies that the cost of waiting to expand, to defer and not execute, the opportunity cost of waiting on executing the option, and the cost of holding the option, is high, then the ability to defer reduces. In addition, increase the *Dividend Rate* to 4.9% and see that the binomial lattice's Custom Option result reverts to $550, (the static, expand-now scenario), indicating that the option is worthless (Figure 31). This result means if the cost-of-waiting as a proportion of the asset value (as measured by the dividend rate) is too high, then execute now and stop wasting time deferring the expansion decision! Of course this decision can be reversed if the volatility is significant enough to compensate for the cost of waiting. That is, it might be worth something to wait and see if the uncertainty is too high even if the cost to wait is high.

Other applications of this option simply abound! To illustrate, here are some additional quick examples of the contraction option (as before, providing some additional sample exercises):

- Suppose a pharmaceutical firm is thinking of developing a new type of insulin that can be inhaled and the drug will directly be absorbed into the blood stream. A novel and honorable idea. Imagine what this means to diabetics who no longer need painful and frequent injections. The problem is, this new type of insulin requires a brand new development effort but if the uncertainties of the market, competition, drug development, and FDA approval are high, perhaps a base insulin drug that can be ingested is first developed. The ingestible version is a required precursor to the inhaled version. The pharmaceutical firm can decide to either take the risk and fast track development into the inhaled version or buy an option to defer, to first wait and see if the ingestible version works. If this precursor works, then the firm has the option to expand into the inhaled version. How much should the firm be willing to spend on performing additional tests on the precursor and under what circumstances should the inhaled version be implemented directly? Suppose the intermediate precursor development work yields an NPV of $100M, but at any time within the next 2 years, an additional $50M can be further invested into the precursor to develop it into the inhaled version, which will triple the NPV. However, after modeling the risk of technical success and uncertainties in the market (competitive threats, sales, and pricing structure), the annualized volatility of the cash flows using the logarithmic present value returns approach comes to 45%. Suppose the risk-free rate is 5% for the 2-year period. *Using the SLS, the analysis results yields $254.95M, indicating that the option value to wait and defer is worth over $4.95M after accounting for the $250M NPV if executing now. In playing with several scenarios, the breakeven point is found when dividend yield is 1.34%. This means that if the cost of waiting (lost net revenues in sales by pursuing the smaller market rather than the larger market, and loss of market share by delaying) exceeds $1.34M per year, then it is not optimal to wait and the pharmaceutical firm should engage in the inhaled version immediately. The loss in returns generated each year does not sufficiently cover the risks incurred.*

- An oil and gas company is currently deciding on a deep-sea exploration and drilling project. The platform provides an expected NPV of $1,000M. This project is wrought with risks (price of oil and production rate are both uncertain) and the annualized volatility is computed to be 55%. The firm is thinking of purchasing an expansion option by spending an additional $10M to build a slightly larger platform that it does not currently need, but if the price of oil is high, or when production rate is low, the firm can execute this expansion option and execute additional drilling to obtain more oil to sell at the higher price, which will cost another $50M, thereby increasing the NPV by 20%. The economic life of this platform is 10 years and the risk-free rate for the corresponding term is 5%. Is obtaining this slightly larger platform worth it? *Using the SLS, the option value is worth $27.12M when applying a 100-step lattice. Therefore, the option cost of $10M is worth it. However, this expansion option will not be worth it if annual dividends exceed 0.75% or $7.5M a year—this is the annual net revenues lost by waiting and not drilling as a percentage of the base case NPV.*

Figure 32 shows a Bermudan Expansion Option with certain vesting and blackout steps, while Figure 33 shows a Customized Expansion Option to account for the expansion factor changing over time. Of course other flavors of customizing the expansion option exist, including changing the implementation cost to expand, and so forth.

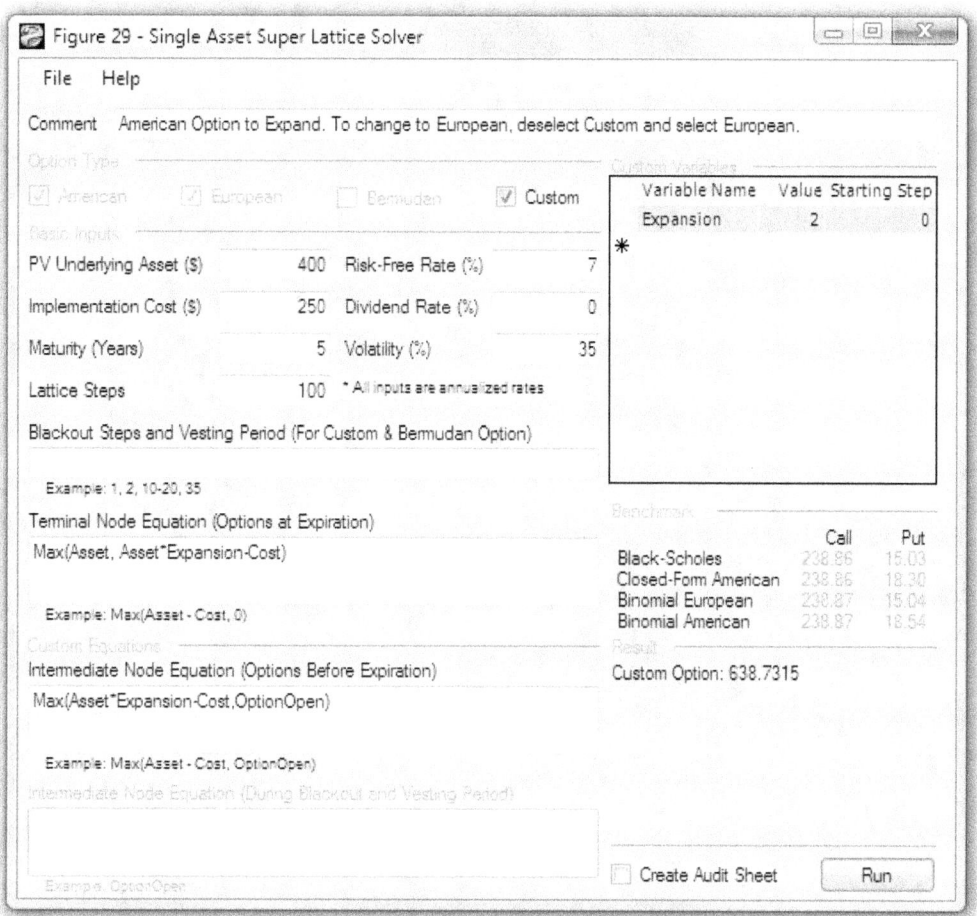

Figure 29 – American and European Options to Expand with a 100-Step Lattice

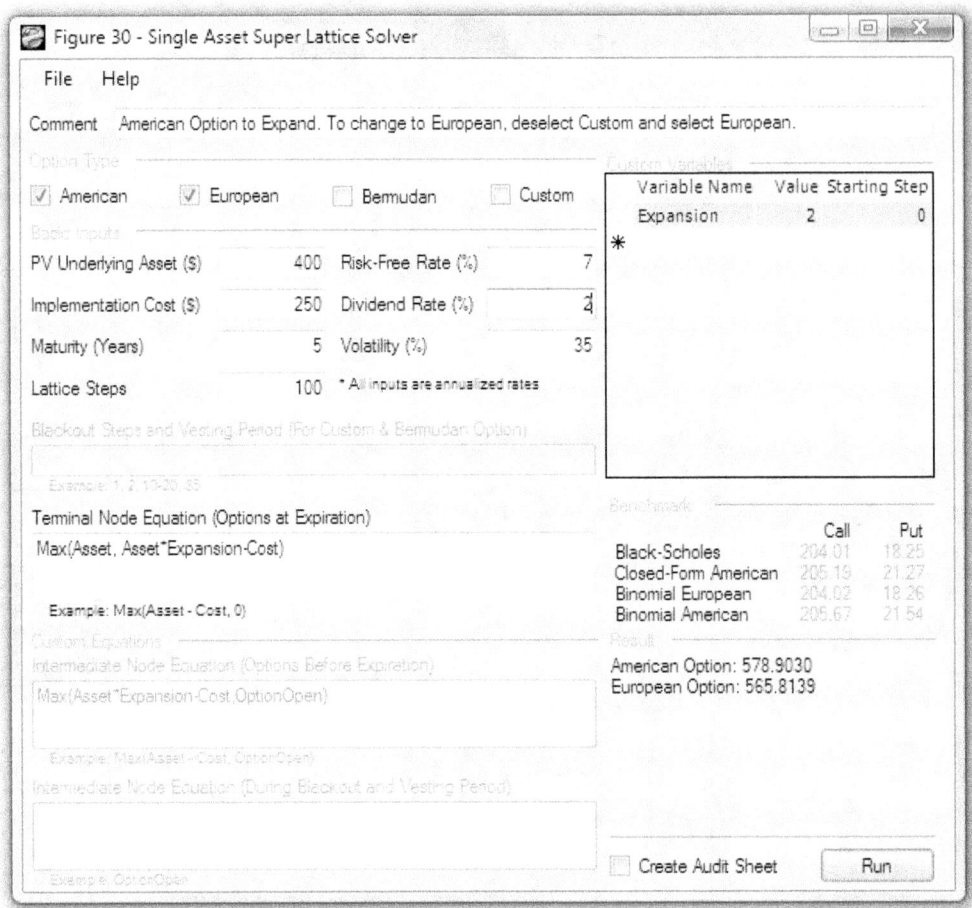

Figure 30 – American and European Options to Expand with a Dividend Rate

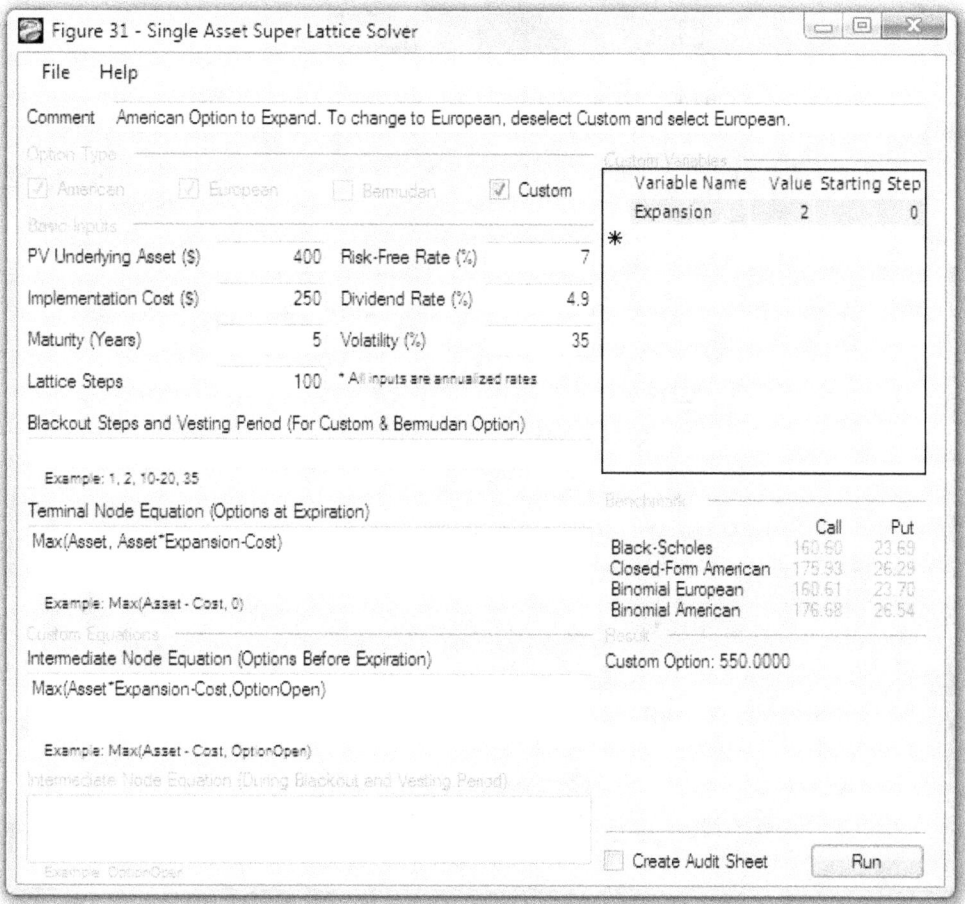

Figure 31 – Dividend Rate Optimal Trigger Value

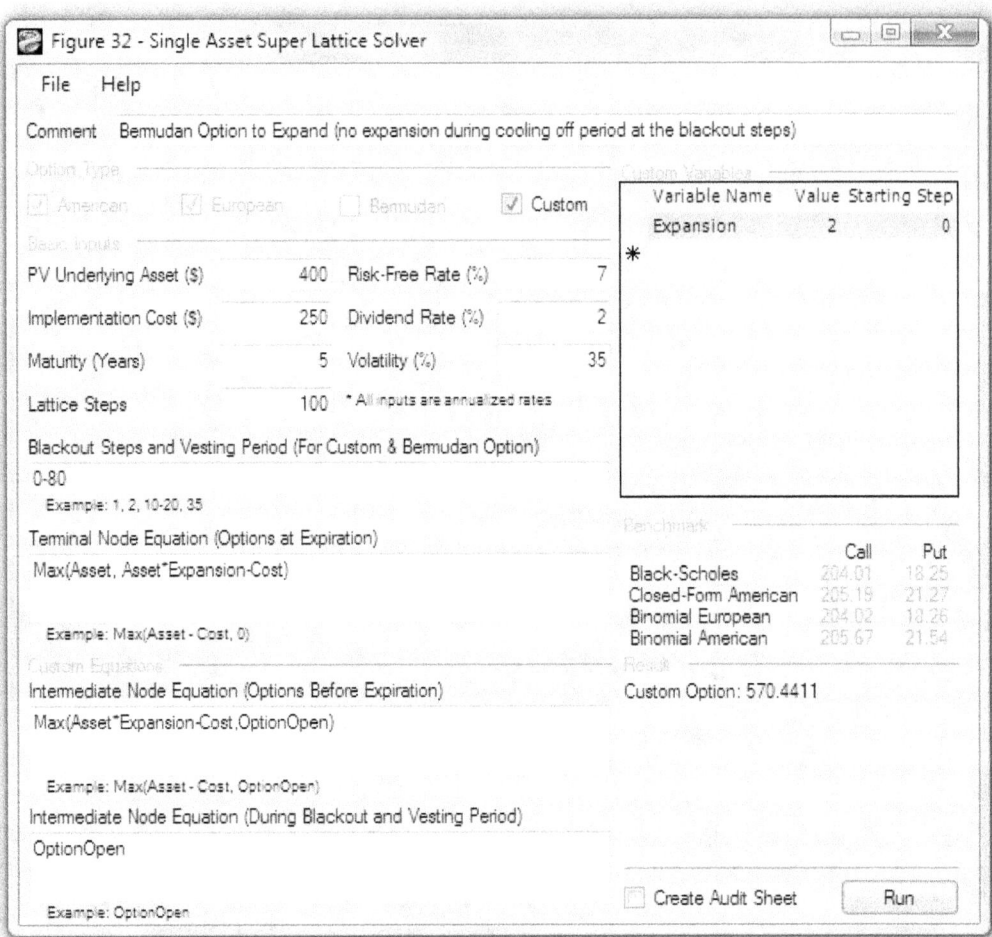

Figure 32 – Bermudan Expansion Option

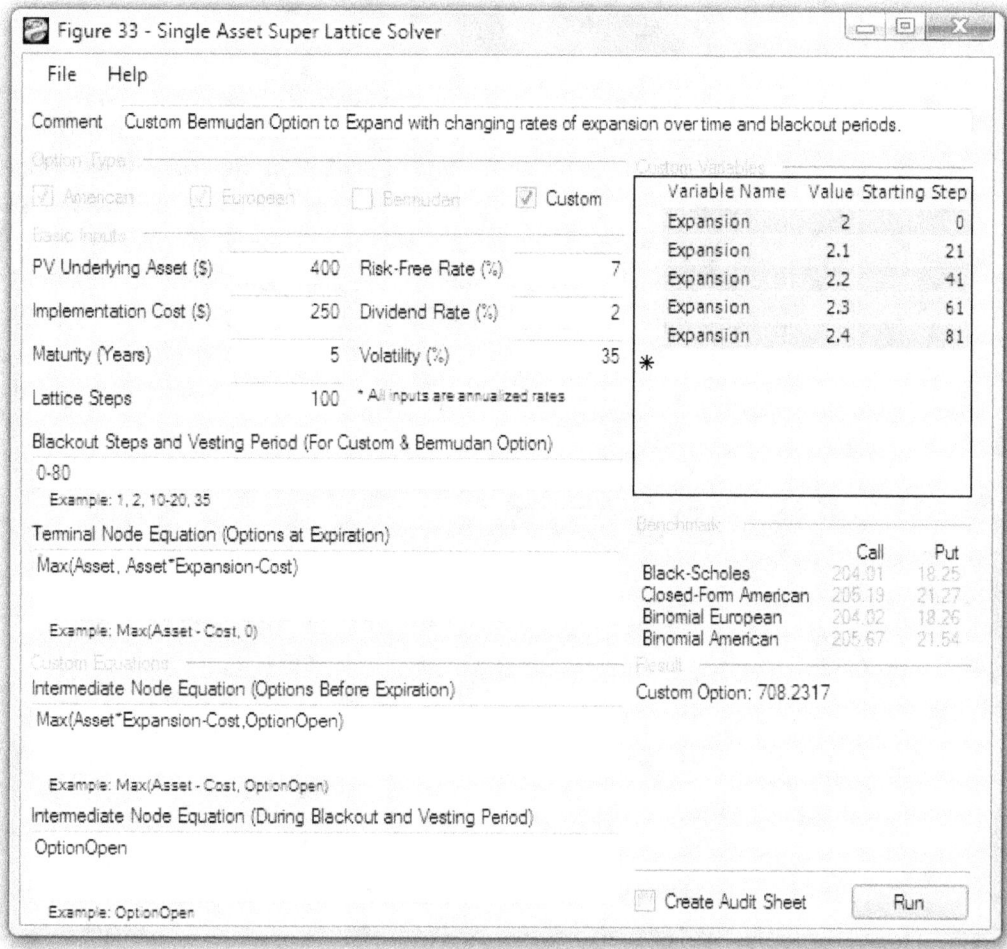

Figure 33 – Customized Expansion Option

2.4 Contraction, Expansion, and Abandonment Options

The *Contraction, Expansion, and Abandonment Option* applies when a firm has three **competing and mutually exclusive** options on a single project to choose from at different times up to the time of expiration. Be aware that this is a mutually exclusive set of options. That is, you cannot execute any combinations of expansion, contraction, or abandonment at the same time. Only one option can be executed at any time. That is, for mutually exclusive options, use a single model to compute the option value as seen in Figure 34 (example file used: *Expand Contract Abandon American and European Option*). However, if the options are non-mutually exclusive, calculate them individually in different models and add up the values for the total value of the strategy.

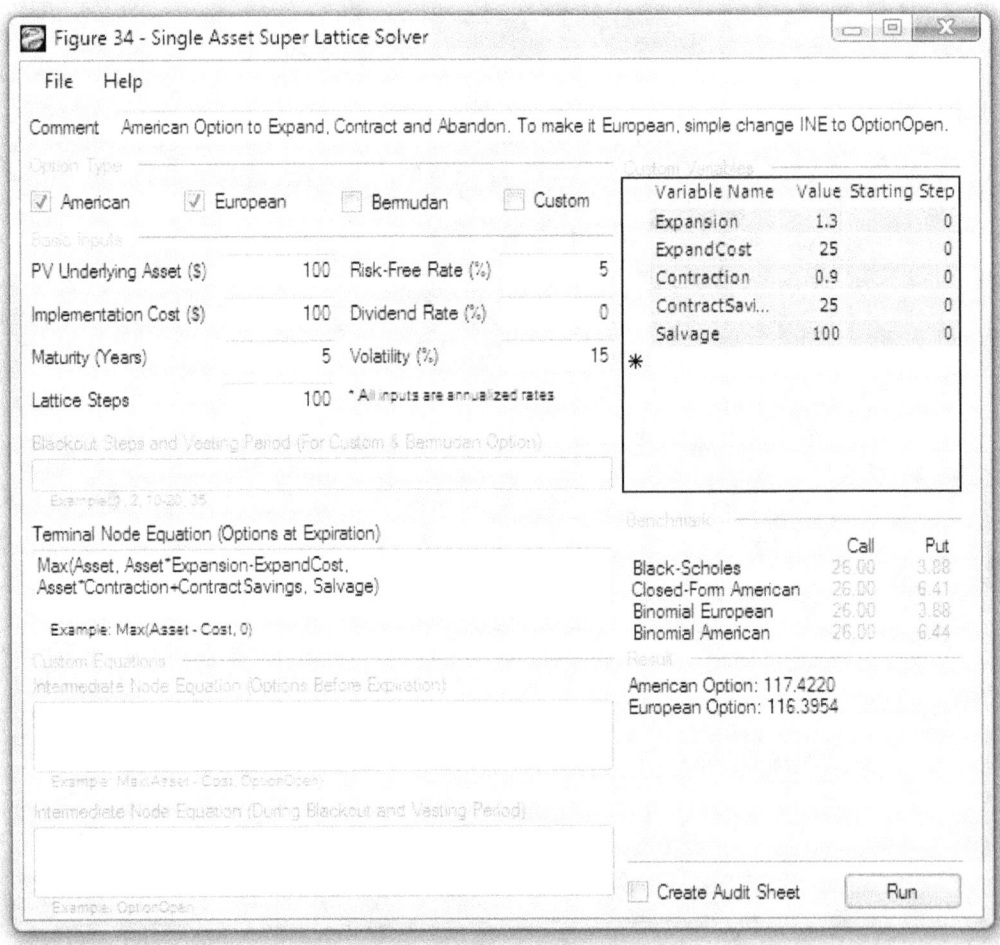

Figure 34 – American, European, and Custom Options to Expand, Contract, and Abandon

Figure 35 illustrates a Bermudan Option with the same parameters but with certain blackout periods (example file used: *Expand Contract Abandon Bermudan Option*), while Figure 36 (example file used: *Expand Contract Abandon Customized Option I*) illustrates a more complex Custom Option where during some earlier period of vesting, the option to expand does not exist yet (perhaps the technology being developed is not yet mature enough in the early stages to be expanded into some spin-off technology). In addition, during the post-vesting period but prior to maturity, the option to contract or abandon does not exist (perhaps the technology is now being reviewed for spin-off opportunities), and so forth. Finally, Figure 37 uses the same example in Figure 36 but now the input parameters (salvage value) are allowed to change over time perhaps accounting for the increase in project, asset, or firm value if abandoned at different times (example file used: *Expand Contract Abandon Customized Option II*).

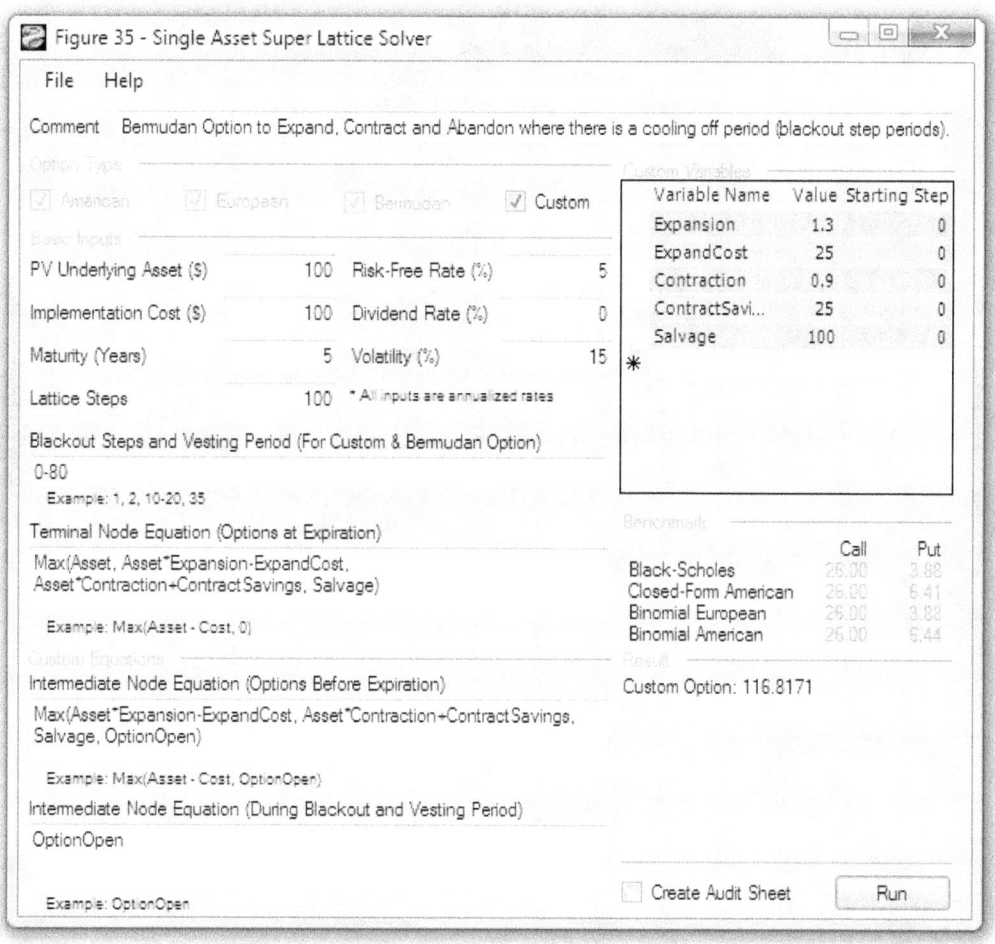

Figure 35 – Bermudan Option to Expand, Contract, and Abandon

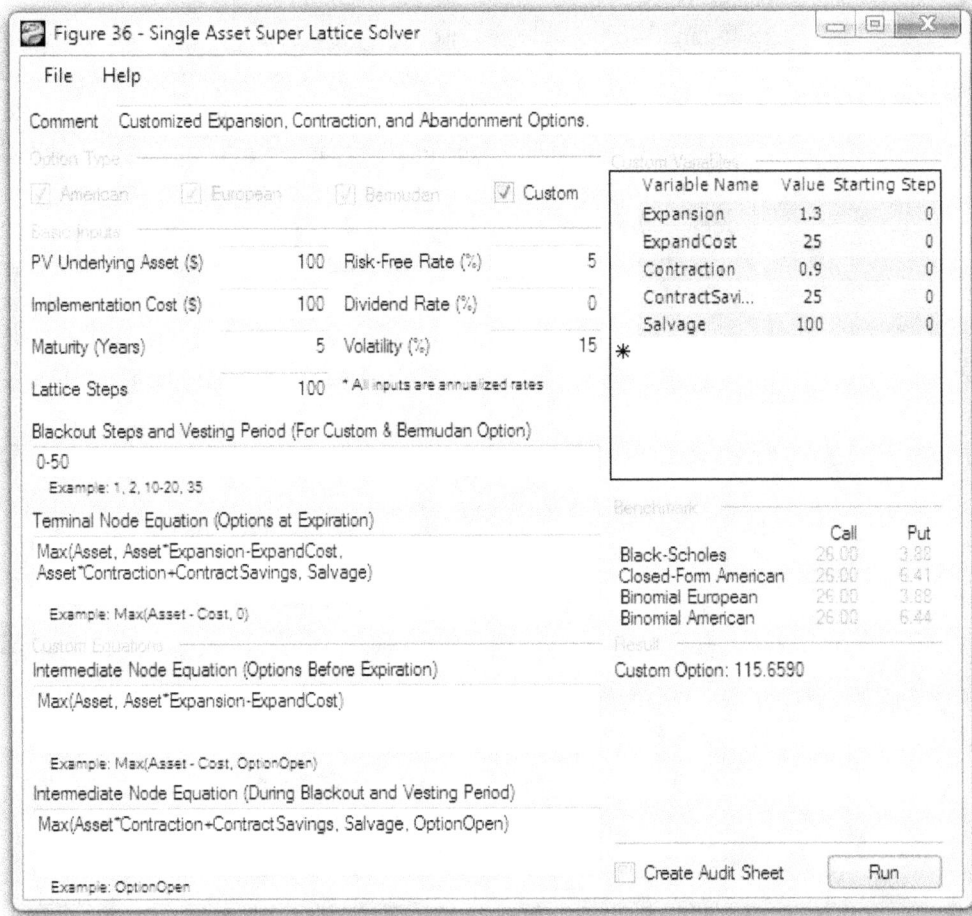

Figure 36 – Custom Options with Mixed Expand, Contract, and Abandon Capabilities

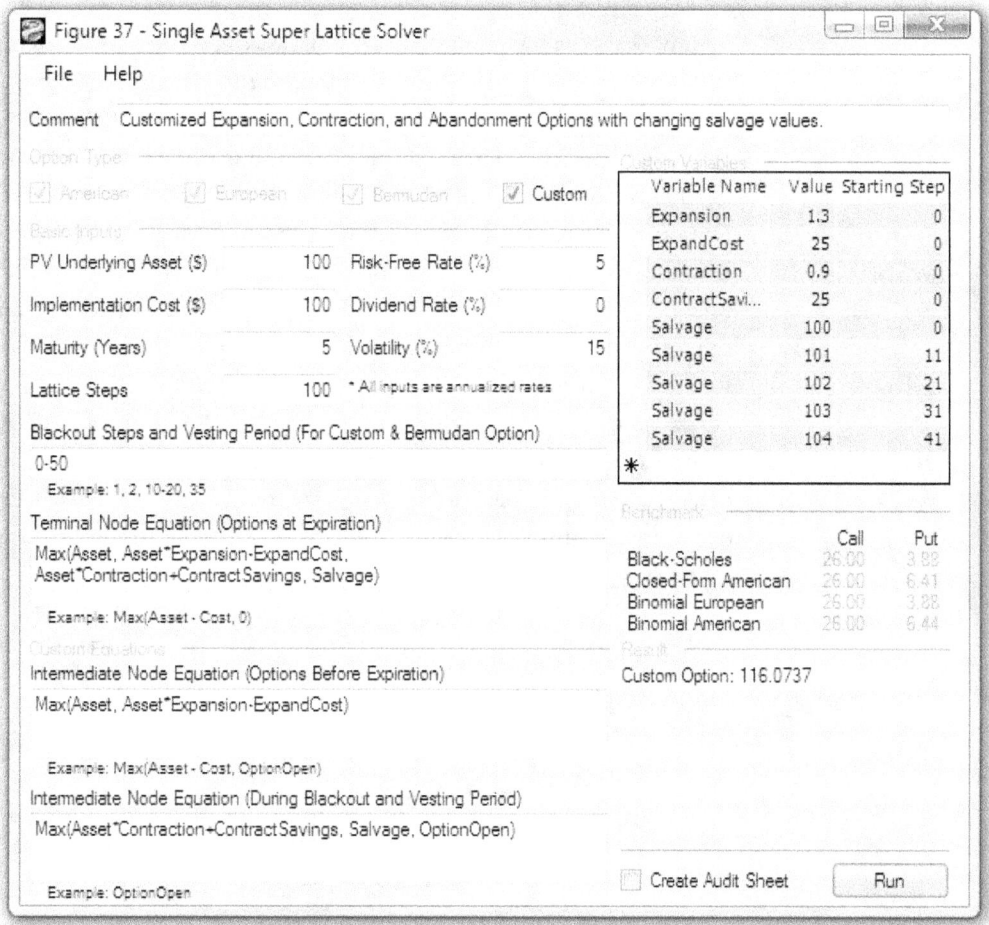

Figure 37 – Custom Options with Mixed Expand, Contract, and Abandon Capabilities with Changing Input Parameters

2.5 Basic American, European, and Bermudan Call Options

Figure 38 shows the computation of basic American, European, and Bermudan Options without dividends (example file used: *Basic American, European, versus Bermudan Call Options*), while Figure 39 shows the computation of the same options but with a dividend yield. Of course, European Options can only be executed at termination and not before, while in American Options, early exercise is allowed, versus a Bermudan Option where early exercise is allowed except during blackout or vesting periods. Notice that the results for the three options without dividends are identical for simple call options, but they differ when dividends exist. When dividends are included, the simple call option values for American $\geq$ Bermudan $\geq$ European in most basic cases, as seen in Figure 39 (insert a 5% dividend rate and blackout steps of 0-50). Of course this generality can be applied only to plain vanilla call options and do not necessarily apply to other exotic options (e.g., Bermudan options with vesting and suboptimal exercise behavior multiples tend to sometimes carry a higher value when blackouts and vesting occur, than regular American options with the same suboptimal exercise parameters.).

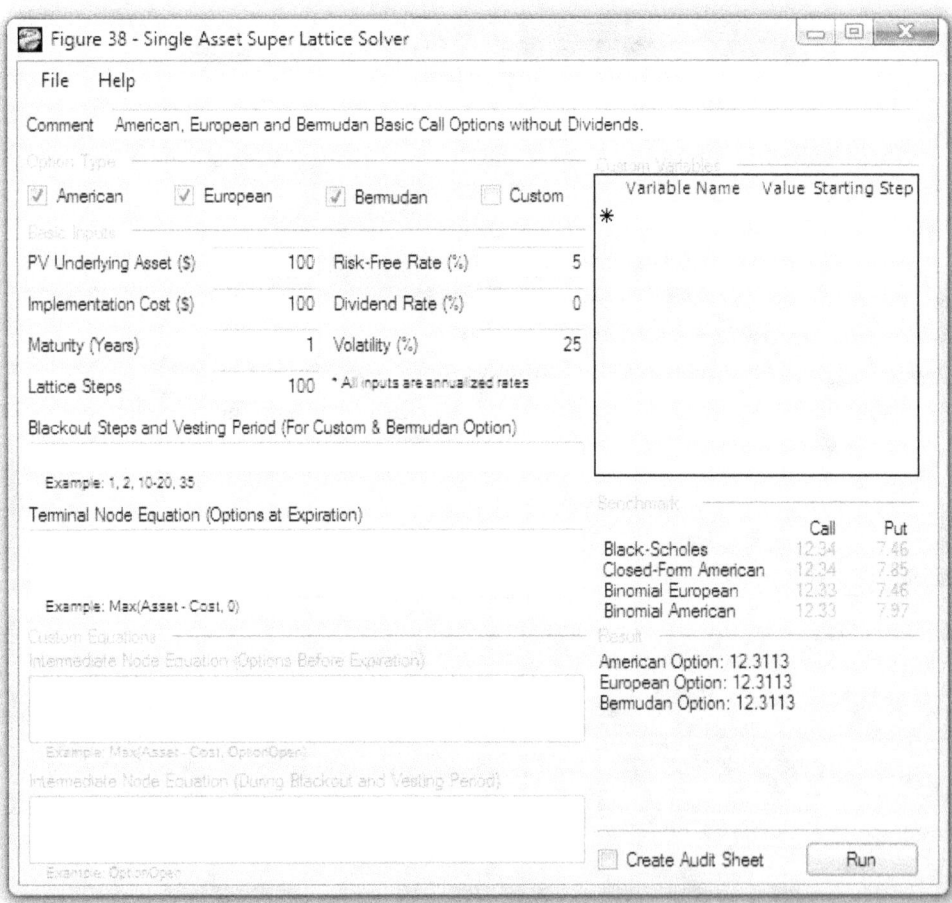

Figure 38 – Simple American, Bermudan, and European Options without Dividends

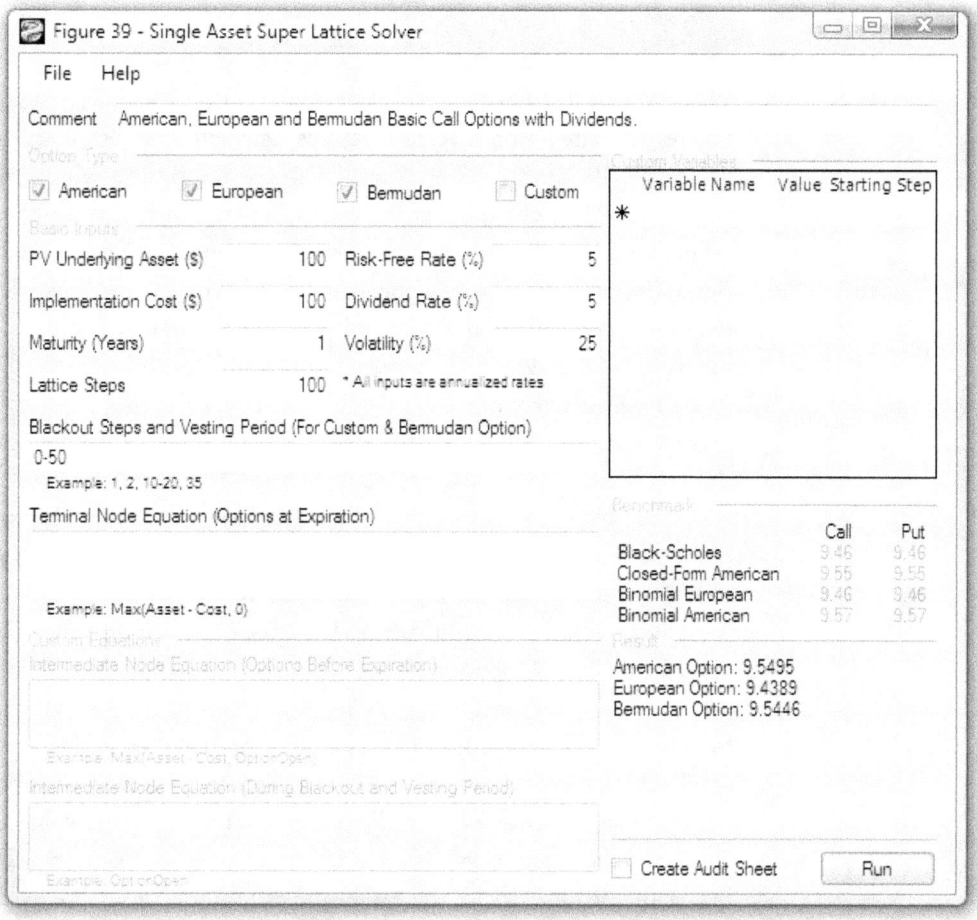

Figure 39 – Simple American, Bermudan, and European Options with Dividends and Blackout Steps

2.6 Basic American, European, and Bermudan Put Options

The *American and European Put Options* without dividends are calculated using the SLS in Figure 40. The sample results of this calculation indicate the strategic value of the project's NPV and provide an option to sell the project within the specified *Maturity* in years. There is a chance that the project value can significantly exceed the single-point estimate of *PV Asset Value* (measured by the present value of all uncertain future cash flows discounted at the risk-adjusted rate of return) or be significantly below it. Hence, the option to **defer** and **wait** until some of the uncertainty becomes resolved through the passage of time is worth more than executing immediately. The value of being able to wait before executing the option and selling the project at the *Implementation Cost* in present values is the value of the option. The NPV of executing immediately is simply the *Implementation Cost* less the *Asset Value* ($0). The option value of being able to wait and defer selling the asset only if the condition goes bad and becomes optimal for selling is the difference between the calculated result (total strategic value) and the NPV or $24.42 for the American Option and $20.68 for the European Option. The American put option is worth more than the European put option even when no dividends exist, contrary to the call options seen previously. For simple call options, when no dividends exist, it is never optimal to exercise early. However, it may sometimes be optimal to exercise early for put options, regardless of whether dividend yields exist. In fact, a dividend yield will decrease the value of a call option but increase the value of a put option. This is because when dividends are paid out, the value of the asset decreases. Thus, the call option will be worth less and the put option will be worth more. The higher the dividend yield, the earlier the call option should be exercised and the later the put option should be exercised.

The put option can be solved by setting the Terminal Node Equation as *Max(Cost–Asset,0)* as seen in Figure 40 (example file used: *Plain Vanilla Put Option*).

Puts have a similar result as calls in that when dividends are included, the basic put option values for American ≥ Bermudan ≥ European in most basic cases. You can confirm this by simply setting the Dividend Rate at 3% and Blackout Steps at 0-80 and re-running the SLS module.

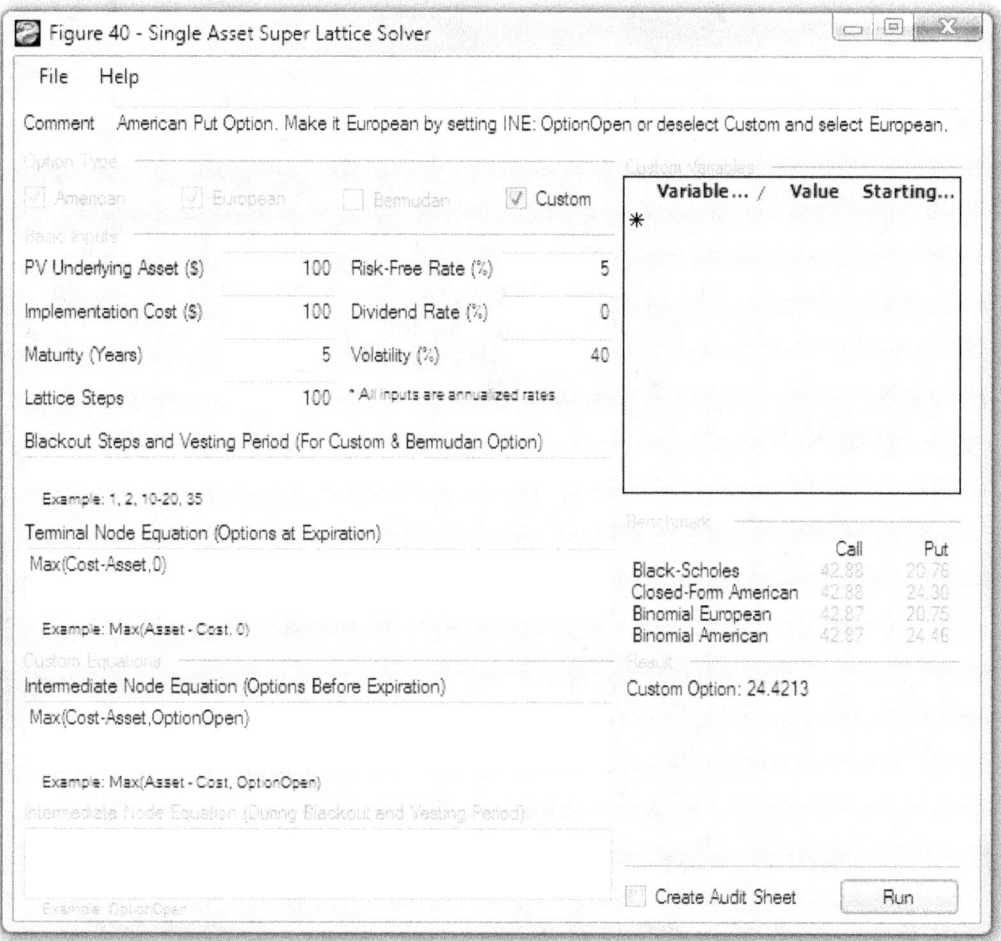

Figure 40 – American and European Put Options using SLS

2.7 Exotic Chooser Options

Many types of user-defined and exotic options can be solved using the SLS and MSLS. For instance, Figure 41 shows a simple Exotic Chooser Option (example file used: *Exotic Chooser Option*). In this simple analysis, the option holder has two options, a call and a put. Instead of having to purchase or obtain two separate options, one single option is obtained, which allows the option holder to choose whether the option will be a call or a put, thereby reducing the total cost of obtaining two separate options. For instance, with the same input parameters in Figure 41, the American Chooser Option is worth $6.7168, as compared to $4.87 for the call and $2.02 for the put ($6.89 total cost for two separate options).

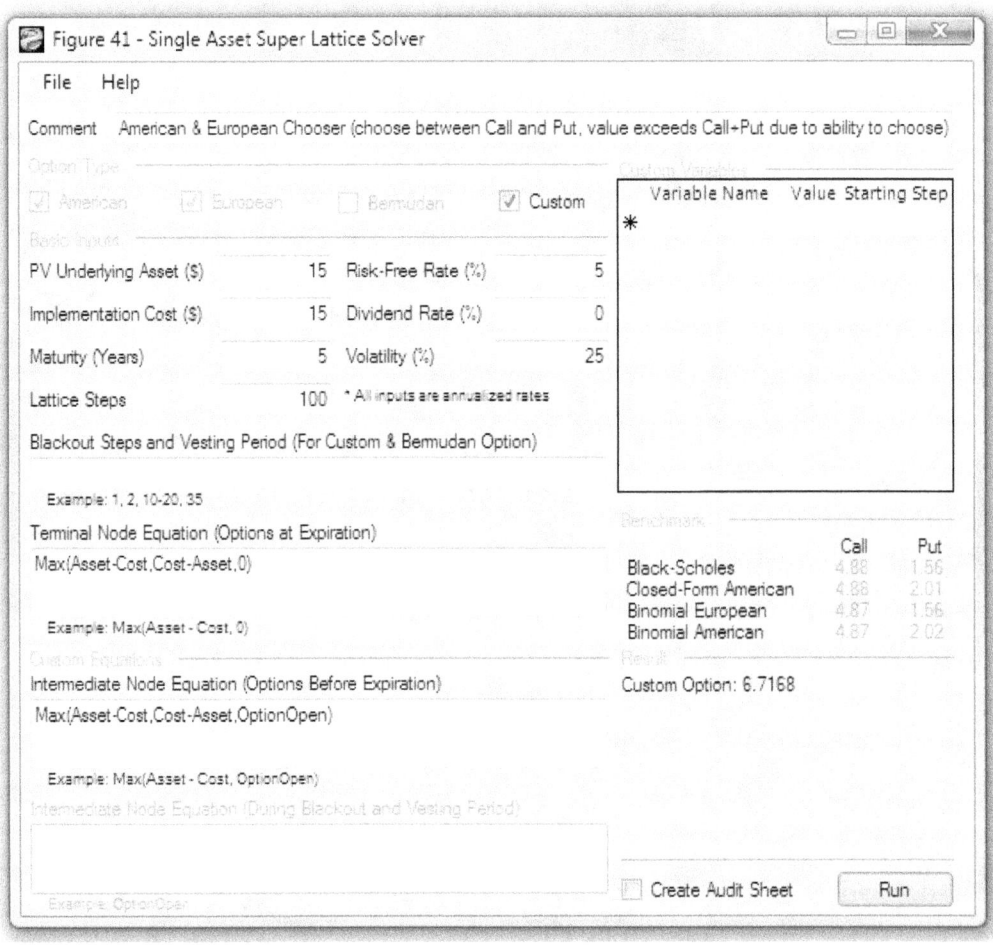

Figure 41 – American and European Exotic Chooser Option using SLS

A more complex Chooser Option can be constructed using the MSLS as seen in Figure 42 (example Multiple Asset Option Module file used: *Exotic Complex Floating European Chooser*) and Figure 43 (example file used: *Exotic Complex Floating American Chooser*). In these examples, the execution costs of the call versus put are set at different levels. An interesting example of a Complex Chooser Option is a firm developing a new technology that is highly uncertain and risky. The firm tries to hedge its downside as well as capitalize its upside by creating a Chooser Option. That is, the firm can decide to build the technology itself once the research and development phase is complete versus selling the intellectual property of the technology, both at different costs. To further complicate matters, you can use the MSLS to easily and quickly solve the situation where building versus selling off the option each has a different volatility and time to choose.

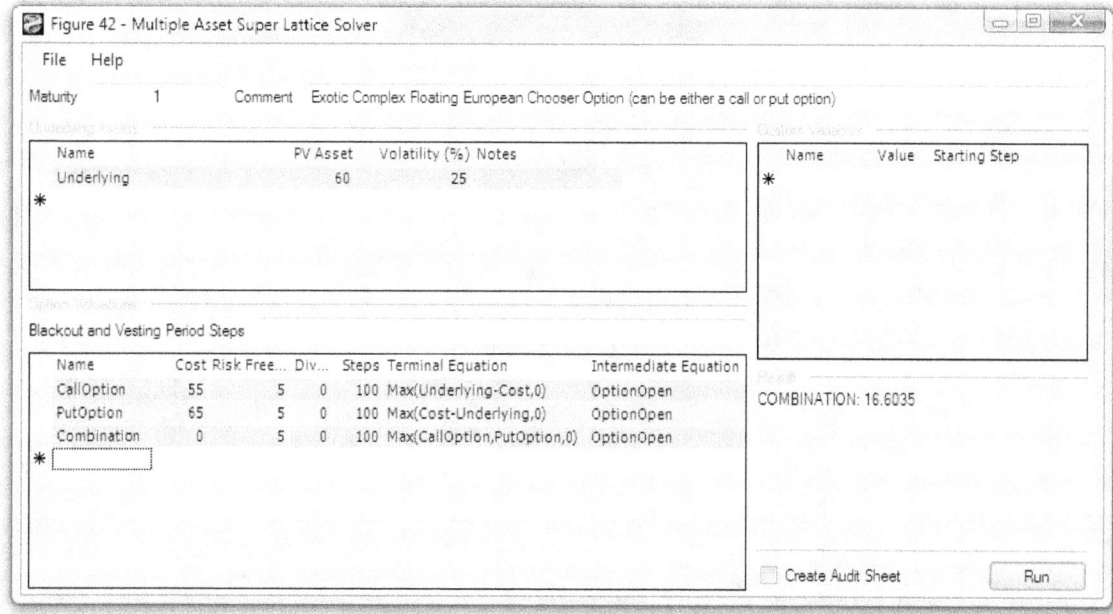

Figure 42 – Complex European Exotic Chooser Option using MSLS

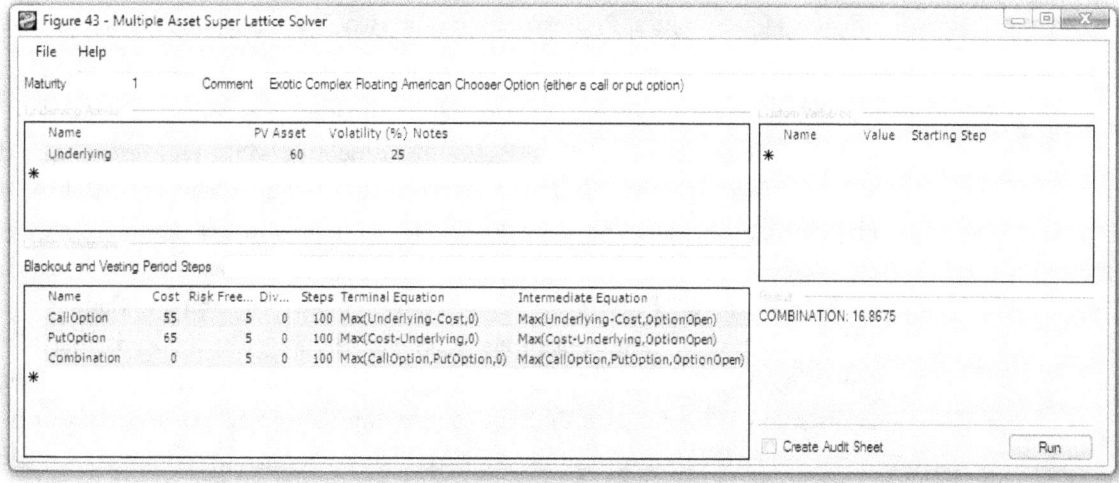

Figure 43 – Complex American Exotic Chooser Option using MSLS

2.8 Sequential Compound Options

Sequential Compound Options are applicable for research and development investments or any other investments that have multiple stages. The MSLS is required for solving Sequential Compound Options. The easiest way to understand this option is to start with a two-phased example as seen in Figure 44. In the two-phased example, management has the ability to decide if Phase II (PII) should be implemented after obtaining the results from Phase I (PI). For example, a pilot project or market research in PI indicates that the market is not yet ready for the product, hence PII is not implemented. All that is lost is the PI sunk cost, not the entire investment cost of both PI and PII. An example below illustrates how the option is analyzed.

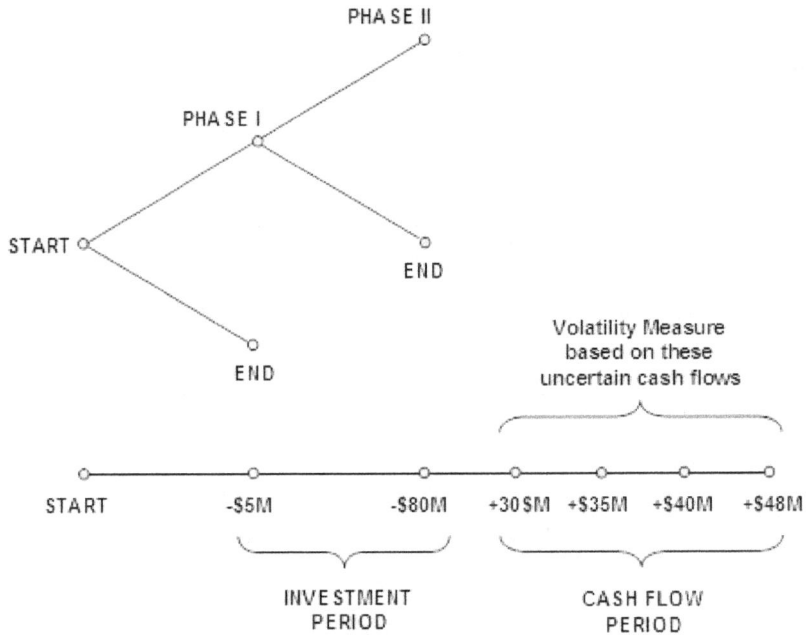

Figure 44 – Graphical Representation of a Two-Phased Sequential Compound Option

The illustration in Figure 44 is valuable in explaining and communicating to senior management the aspects of an American Sequential Compound Option and its inner workings. In the illustration, the *Phase I* investment of –$5M (in present value dollars) in Year 1 is followed by *Phase II* investment of –$80M (in present value dollars) in Year 2. Hopefully, positive net free cash flows (CF) will follow in Years 3 to 6, yielding a sum of *PV Asset* of $100M (CF discounted at, say, a 9.7% discount or hurdle rate), and the *Volatility* of these CFs is 30%. At a 5% risk-free rate, the strategic value is calculated at $27.67 as seen in Figure 45 using a 100-step lattice, which means that the strategic option value of being able to **defer** investments and to **wait and see** until more information becomes available and uncertainties become resolved is worth $12.67M because the NPV is worth $15M ($100M – $5M – $85M). In other words, the **Expected Value of Perfect Information** is worth $12.67M, which indicates that assuming market research can be used to obtain credible information to decide if this project is a good one, the maximum the firm should be willing to spend in Phase I is *on average no more than* $17.67M (i.e., $12.67M + $5M) if PI is part of the market research initiative, or simply $12.67M otherwise. If the cost to obtain the credible information exceeds this value, then it is optimal to take the risk and execute the entire project immediately at $85M. The Multiple Asset module example file used is: *Simple Two Phased Sequential Compound Option.*

In contrast, if the volatility decreases (uncertainty and risk are lower), the strategic option value decreases. In addition, when the cost of waiting (as described by the *Dividend Rate* as a percentage of the *Asset Value*) increases, it is better not to defer and wait that long. Therefore, the higher the dividend rate, the lower the strategic option value. For instance, at an 8% dividend rate and 15% volatility, the resulting value reverts to the NPV of $15M, which means that the option value is zero, and that it is better to execute immediately as the cost of waiting far outstrips the value of being able to wait given the level of volatility (uncertainty and risk). Finally, if risks and uncertainty increase significantly even with a high cost of waiting (e.g., 7% dividend rate at 30% volatility) it is still valuable to wait.

This model provides the decision-maker with a view into the optimal balancing between *waiting for more information* (Expected Value of Perfect Information) and the *cost of waiting.* You can analyze this balance by creating strategic *options to defer* investments through development stages where at every stage the project is reevaluated as to whether it is beneficial to proceed to the next phase. Based on the input assumptions used in this model, the *Sequential Compound Option* results show the strategic value of the project, and the NPV is simply the *PV Asset* less both phases' *Implementation Costs.* In other words, the strategic option value is the difference between the calculated strategic value minus the NPV. It is recommended for your consideration that the volatility and dividend inputs are varied to determine their interactions—specifically, where the breakeven points are for different combinations of volatilities and dividends. Thus, using this information, you can make better go or *no-go decisions* (for instance, breakeven volatility points can be traced back into the discounted cash flow model to estimate the probability of crossing over and that this ability to wait becomes valuable).

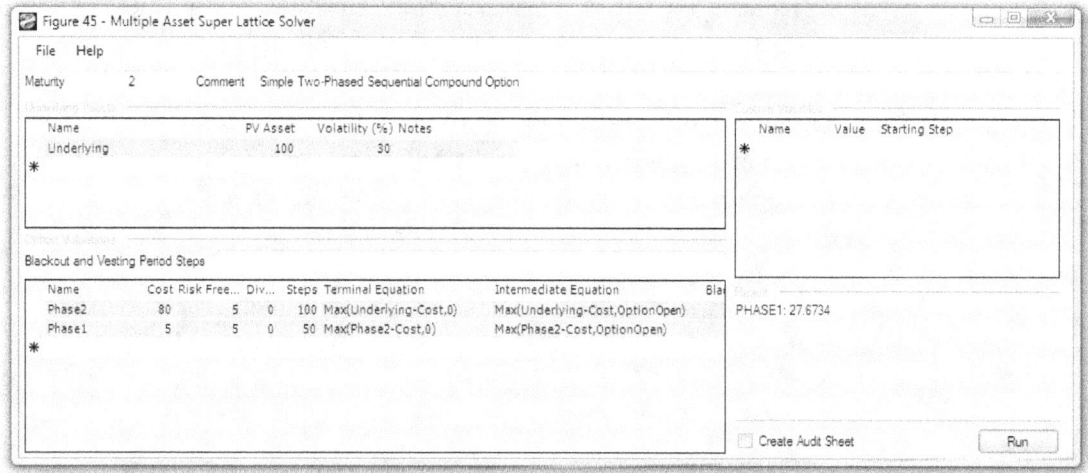

Figure 45 – Solving a Two-Phased Sequential Compound Option using MSLS

2.9 Multiple-Phased Sequential Compound Options

The Sequential Compound Option can similarly be extended to multiple phases with the use of MSLS. A graphical representation of a multi-phased or stage-gate investment is seen in Figure 46. The example illustrates a multi-phase project, where at every phase management has the option and flexibility to either continue to the next phase if everything goes well, or to terminate the project otherwise. Based on the input assumptions, the results in the MSLS indicate the calculated strategic value of the project, while the NPV of the project is simply the *PV Asset* less all *Implementation Costs* (in present values) if implementing all phases immediately. Therefore, with the strategic option value of being able to defer and wait before implementing future phases because due to the volatility, there is a possibility that the asset value will be significantly higher. Hence, the ability to wait before making the investment decisions in the future is the option value or the strategic value of the project less the NPV.

Figure 47 shows the results using the MSLS. Notice that due to the backward induction process used, the analytical convention is to start with the last phase and going all the way back to the first phase (the Multiple Asset module's example file used: *Sequential Compound Option for Multiple Phases*). In NPV terms the project is worth –$500. However, the total strategic value of the stage-gate investment option is worth $41.78. This means that although on an NPV basis the investment looks bad, but in reality, by hedging the risks and uncertainties through sequential investments, the option holder can pull out at any time and not have to keep investing unless things look promising. If after the first phase things look bad, pull out and stop investing and the maximum loss will be $100 (Figure 47) and not the entire $1,500 investment. If however, things look promising, the option holder can continue to invest in stages. The expected value of the investments in present values after accounting for the probabilities that things will look bad (and hence stop investing) versus things looking great (and hence continuing to invest), is worth an average of $41.78M.

Notice that the option valuation result will always be greater than or equal to zero (e.g., try reducing the volatility to 5% and increasing the dividend yield to 8% for all phases). When the option value is very low or zero, this means that it is not optimal to defer investments and that this stage-gate investment process is not optimal here. The cost of waiting is too high (high dividend) or that the uncertainties in the cash flows are low (low volatility), hence, invest if the NPV is positive. In such a case, although you obtain a zero value for the option, the analytical interpretation is significant! A zero or very low value is indicative of an optimal decision not to wait.

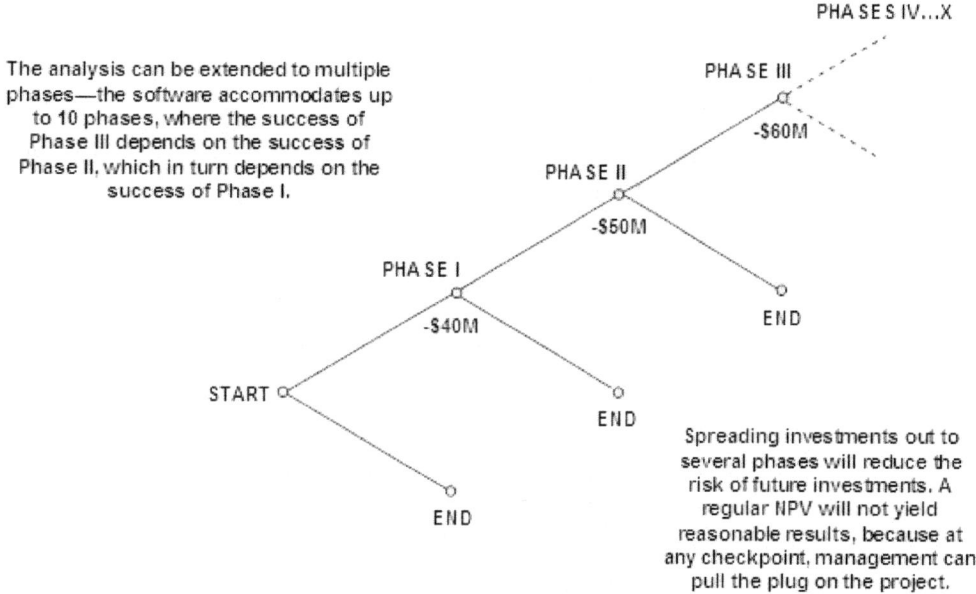

Figure 46 – Graphical Representation of a Multi-Phased Sequential Compound Option

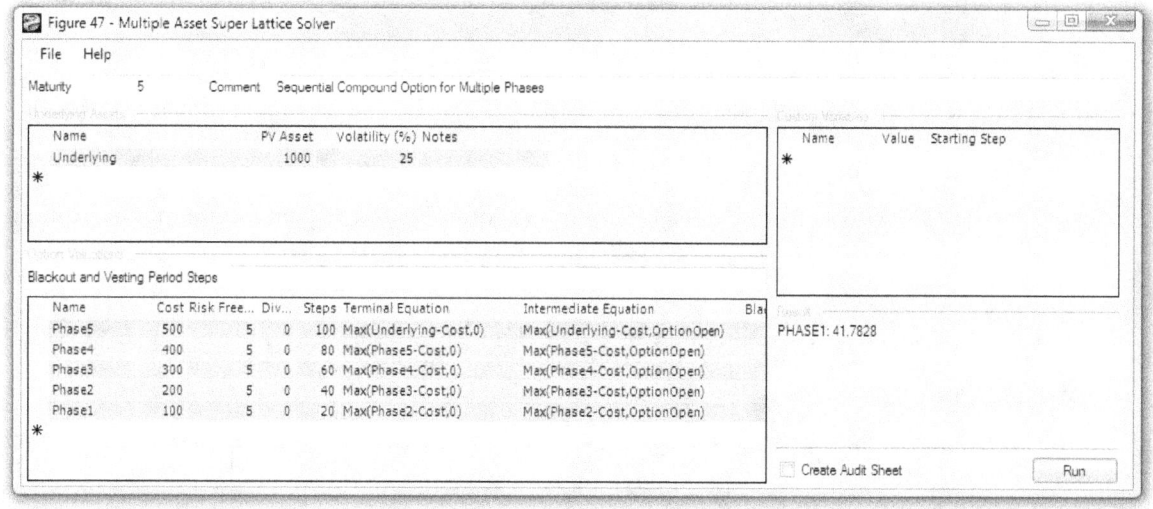

Figure 47 – Solving a Multi-Phased Sequential Compound Option using MSLS

2.10 Customizing Sequential Compound Options

The Sequential Compound Option can be further complicated by adding customized options at each phase as illustrated in Figure 48, where at every phase, there may be different combinations of mutually exclusive options including the flexibility to stop investing, *abandon* and *salvage* the project in return for some value, *expand* the scope of the project into another project (e.g., spin-off projects and expand into different geographical locations), *contract* the scope of the project resulting in some savings, or continue on to the next phase. The seemingly complicated option can be very easily solved using MSLS as seen in Figure 49 (example file used: *Multiple Phased Complex Sequential Compound Option*).

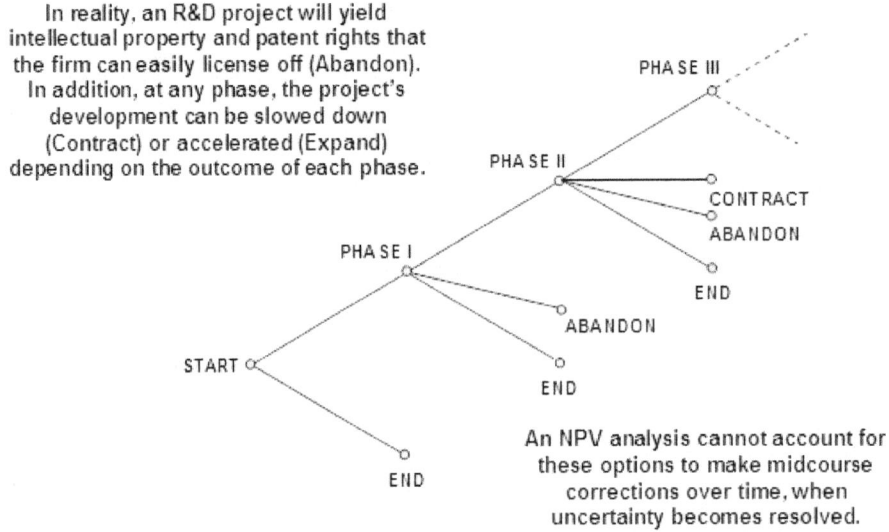

Figure 48 – Complex Multi-Phased Sequential Compound Option

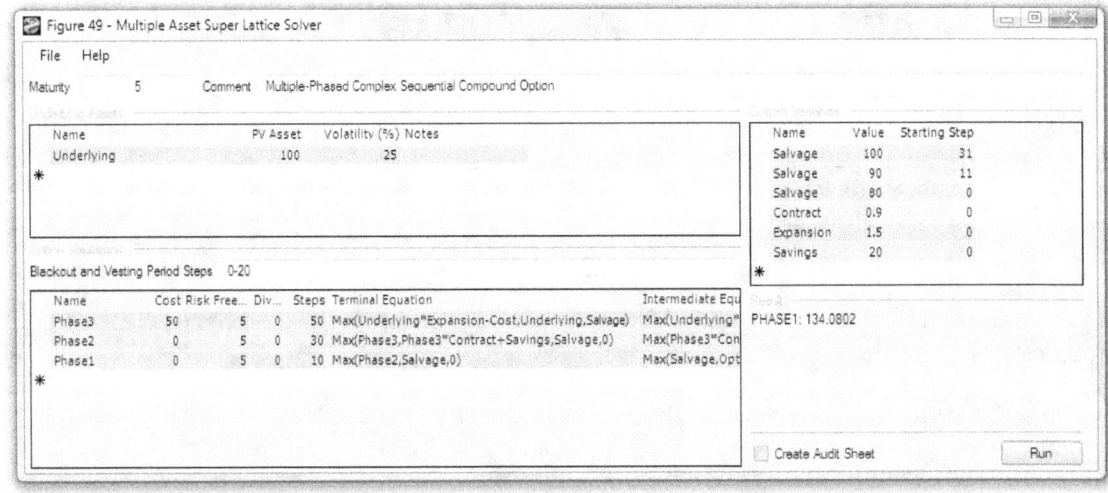

Figure 49 – Complex Multi-Phased Sequential Compound Option using MSLS

To illustrate, Figure 49's MSLS path-dependent sequential option uses the following inputs:

Phase 3:	Terminal:	Max(Underlying*Expansion-Cost,Underlying,Salvage)
	Intermediate:	Max(Underlying*Expansion-Cost,Salvage,OptionOpen)
	Steps:	50
Phase 2:	Terminal:	Max(Phase3,Phase3*Contract+Savings,Salvage,0)
	Intermediate:	Max(Phase3*Contract+Savings,Salvage,OptionOpen)
	Steps:	30
Phase 1:	Terminal:	Max(Phase2,Salvage,0)
	Intermediate:	Max(Salvage,OptionOpen)
	Steps:	10

2.11 Path-Dependent, Path-Independent, Mutually Exclusive, Non-Mutually Exclusive, and Complex Combinatorial Nested Options

Sequential Compound Options are **path-dependent options**, where one phase depends on the success of another, in contrast to **path-independent options** like those solved using SLS. Figure 49 shows that in a complex strategy tree, at certain phases, different combinations of options exist. These options can be **mutually exclusive** or **non-mutually exclusive**. In all these types of options, there might be multiple underlying assets (e.g., Japan has a different risk-return or profitability-volatility profile than the U.K. or Australia). You can build multiple underlying asset lattices this way using the MSLS, and combine them in many various ways depending on the options. The following are some examples of path-dependent versus path-independent and mutually exclusive versus non-mutually exclusive options.

- **Path Independent and Mutually Exclusive Options**: Use the SLS to solve these types of options by combining all the options into a single valuation lattice. Examples include the option to expand, contract, and expand. These are mutually exclusive if you cannot both expand into a different country while at the same time abandoning and selling the company. These are path independent if there are no restrictions on timing, that is, you can expand, contract, and abandon at any time within the confines of the maturity period.

- **Path Independent and Non-Mutually Exclusive Options**: Use the SLS to solve these types of options by running each of the options that are non-mutually exclusive one at a time in SLS. Examples include the option to expand your business into Japan, U.K., and Australia. These are not mutually exclusive if you can choose to expand to any combinations of countries (e.g., Japan only, Japan and U.K., U.K. and Australia, and so forth). These are path independent if there are no restrictions on timing, that is, you can expand to any country at any time within the maturity of the option. Add the individual option values and obtain the total option value for expansion.

- **Path Dependent and Mutually Exclusive Options**: Use the MSLS to solve these types of options by combining all the options into one valuation lattice. Examples include the option to expand into the three countries, Japan, U.K. and Australia. However, this time, the expansions are mutually exclusive and path dependent. That is, you can only expand into one country at a time, but at certain periods, you can only expand into certain countries (e.g., Japan is only optimal in three years due to current economic conditions, export restrictions, and so forth, as compared to the U.K. expansion, which can be executed right now).

- **Path Dependent and Non-Mutually Exclusive Options**: Use MSLS to solve these. These are typically simple Sequential Compound Options with multiple phases. If more than one non-mutually exclusive option exists, re-run the MSLS for each option. Examples include the ability to enter Japan from Years 0-3, Australia in Years 3-6, and U.K. at any time between Years 0-10. Each entry strategy is not mutually exclusive if you can enter more than one country, and are path dependent as they are time dependent.

- **Nested Combinatorial Options**: These are the most complicated and can take a combination of any of the four types above. In addition, the options are nested within one another in that the expansion into Japan must come only after Australia, and cannot be executed without heading to Australia first. In addition, Australia and U.K. are okay but you cannot expand to U.K. and Japan (e.g., certain trade restrictions, anti-trust issues, competitive considerations, strategic issues, restrictive agreements with alliances, and so forth). For such options, draw all the scenarios on a strategy tree and use IF, AND, OR, and MAX statements in MSLS to solve the option. That is, if you enter into U.K., that's it, but *if* you enter into Australia, you can still enter into Japan *or* U.K. but *not* Japan and U.K.

2.12 Simultaneous Compound Options

The Simultaneous Compound Option evaluates a project's strategic value when the value of the project depends on the success of *two or more* investment initiatives executed *simultaneously in time*. The Sequential Compound Option evaluates these investments in stages, one after another over time, while the simultaneous option evaluates these options in concurrence. Clearly, the sequential compound is worth more than the simultaneous compound option by virtue of staging the investments. Note that the simultaneous compound option acts like a regular execution call option. Hence, the *American Call Option* is a good benchmark for such an option. Figure 50 shows how a Simultaneous Compound Option can be solved using the MSLS (example file used: *Simple Two Phased Simultaneous Compound Option*). Similar to the sequential compound option analysis, the existence of an option value implies that the ability to defer and wait for additional information prior to executing is valuable due to the significant uncertainties and risks as measured by *Volatility*. However, when the cost of waiting as measured by the *Dividend Rate* is high, the option to wait and defer becomes less valuable, until the breakeven point where the option value equals zero and the strategic project value equals the NPV of the project. This breakeven point provides valuable insights for the decision maker into the interactions between the levels of uncertainty inherent in the project and the cost of waiting to execute. The same analysis can be extended to Multiple Investment Simultaneous Compound Options as seen in Figure 51 (example file used: *Multiple Phased Simultaneous Compound Option*).

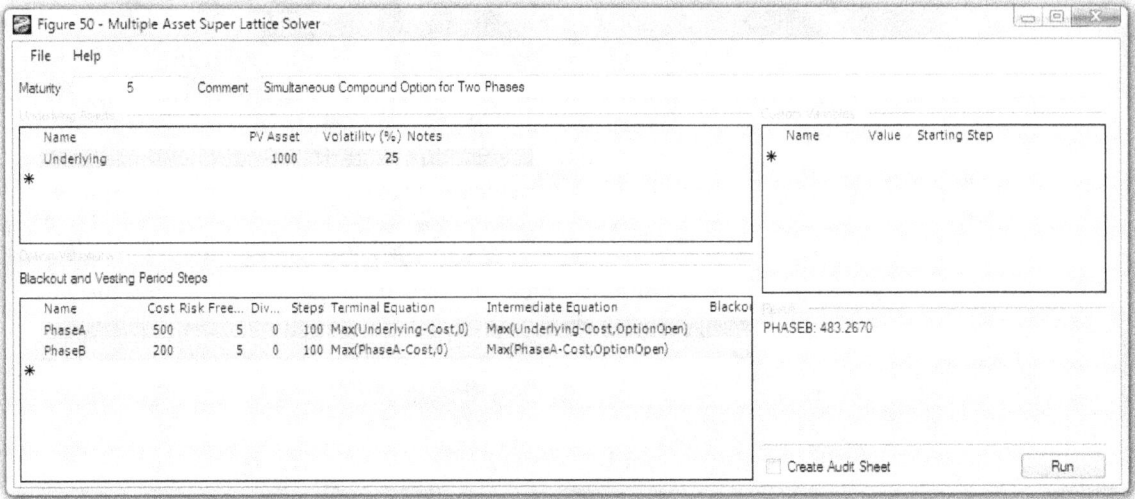

Figure 50 – Solving a Simultaneous Compound Option using MSLS

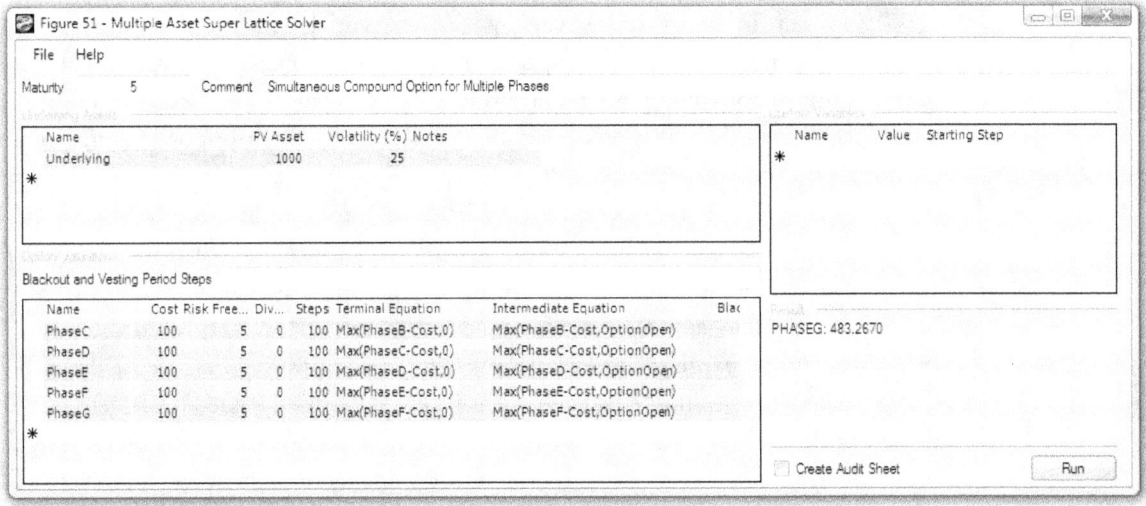

Figure 51 – Solving a Multiple Investment Simultaneous Compound Option using MSLS

2.13 American and European Options Using Trinomial Lattices

Building and solving trinomial lattices is similar to building and solving binomial lattices, complete with the up/down jumps and risk-neutral probabilities, but it is more complicated due to more branches stemming from each node. At the limit, both the binomial and trinomial lattices yield the same result, as seen in the following table. However, the lattice-building complexity is much higher for trinomial or multinomial lattices. The only reason to use a trinomial lattice is because the level of convergence to the correct option value is achieved more quickly than by using a binomial lattice. In the sample table, notice how the trinomial lattice yields the correct option value with fewer steps than it takes for a binomial lattice (1,000 as compared to 5,000). Because both yield identical results at the limit but trinomials are much more difficult to calculate and take a longer computation time, the binomial lattice is usually used instead. However, a trinomial is required only when the underlying asset follows a **mean-reverting process**. An illustration of the convergence of trinomials and binomials can be seen in the following example:

Steps	5	10	100	1,000	5,000
Binomial Lattice	$30.73	$29.22	$29.72	$29.77	$29.78
Trinomial Lattice	$29.22	$29.50	$29.75	$29.78	$29.78

Figure 52 shows another example using the Multinomial Option. The computed American Call is $31.99 using a 5-step trinomial, and is identical to a 10-step binomial lattice seen in Figure 53. Therefore, due to the simpler computation and the speed of computation, the SLS and MSLS use binomial lattices instead of trinomials or other multinomial lattices. The only time a trinomial lattice is truly useful is when the underlying asset of the option follows a mean-reversion tendency. In that case, use the MNLS module instead. When using this MNLS module, just like in the single asset lattices, you can modify and add in your own customized equations and variables, and the concepts are identical to that of the SLS examples throughout this user manual.

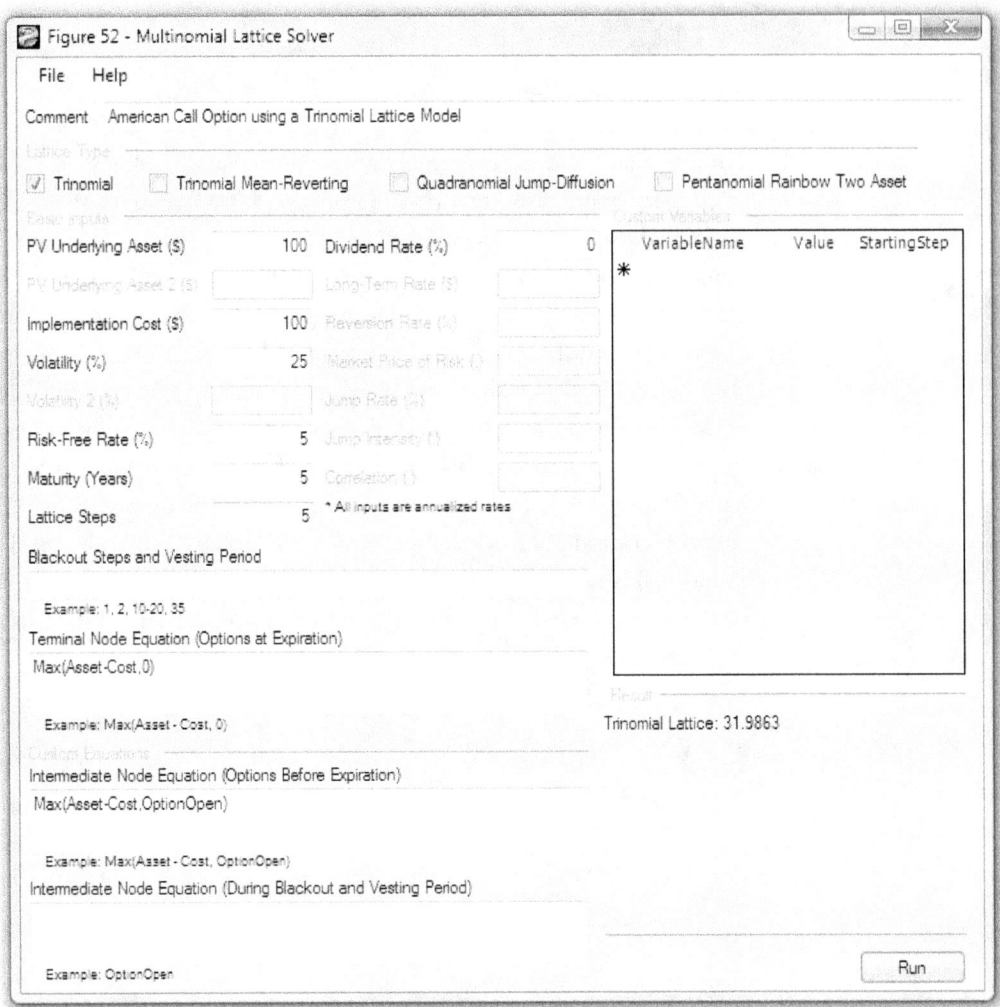

Figure 52 – Simple Trinomial Lattice Solution

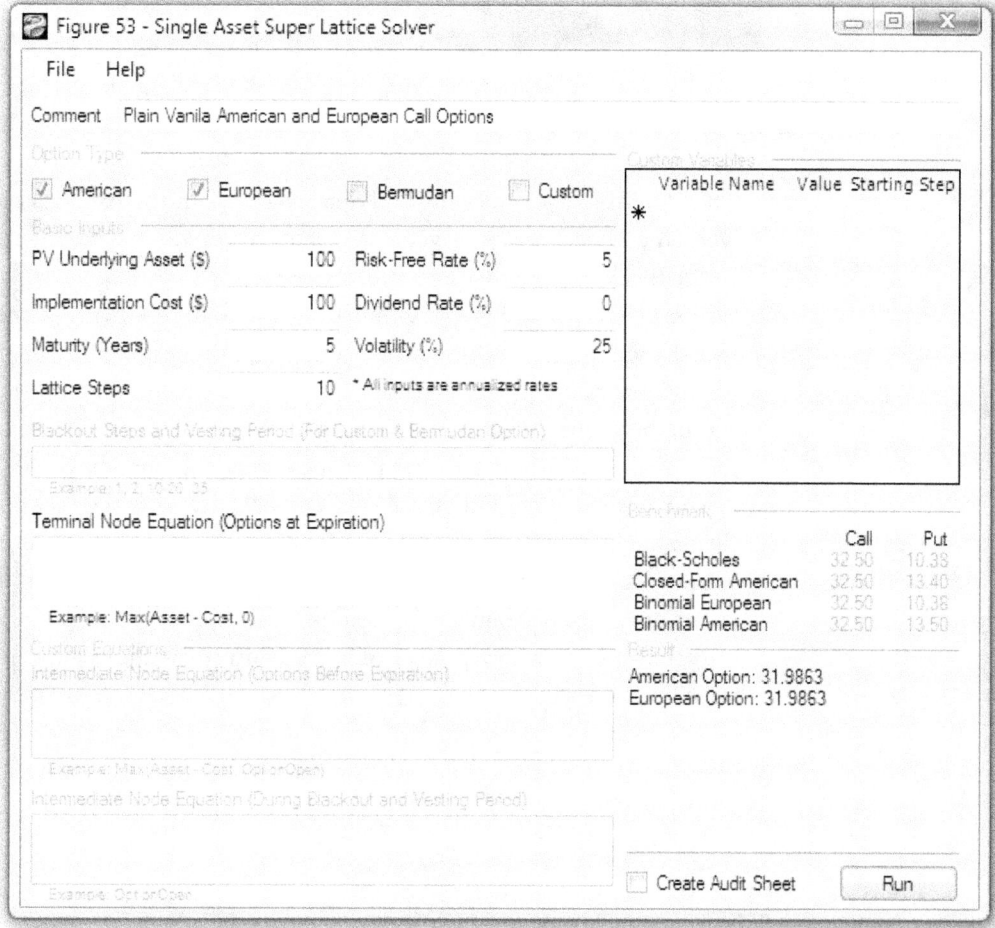

Figure 53 – 10-Step Binomial Lattice Comparison Result

2.14 American and European Mean-Reversion Options Using Trinomial Lattices

The *Mean-Reversion Option* in MNLS calculates both the American and European options when the underlying asset value is mean-reverting. A mean-reverting stochastic process reverts back to the long-term mean value (*Long-Term Rate Level*) at a particular speed of reversion (*Reversion Rate*). Examples of variables following a mean-reversion process include inflation rates, interest rates, gross domestic product growth rates, optimal production rates, price of natural gas, and so forth. Certain variables such as these succumb to either natural tendencies or economic/business conditions to revert to a long-term level when the actual values stray too far above or below this level. For instance, monetary and fiscal policy will prevent the economy from significant fluctuations, while policy goals tend to have a specific long-term target rate or level. Figure 54 illustrates a regular stochastic process (dotted red line) versus a mean-reversion process (solid line). Clearly the mean-reverting process with its dampening effects will have a lower level of uncertainty than the regular process with the same volatility measure.

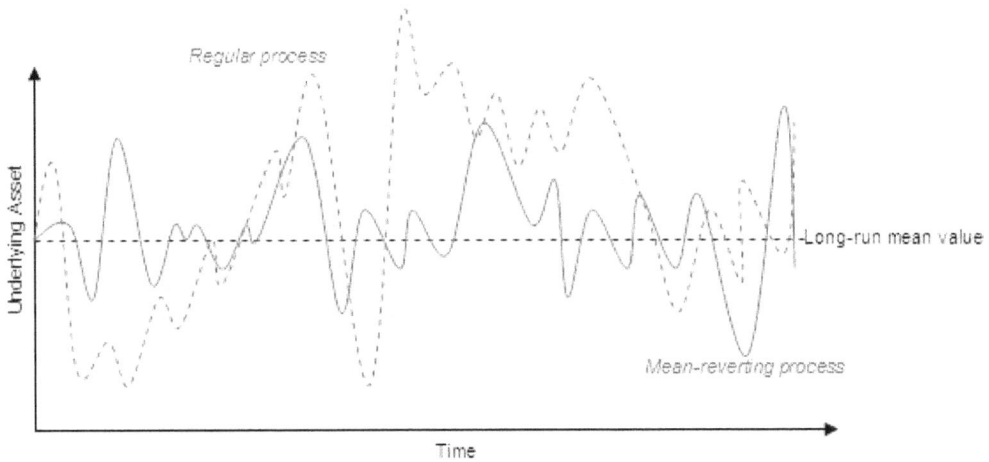

Figure 54 – Mean-Reversion in Action

Figure 55 shows the call and put results from a regular option modeled using the Trinomial Lattice versus calls and puts assuming a mean-reverting (MR) tendency of the underlying asset using the Mean-Reverting Trinomial Lattice. Several items are worthy of attention:

- The MR Call < regular Call because of the dampening effect of the mean-reversion asset. The MR asset value will not increase as high as the regular asset value.

- Conversely, the MR Put > regular Put because the asset value will not rise as high, indicating that there will be a higher chance that the asset value will hover around the PV Asset, and a higher probability it will be below the PV Asset, making the put option more valuable.

- With the dampening effect, the MR Call and MR Put ($18.62 and $18.76) are more symmetrical in value than with a regular call and put ($31.99 and $13.14).

- The regular American Call = regular European Call because without dividends, it is never optimal to execute early. However, because of the mean-reverting tendencies, being able to execute early is valuable, especially before the asset value decreases. So, we see that MR American Call > MR European Call but of course both are less than the regular Call.

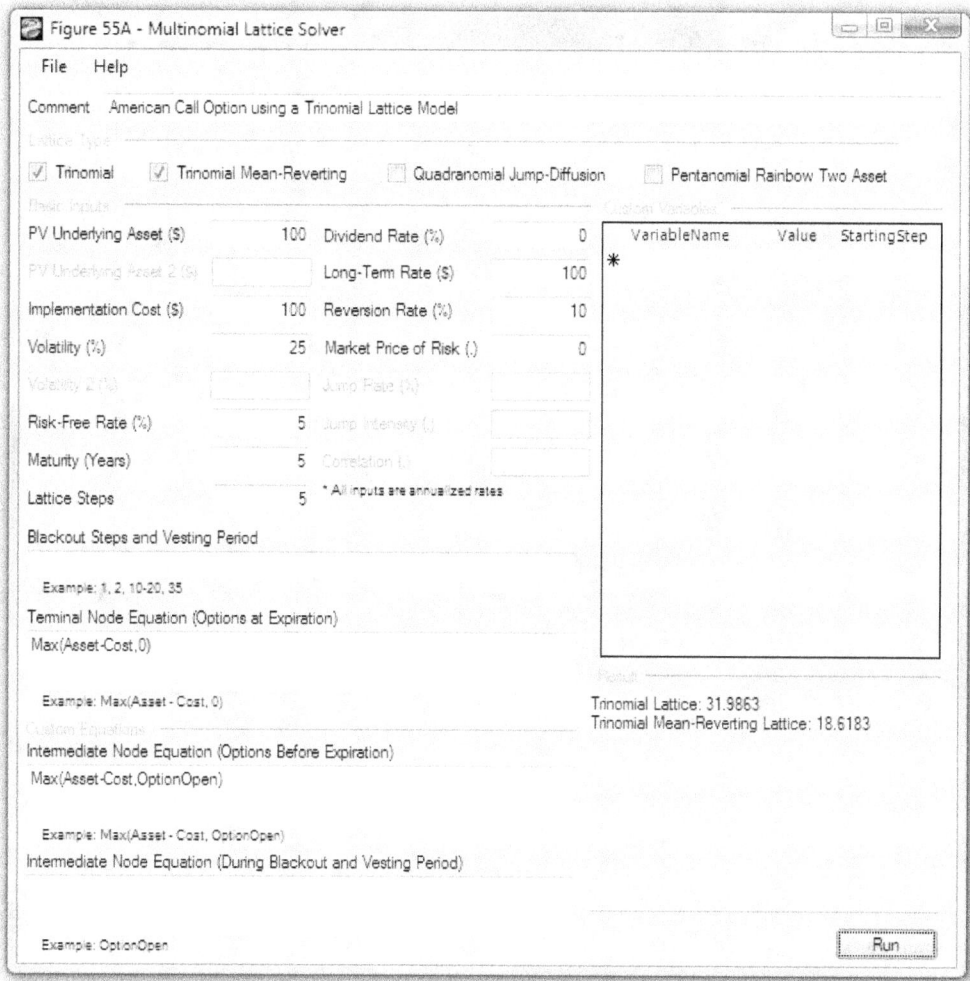

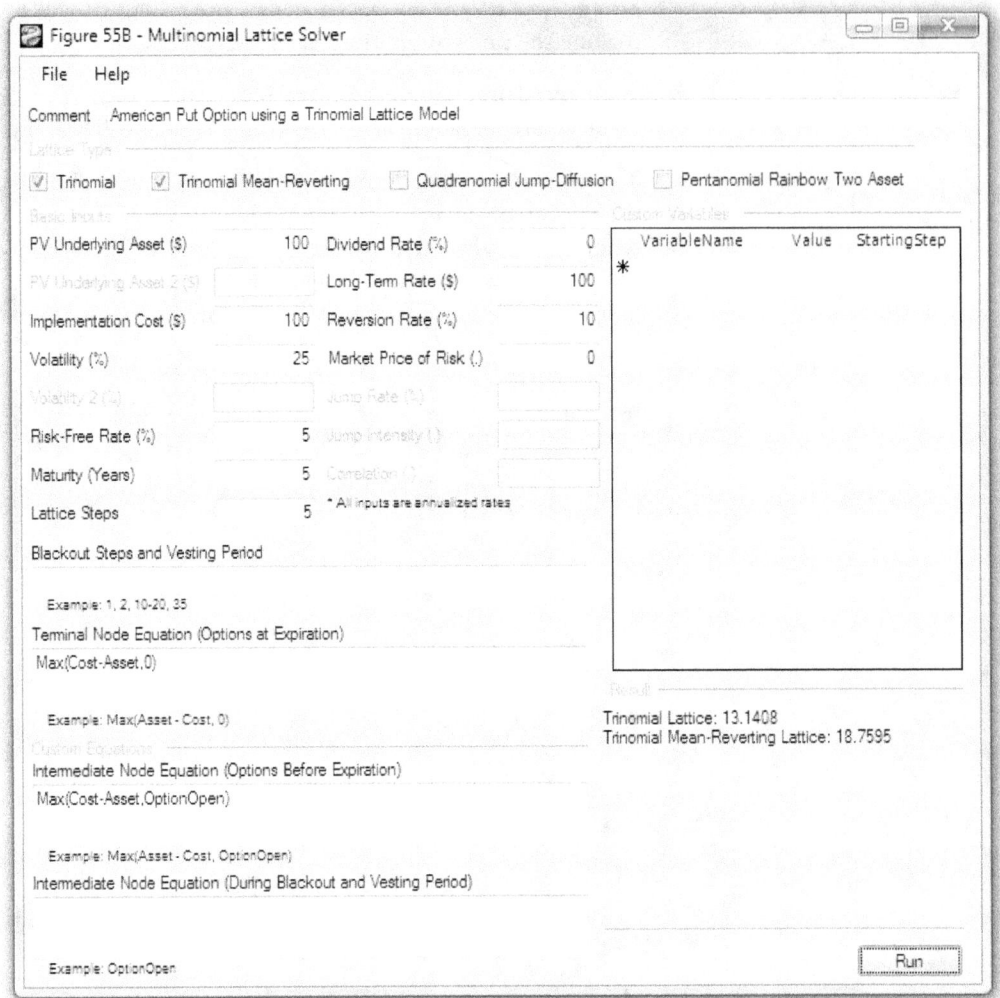

Figure 55A and 55B – Comparing Mean-Reverting Calls and Puts to
Regular Calls and Puts

Other items of interest in mean-reverting options include:

- The higher (lower) the long-term rate level, the higher (lower) the call options

- The higher (lower) the long-term rate level, the lower (higher) the put options

Finally, be careful when modeling mean-reverting options as higher lattice steps are usually required and certain combinations of reversion rates, long-term rate level, and lattice steps may yield unsolvable trinomial lattices. When this occurs, the MNLS will return error messages.

2.15 Jump-Diffusion Options Using Quadranomial Lattices

The *Jump-Diffusion Calls and Puts* for both American and European options applies the *Quadranomial Lattice* approach. This model is appropriate when the underlying variable in the option follows a jump-diffusion stochastic process. Figure 56 illustrates an underlying asset modeled using a jump-diffusion process. Jumps are commonplace in certain business variables such as price of oil and price of gas where prices take sudden and unexpected jumps (e.g., during a war). The underlying variable's frequency of jump is denoted as its *Jump Rate*, and the magnitude of each jump is its *Jump Intensity*.

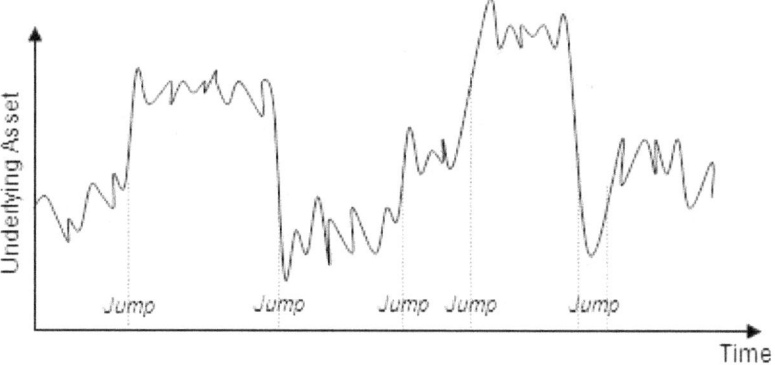

Figure 56 – Jump Diffusion Process

The binomial lattice is only able to capture a stochastic process without jumps (e.g., Brownian Motion and Random Walk processes) but when there is a probability of jump (albeit a small probability that follows a Poisson distribution), additional branches are required. The quadranomial lattice (four branches on each node) is used to capture these jumps as seen in Figure 57.

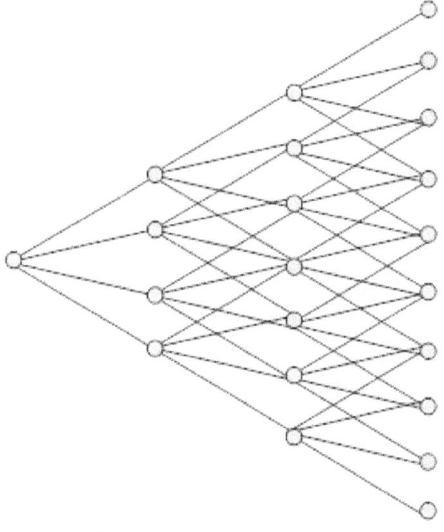

Figure 57 – Quadranomial Lattice

Be aware that due to the complexity of the models, some calculations with higher lattice steps may take slightly longer to compute. Furthermore, certain combinations of inputs may yield negative implied risk-neutral probabilities and result in a noncomputable lattice. In that case, make sure the inputs are correct (e.g., *Jump Intensity* has to exceed 1, where 1 implies no jumps; check for erroneous combinations of *Jump Rates*, *Jump Sizes*, and *Lattice Steps*). The probability of a jump can be computed as the product of the *Jump Rate* and time-step *δt*. Figure 58 illustrates a sample Quadranomial Jump-Diffusion Option analysis (example file used: *MNLS – Jump Diffusion Calls and Puts Using Quadranomial Lattices*). Notice that the Jump Diffusion call and put options are worth more than regular calls and puts. This is because with the positive jumps (10% probability per year with an average jump size of 1.50 times the previous values) of the underlying asset, the call and put options are worth more, even with the same volatility. If a real options problem has more than 2 underlying assets, either use the MSLS and/or Risk Simulator to simulate the underlying asset's trajectories and capture their interacting effects in a DCF model.

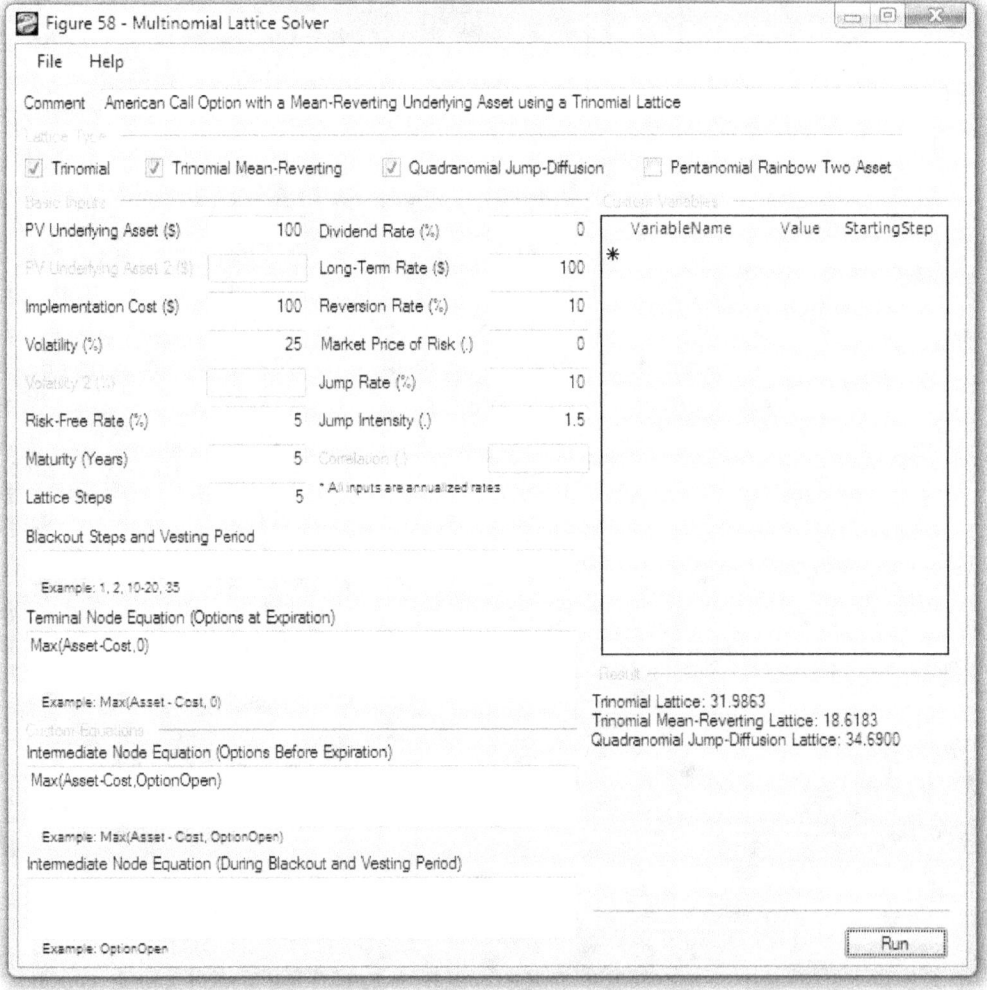

Figure 58 – Quadranomial Lattice Results on Jump-Diffusion Options

2.16 Dual Variable Rainbow Options
Using Pentanomial Lattices

The *Dual Variable Rainbow Option* for both American and European options requires the *Pentanomial Lattice* approach. Rainbows on the horizon after a rainy day comprise various colors of the light spectrum, and although rainbow options aren't as colorful as their physical counterparts, they get their name from the fact that they have two or more underlying assets rather than one. In contrast to standard options, the value of a rainbow option is determined by the behavior of two or more underlying elements and by the correlation between these underlying elements. That is, the value of a rainbow option is determined by the performance of two or more underlying asset elements. This particular model is appropriate when there are two underlying variables in the option (e.g., *Price of Asset* and *Quantity*) where each fluctuates at different rates of volatilities but at the same time might be correlated (Figure 59). These two variables are usually correlated in the real world, and the underlying asset value is the product of price and quantity. Due to the different volatilities, a pentanomial or five-branch lattice is used to capture all possible combinations of products (Figure 60). Be aware that certain combinations of inputs may yield an unsolvable lattice with negative implied probabilities. If that result occurs, a message will appear. Try a different combination of inputs as well as higher lattice steps to compensate.

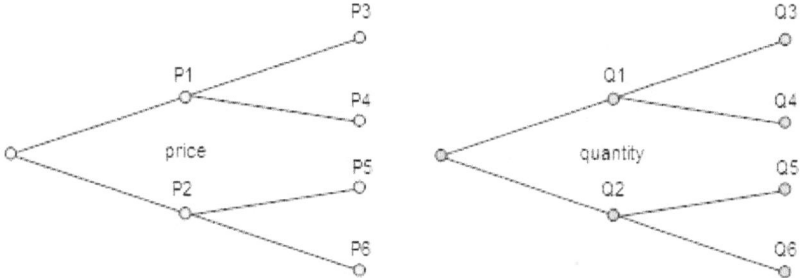

Figure 59 – Two Binomial Lattices (Asset Prices and Quantity)

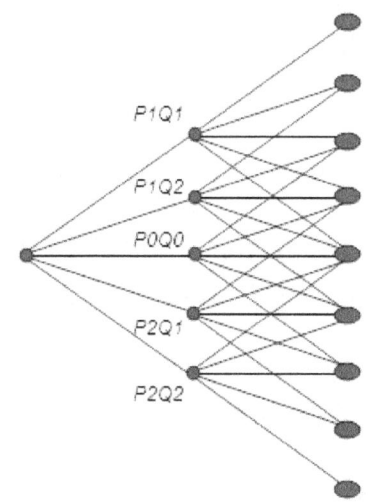

Figure 60 – Pentanomial Lattice (Combining Two Binomial Lattice)

Figure 61 shows an example Dual-Asset Rainbow Option (example file used: *MNLS – Dual-Asset Rainbow Option Pentanomial Lattice*). Notice that a high positive correlation will increase both the call option and put option values. This is because if both underlying elements move in the same direction, there is a higher overall portfolio volatility (price and quantity can fluctuate at high-high and low-low levels, generating a higher overall underlying asset value). In contrast, negative correlations will reduce both the call option and put option values for the opposite reason due to the portfolio diversification effects of negatively correlated variables. Of course correlation here is bounded between –1 and +1 inclusive.

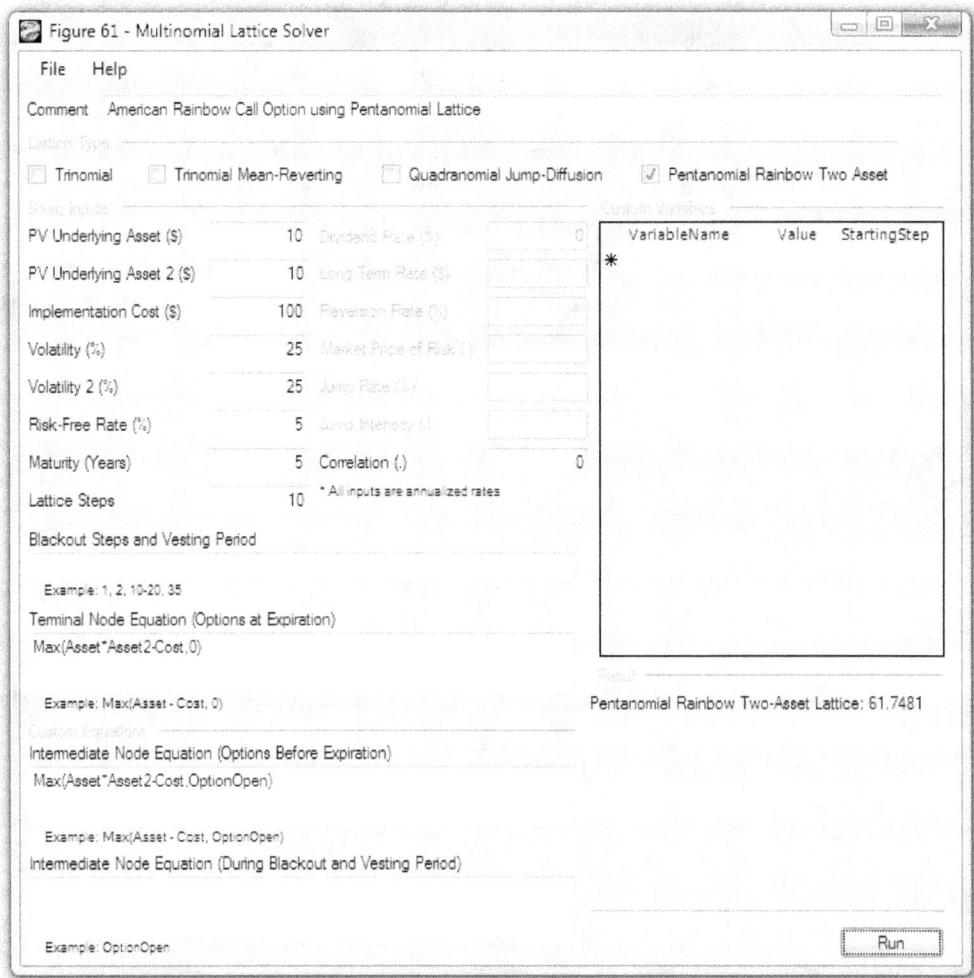

Figure 61 – Pentanomial Lattice Solving a Dual Asset Rainbow Option

2.17 American and European Lower Barrier Options

The *Lower Barrier Option* measures the strategic value of an option (this applies to both calls and puts) that comes either in-the-money or out-of-the-money when the *Asset Value* hits an artificial *Lower Barrier* that is currently lower than the asset value. Therefore, a *Down-and-In* option (for both calls and puts) indicates that the option becomes live if the asset value hits the lower barrier. Conversely, a *Down-and-Out* option is live only when the lower barrier is not breached.

Examples of this option include contractual agreements whereby if the lower barrier is breached some event or clause is triggered. The value of a barrier option is lower than standard options, as the barrier option will be valuable only within a smaller price range than the standard option. The holder of a barrier option loses some of the traditional option value and therefore such options should be worth less than a standard option. An example would be a contractual agreement whereby the writer of the contract can get into or out of certain obligations if the asset or project value breaches a barrier.

Figure 62 shows a Lower Barrier Option for a Down-and-In-Call. Notice that the value is only $7.3917, much lower than a regular American call option of $42.47. This is because the barrier is set low, at $90. This means that all of the upside potential that the regular call option can have will be reduced significantly, and the option can only be exercised if the asset value falls below this lower barrier of $90 (example file used: *Barrier Option – Down and In Lower Barrier Call*). To make such a Lower Barrier option *binding*, the *lower barrier level must be below the starting asset value but above the implementation cost.* If the barrier level is above the starting asset value, then it becomes an upper barrier option. If the lower barrier is below the implementation cost, then the option will be worthless under all conditions. It is when the lower barrier level is between the implementation cost and starting asset value that the option is potentially worth something. However, the value of the option is dependent on volatility. Using the same parameters in Figure 62 and changing the volatility and risk-free rates, the following examples illustrate what happens:

- At a volatility of 75%, the option value is $4.34
- At a volatility of 25%, the option value is $3.14
- At a volatility of 5%, the option value is $0.01

The lower the volatility, the lower the probability that the asset value will fluctuate enough to breach the lower barrier such that the option will be executed. By balancing volatility with the threshold lower barrier, you can create optimal trigger values for barriers.

In contrast, the Lower Barrier Option for Down-and-Out Call option is shown in Figure 63. Here, if the asset value breaches this lower barrier, the option is worthless, but is only valuable when it does not breach this lower barrier. As call options have higher values when the asset value is high, and lower value when the asset is low, this Lower Barrier Down-and-Out Call Option is hence worth almost the same as the regular American option. The higher the barrier, the lower the value of the lower barrier option will be (example file: *Barrier Option – Down and Out Lower Barrier Call*). For instance:

- At a lower barrier of $90, the option value is $42.19

- At a lower barrier of $100, the option value is $41.58

Figures 62 and 63 illustrate American Barrier Options. To change these into European Barrier Options set the Intermediate Node Equation Nodes to *OptionOpen*. In addition, for certain types of contractual options, vesting and blackout periods can be imposed. For solving such Bermudan Barrier Options, keep the same Intermediate Node Equation as the American Barrier Options but set the Intermediate Node Equation During Blackout and Vesting Periods to *OptionOpen* and insert the corresponding blackout and vesting period lattice steps. Finally, if the Barrier is a changing target over time, put in several custom variables named Barrier with the different values and starting lattice steps.

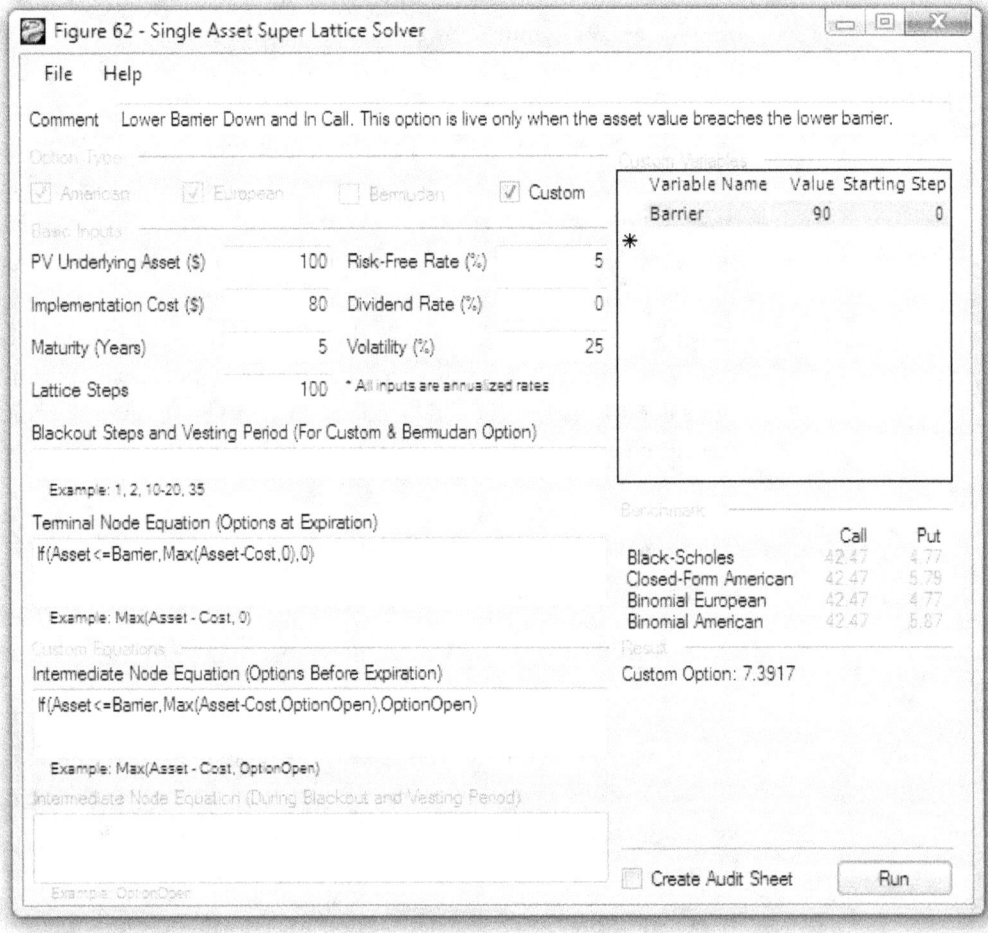

Figure 62 – Down and In Lower American Barrier Option

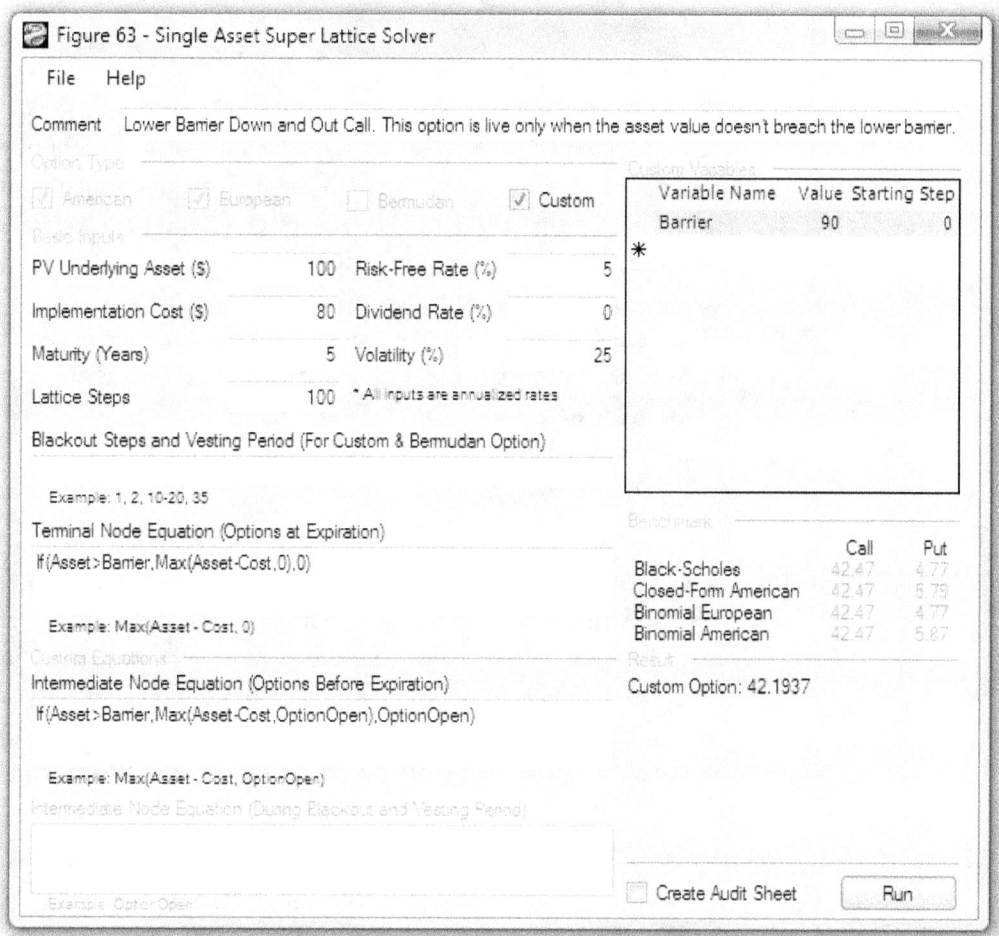

Figure 63 – Down and Out Lower American Barrier Option

2.18 American and European Upper Barrier Options

The *Upper Barrier Option* measures the strategic value of an option (this applies to both calls and puts) that comes either in-the-money or out-of-the-money when the *Asset Value* hits an artificial *Upper Barrier* that is currently higher than the asset value. Therefore, an *Up-and-In* option (for both calls and puts) indicates that the option becomes live if the asset value hits the upper barrier. Conversely, for the *Up-and-Out* option, the option is live only when the upper barrier is not breached. This is very similar to the Lower Barrier Option but now the barrier is above the starting asset value, and for a binding barrier option, the implementation cost is typically lower than the upper barrier. That is, the *upper barrier is usually > implementation cost and the upper barrier is also > starting asset value.*

Examples of this option include contractual agreements whereby if the upper barrier is breached some event or clause is triggered. The values of barrier options are typically lower than standard options, as the barrier option will have value within a smaller price range than the standard option. The holder of a barrier option loses some of the traditional option value and therefore a barrier option should sell at a lower price than a standard option. An example would be a contractual agreement whereby the writer of the contract can get into or out of certain obligations if the asset or project value breaches a barrier.

The Up-and-In Upper American Barrier Option has slightly lower value than a regular American call option as seen in Figure 64. This is because some of the option value when the asset is less than the barrier but greater than the implementation cost is lost. Clearly, the *higher the upper barrier, the lower the up-and-in barrier option value* will be as more of the option value is lost due to the inability to execute when the asset value is below the barrier (example file used: *Barrier Option – Up and In Upper Barrier Call*). For instance:

- When the upper barrier is $110, the option value is $41.22
- When the upper barrier is $120, the option value is $39.89

In contrast, an Up-and-Out Upper American Barrier Option is worth a lot less because this barrier truncates the option's upside potential. Figure 65 shows the computation of such an option. Clearly, the *higher the upper barrier, the higher the option value* will be (example file used: *Barrier Option – Up and Out Upper Barrier Call*). For instance:

- When the upper barrier is $110, the option value is $23.69
- When the upper barrier is $120, the option value is $29.59

Finally, note the issues of nonbinding barrier options. Examples of ***nonbinding options*** are:

- Up-and-Out Upper Barrier Calls when the Upper Barrier ≤ Implementation Cost, then the option will be worthless

- Up-and-In Upper Barrier Calls when Upper Barrier ≤ Implementation Cost, then the option value reverts to a simple call option

Examples of Upper Barrier Options are contractual options. Typical examples are:

- A manufacturer contractually agrees not to sell its products at prices higher than a pre-specified upper barrier price level.

- A client agrees to pay the market price of a good or product until a certain amount and then the contract becomes void if it exceeds some price ceiling.

Figures 64 and 65 illustrate American Barrier Options. To change these into European Barrier Options set the Intermediate Node Equation Nodes to *OptionOpen*. In addition, for certain types of contractual options, vesting and blackout periods can be imposed. For solving such Bermudan Barrier Options, keep the same Intermediate Node Equation as the American Barrier Options but set the Intermediate Node Equation During Blackout and Vesting Periods to *OptionOpen* and insert the corresponding blackout and vesting period lattice steps. Finally, if the Barrier is a changing target over time, put in several custom variables named Barrier with the different values and starting lattice steps.

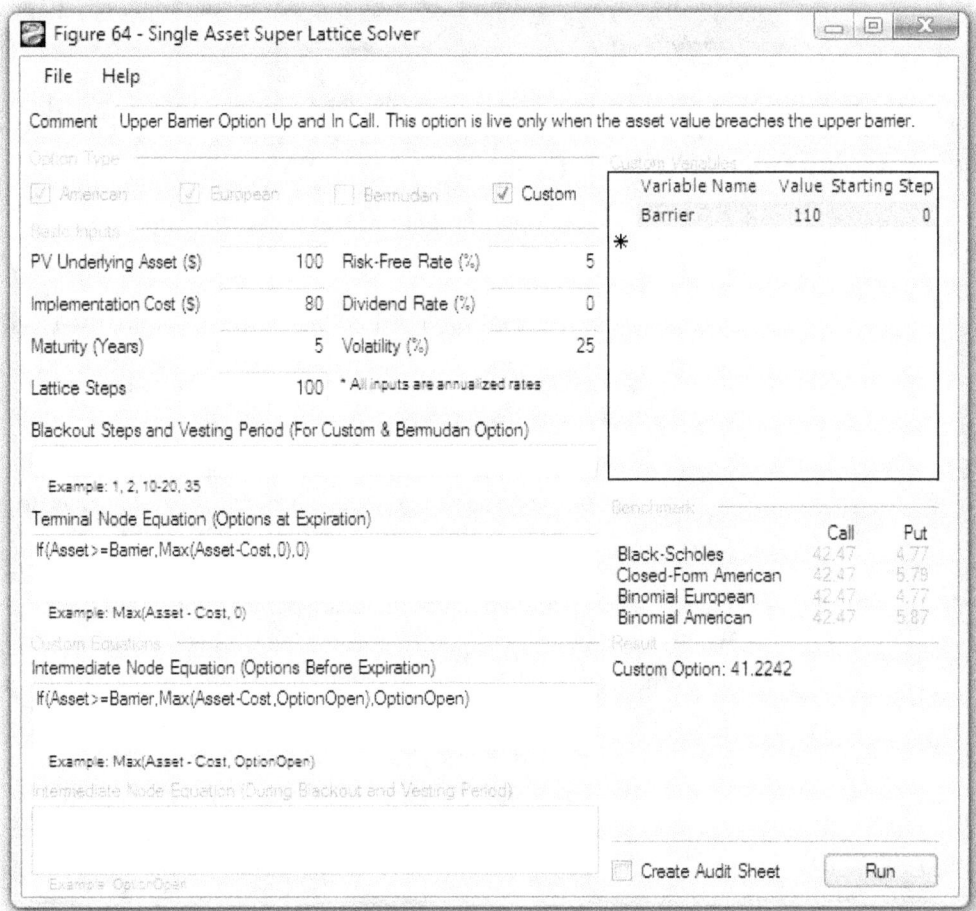

Figure 64 – Up and In Upper American Barrier Option

User Manual

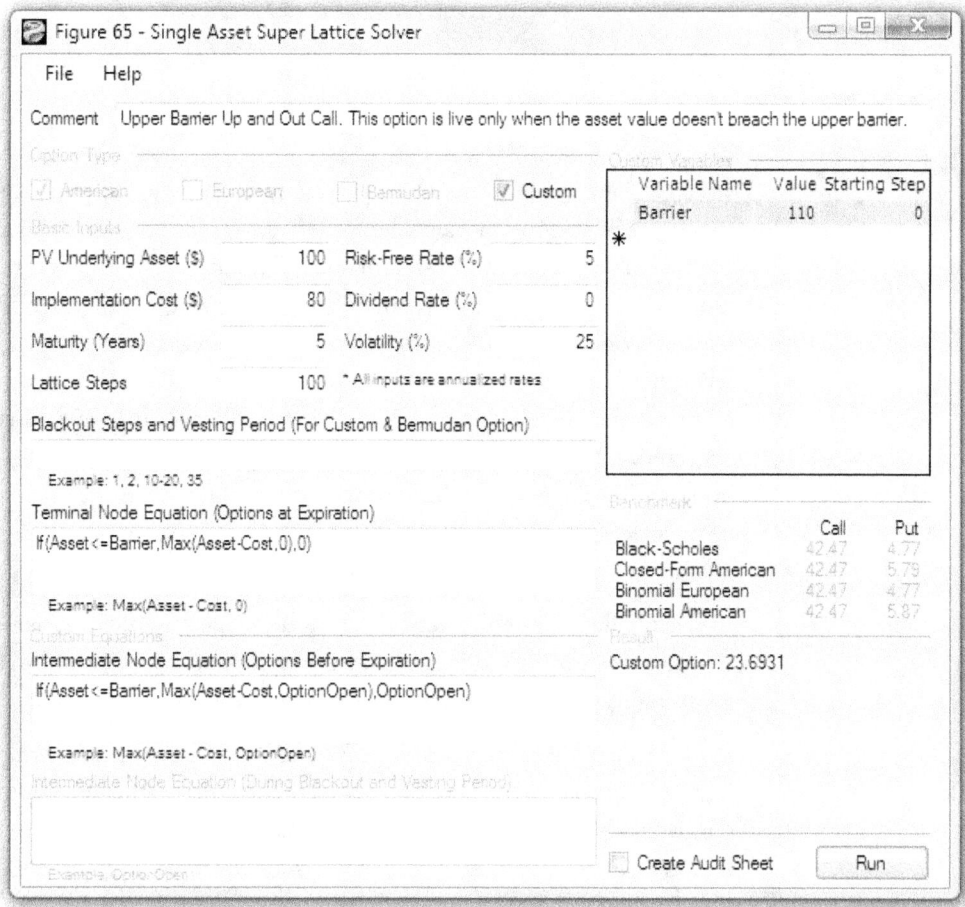

Figure 65 – Up and Out Upper American Barrier Option

2.19 American and European Double Barrier Options and Exotic Barriers

The *Double Barrier Option* is solved using the binomial lattice. This model measures the strategic value of an option (this applies to both calls and puts) that comes either in-the-money or out-of-the-money when the *Asset Value* hits either the artificial *Upper* or *Lower Barriers*. Therefore, an *Up-and-In* and *Down-and-In* option (for both calls and puts) indicates that the option becomes live if the asset value either hits the upper or lower barrier. Conversely, for the *Up-and-Out* and *Down-and-Out* option, the option is live only when neither the upper nor lower barrier is breached. Examples of this option include contractual agreements whereby if the upper barrier is breached some event or clause is triggered. The value of barrier options is lower than standard options, as the barrier option will have value within a smaller price range than the standard option. The holder of a barrier option loses some of the traditional option value and therefore should sell it at a lower price than a standard option.

Figure 66 illustrates an American Up-and-In, Down-and-In Double Barrier Option. This is a combination of the Upper and Lower Barrier Options shown previously. The same exact logic applies to this Double Barrier Option.

Figure 66 illustrates the American Barrier Option solved using the SLS. To change these into a European Barrier Option set the Intermediate Node Equation Nodes to *OptionOpen*. In addition, for certain types of contractual options, vesting and blackout periods can be imposed. For solving such Bermudan Barrier Options, keep the same Intermediate Node Equation as the American Barrier Options but set the Intermediate Node Equation During Blackout and Vesting Periods to *OptionOpen* and insert the corresponding blackout and vesting period lattice steps. Finally, if the Barrier is a changing target over time, put in several custom variables named Barrier with the different values and starting lattice steps.

Exotic Barrier Options exist when other options are combined with barriers. For instance, an option to expand can only be executed if the PV Asset exceeds some threshold, or a contraction option to outsource manufacturing can only be executed when it falls below some breakeven point. Again, such options can be easily modeled using the SLS.

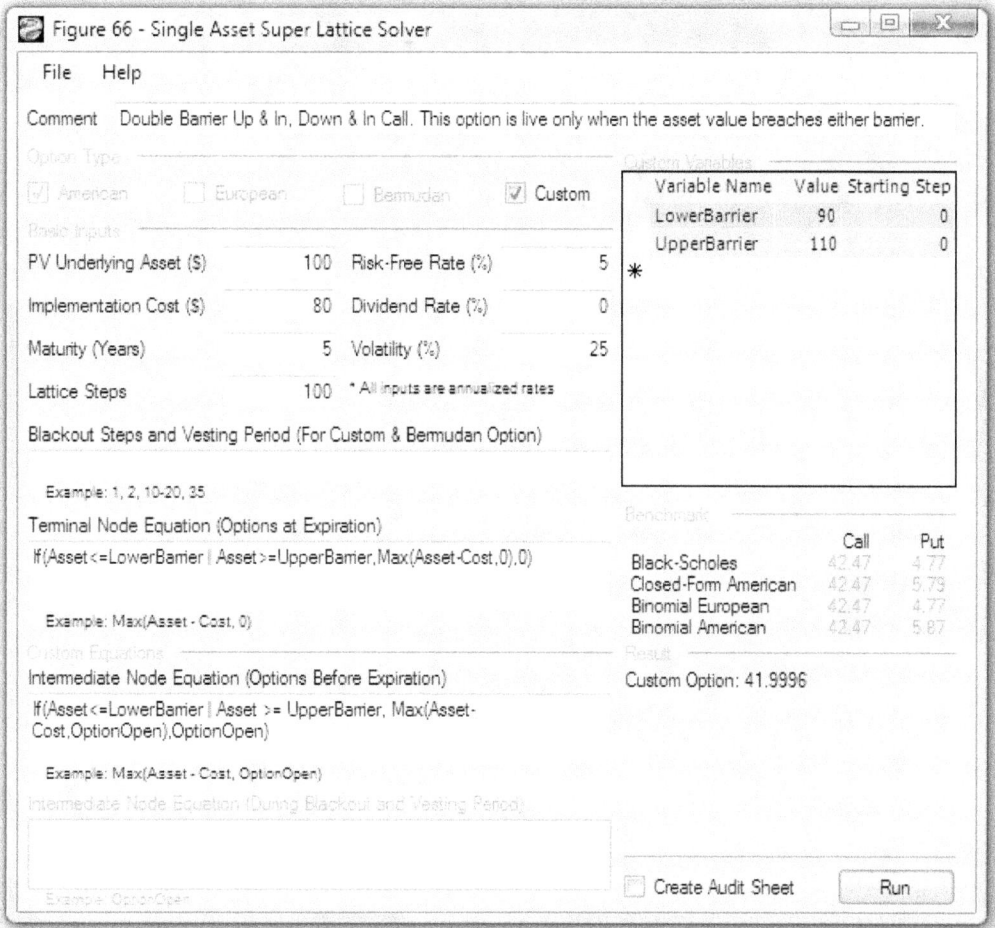

Figure 66 – Up and In, Down and In Double Barrier Option

SECTION III – EMPLOYEE STOCK OPTIONS

3.1 American ESO with Vesting Period

Figure 67 illustrates how an employee stock option (ESO) with a vesting period and blackout dates can be modeled. Enter the blackout steps (0-39). Because the blackout dates input box has been used, you will need to enter the Terminal Node Equation (TE), Intermediate Node Equation (IE), and Intermediate Node Equation During Vesting and Blackout Periods (IEV). Enter *Max(Stock-Strike,0)* for the TE; *Max(Stock-Strike,0,OptionOpen)* for the IE; and *OptionOpen* for IEV (example file used: *ESO Vesting*). This means the option is executed or left to expire worthless at termination; execute early or keep the option open during the intermediate nodes; and keep the option open only and no executions are allowed during the intermediate steps when blackouts or vesting occurs. The result is $49.73 (Figure 67) which can be corroborated with the use of the ESO Valuation Toolkit (Figure 68). ESO Valuation Toolkit is another software tool developed by Real Options Valuation, Inc., specifically designed to solve ESO problems following the 2004 FAS 123. In fact, this software was used by the Financial Accounting Standards Board to model the valuation example in their final FAS 123 Statement in December 2004. Before starting with ESO valuations, it is suggested that the user read Dr. Johnathan Mun's book *Valuing Employee Stock Options* (Wiley 2004) as a primer.

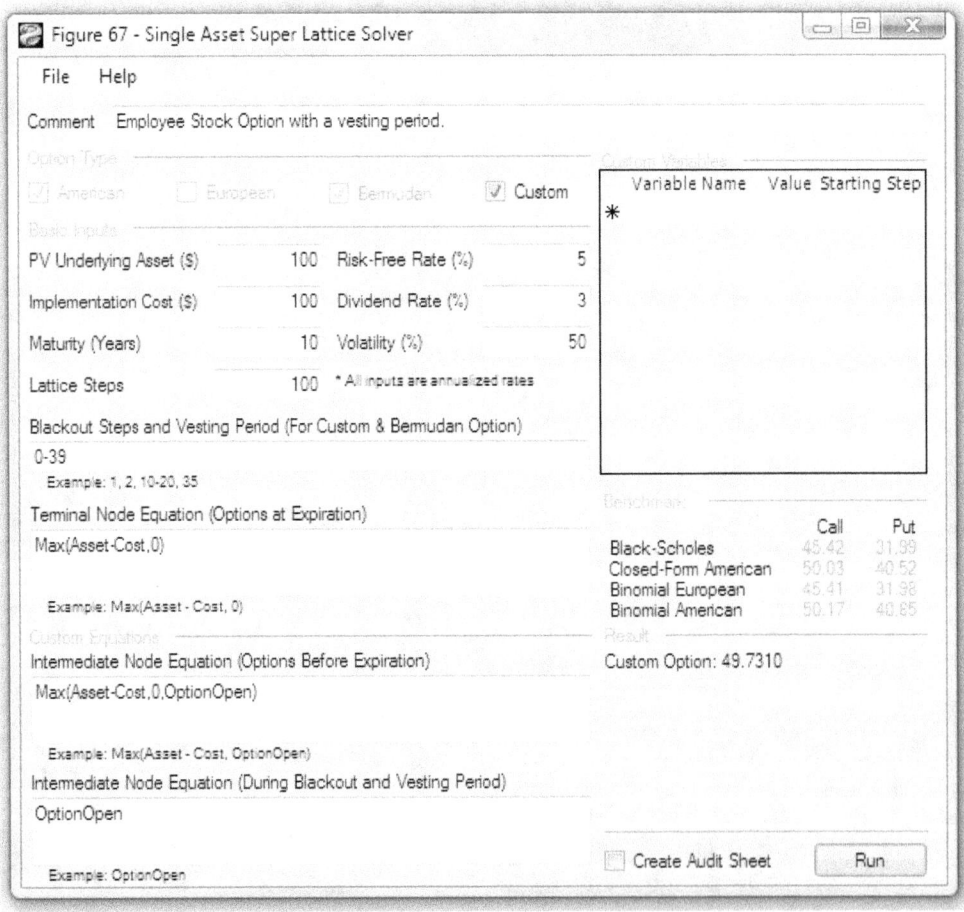

Figure 67 – SLS Results of a Vesting Call Option

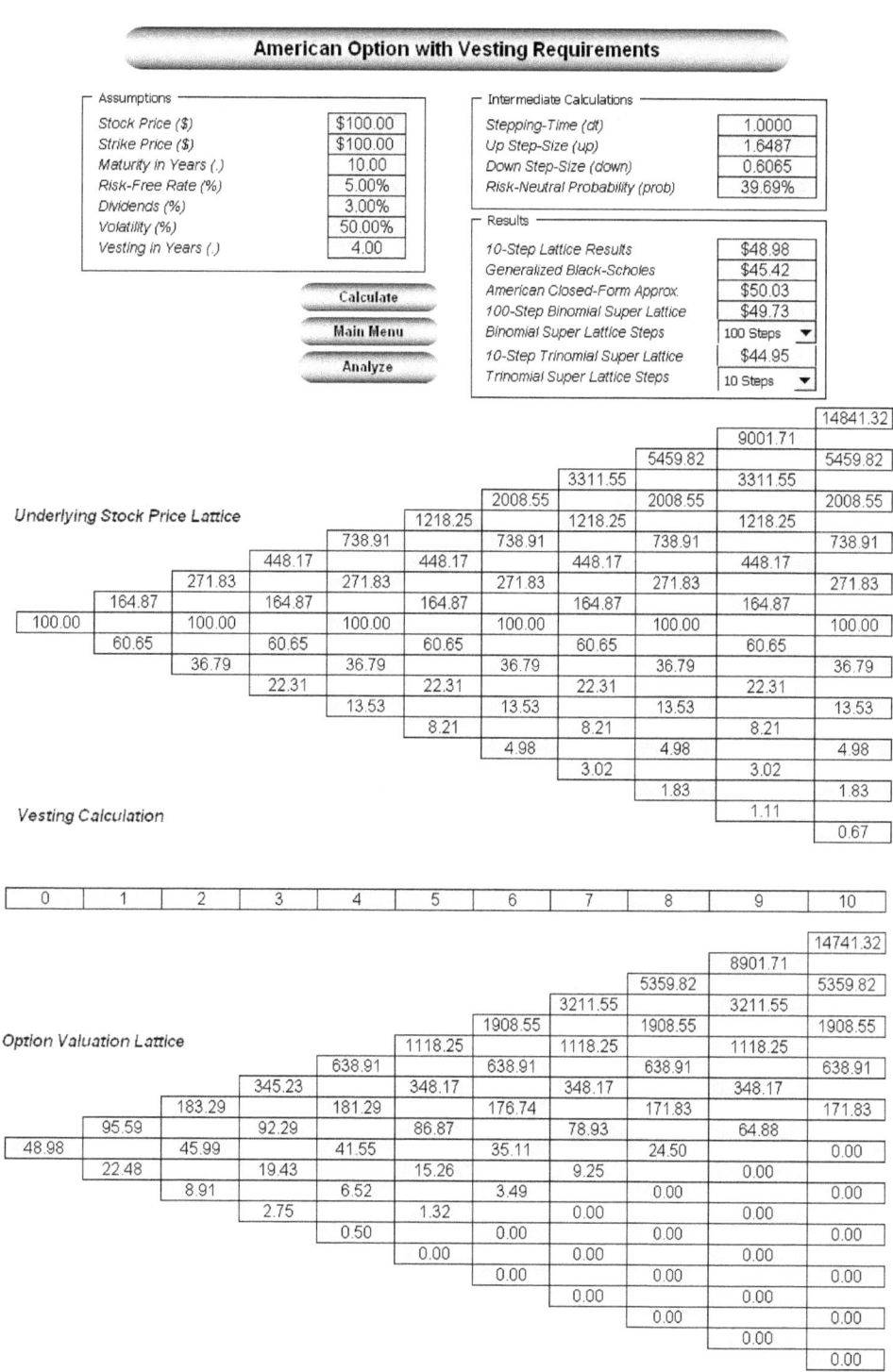

Figure 68 – ESO Valuation Toolkit Results of a Vesting Call Option

3.2 American ESO with Suboptimal Exercise Behavior

This example shows how suboptimal exercise behavior multiples can be included into the analysis and how the custom variables list can be used as seen in Figure 69 (example file used: *ESO Suboptimal Behavior* and steps was changed to 100 in this example). The TE is the same as the previous example but the IE assumes that the option will be suboptimally executed if the stock price in some future state exceeds the suboptimal exercise threshold times the strike price. Notice that the IEV is not used because we did not assume any vesting or blackout periods. Also, the *Suboptimal* exercise multiple variable is listed on the customs variable list with the relevant value of 1.85 and a starting step of 0. This means that 1.85 is applicable starting from step 0 in the lattice all the way through to step 100. The results again are verified through the ESO Toolkit (Figure 70).

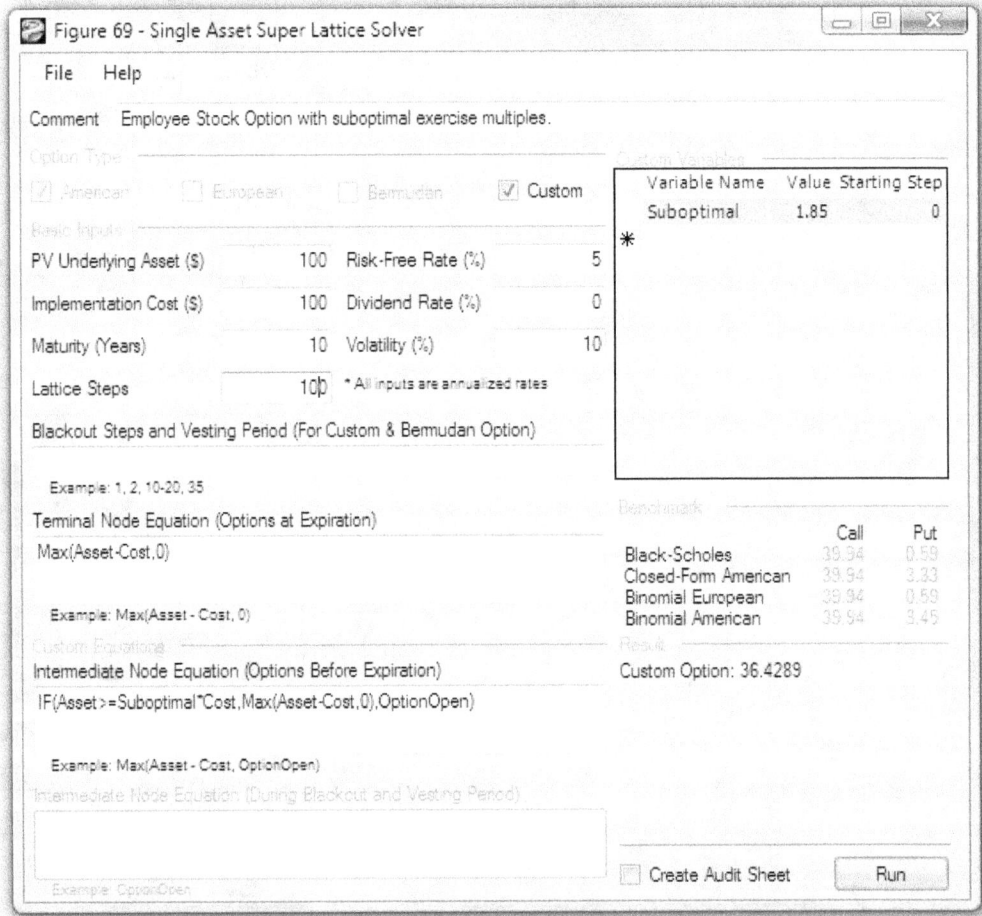

Figure 69 – SLS Results of a Call Option with Suboptimal Behavior

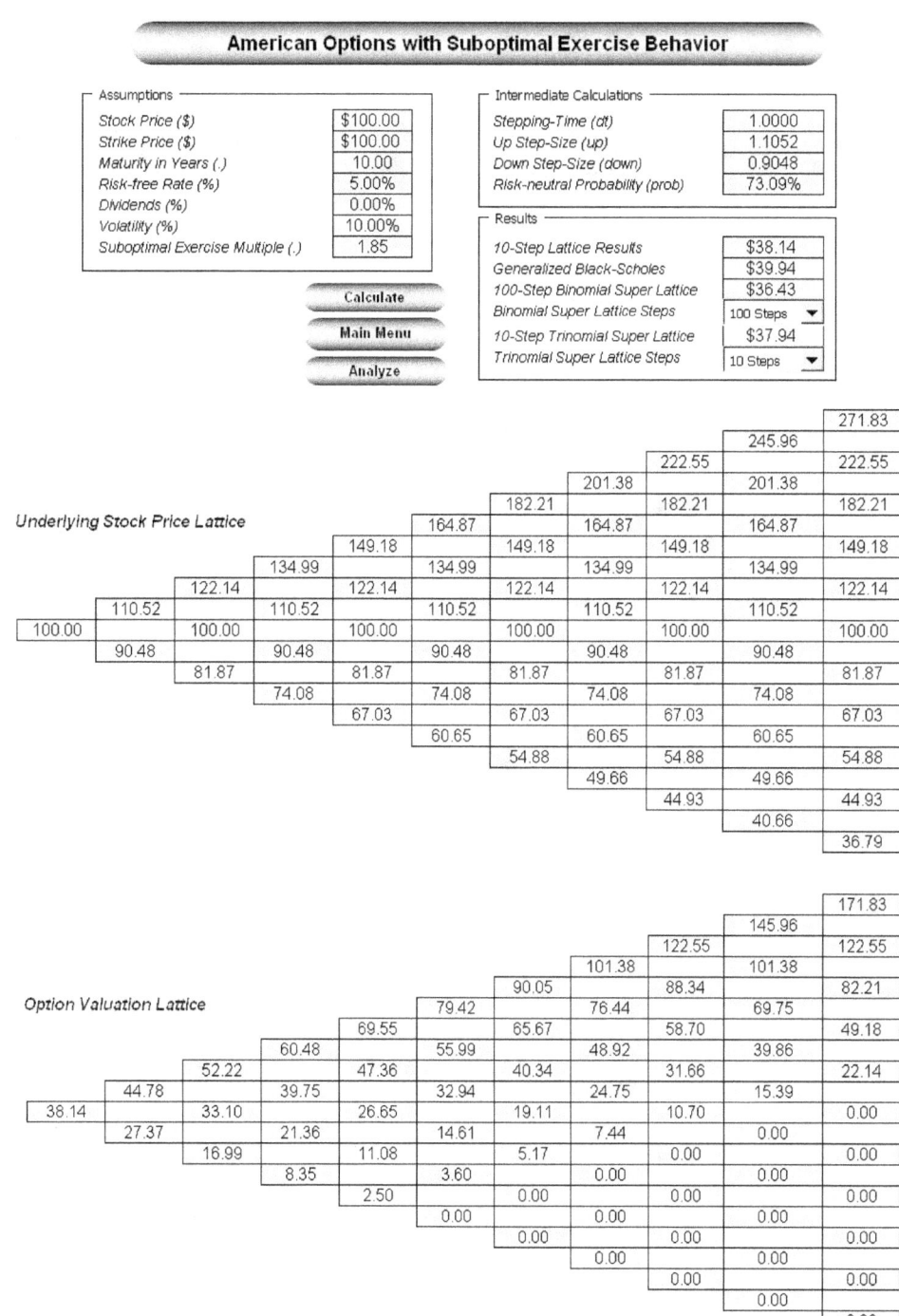

Figure 70 – ESO Toolkit Results of a Call Option accounting for Suboptimal Behavior

3.3 American ESO with Vesting and Suboptimal Exercise Behavior

Next, we have the ESO with vesting and suboptimal exercise behavior. This is simply the extension of the previous two examples. Again, the result of $9.22 (Figure 71) is verified using the ESO Toolkit as seen in Figure 72 (example file used: *ESO Vesting with Suboptimal Behavior*).

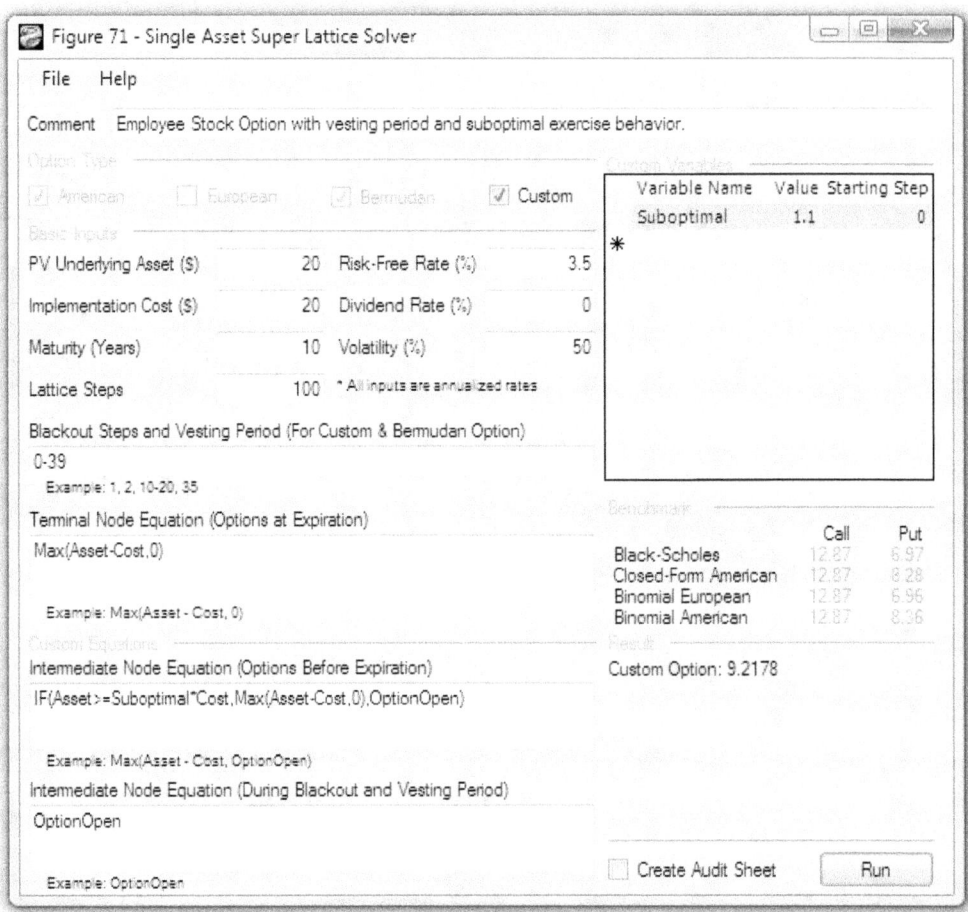

Figure 71 – SLS Results of a Call Option accounting for Vesting and Suboptimal Behavior

American Option with Vesting and Suboptimal Behavior

Assumptions

Stock Price ($)	$20.00
Strike Price ($)	$20.00
Maturity in Years (.)	10.00
Risk-free Rate (%)	3.50%
Dividends (%)	0.00%
Volatility (%)	50.00%
Suboptimal Exercise Multiple (.)	1.10
Vesting in Years (.)	4.00

Intermediate Calculations

Stepping-Time (dt)	1.0000
Up Step-Size (up)	1.6487
Down Step-Size (down)	0.6065
Risk-neutral Probability (prob)	41.17%

Results

10-Step Lattice Results	$10.61
Generalized Black-Scholes	$12.87
100-Step Binomial Super Lattice	$9.22
Binomial Super Lattice Steps	100 Steps ▼
100-Step Trinomial Super Lattice	$9.43
Trinomial Super Lattice Steps	100 Steps ▼

Calculate

Main Menu

Analyze

Underlying Stock Price Lattice

										2968.26
									1800.34	
								1091.96		1091.96
							662.31		662.31	
						401.71		401.71		401.71
					243.65		243.65		243.65	
				147.78		147.78		147.78		147.78
			89.63		89.63		89.63		89.63	
		54.37		54.37		54.37		54.37		54.37
	32.97		32.97		32.97		32.97		32.97	
20.00		20.00		20.00		20.00		20.00		20.00
	12.13		12.13		12.13		12.13		12.13	
		7.36		7.36		7.36		7.36		7.36
			4.46		4.46		4.46		4.46	
				2.71		2.71		2.71		2.71
					1.64		1.64		1.64	
						1.00		1.00		1.00
							0.60		0.60	
								0.37		0.37
									0.22	
										0.13

Option Valuation Lattice

										2948.26
									1780.34	
								1071.96		1071.96
							642.31		642.31	
						381.71		381.71		381.71
					223.65		223.65		223.65	
				127.78		127.78		127.78		127.78
			70.32		69.63		69.63		69.63	
		37.93		34.37		34.37		34.37		34.37
	20.17		17.55		12.97		12.97		12.97	
10.61		8.97		6.85		6.32		5.16		0.00
	4.55		3.50		2.98		2.05		0.00	
		1.74		1.37		0.82		0.00		0.00
			0.62		0.32		0.00		0.00	
				0.13		0.00		0.00		0.00
					0.00		0.00		0.00	
						0.00		0.00		0.00
							0.00		0.00	
								0.00		0.00
									0.00	
										0.00

Figure 72 – ESO Toolkit Results of a Call Option accounting for Vesting and Suboptimal Behavior

3.4 American ESO with Vesting, Suboptimal Exercise Behavior, Blackout Periods, and Forfeiture Rate

This example now incorporates the element of forfeiture into the model as seen in Figure 73 (example file used: *ESO Vesting, Blackout, Suboptimal, Forfeiture*). This means that if the option is vested and the prevailing stock price exceeds the suboptimal threshold above the strike price, the option will be summarily and suboptimally executed. If vested but not exceeding the threshold, the option will be executed only if the post-vesting forfeiture occurs, but the option is kept open otherwise. This means that the intermediate step is a probability weighted average of these occurrences. Finally, when an employee forfeits the option during the vesting period, all options are forfeited, with a pre-vesting forfeiture rate. In this example, we assume identical pre- and post-vesting forfeitures so that we can verify the results using the ESO Toolkit (Figure 74). In certain other cases, a different rate may be assumed.

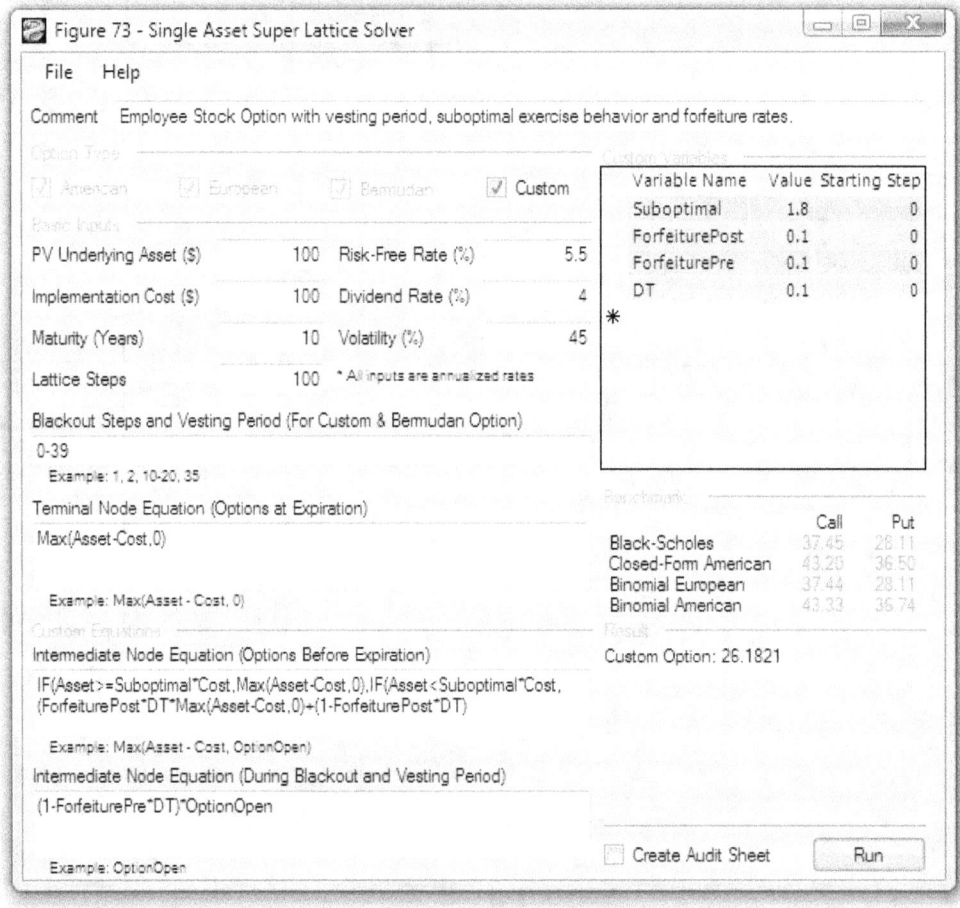

Figure 73 – SLS Results of a Call Option accounting for Vesting, Forfeiture, Suboptimal Behavior, and Blackout Periods

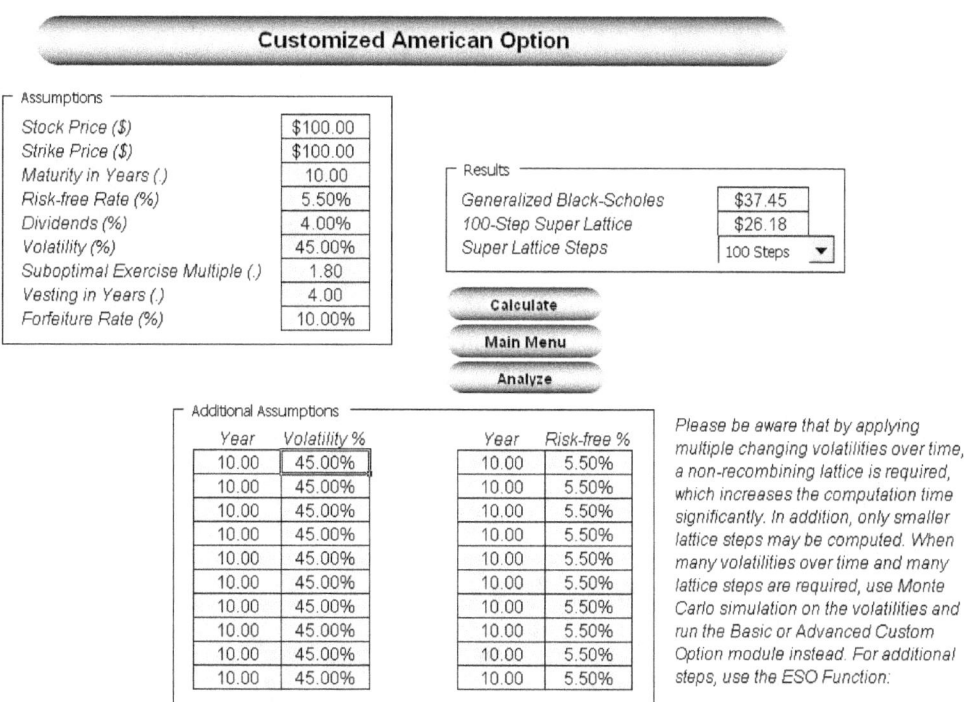

Figure 74 – ESO Toolkit Results after accounting for Vesting, Forfeiture, Suboptimal Behavior, and Blackout Periods

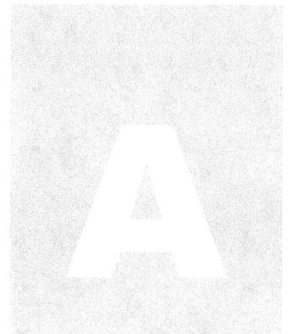

Appendix A: Lattice Convergence

The higher the number of lattice steps, the higher the precision of the results. Figure A1 illustrates the convergence of results obtained using a BSM closed-form model on a European call option without dividends, and comparing its results to the basic binomial lattice. Convergence is generally achieved at between 500-1,000 steps. Due to the high number of steps required to generate the results, software-based mathematical algorithms are used.[4] For instance, a nonrecombining binomial lattice with 1,000 steps has a total of 2×10^{301} nodal calculations to perform, making manual computation impossible without the use of specialized algorithms.[5] Figure A1 also illustrates the binomial lattice results with different steps and notes the convergence of the binomial for a simple European call option using the Black-Scholes model.

---

[4] This proprietary algorithm was developed by Dr. Johnathan Mun based on his analytical work with FASB in 2003-2004; his books: "Valuing Employee Stock Options Under the 2004 FAS 123 Requirements" (Wiley, 2004), "Real Options Analysis: Tools and Techniques" (Wiley, 2002), "Real Options Analysis Course" (Wiley, 2003), "Applied Risk Analysis: Moving Beyond Uncertainty" (Wiley, 2003); creation of his software, "Real Options Analysis Toolkit" (versions 1.0 and 2.0); academic research; and previous valuation consulting experience at KPMG Consulting.

[5] A nonrecombining binomial lattice bifurcates (splits into two) every step it takes, so starting from one value, it branches out to two values on the first step (2^1), two becomes four in the second step (2^2), and four becomes eight in the third step (2^3) and so forth, until the 1,000th step (2^{1000} or over 10^{301} values to calculate, and the world's fastest supercomputer won't be able to calculate the result within our lifetimes).

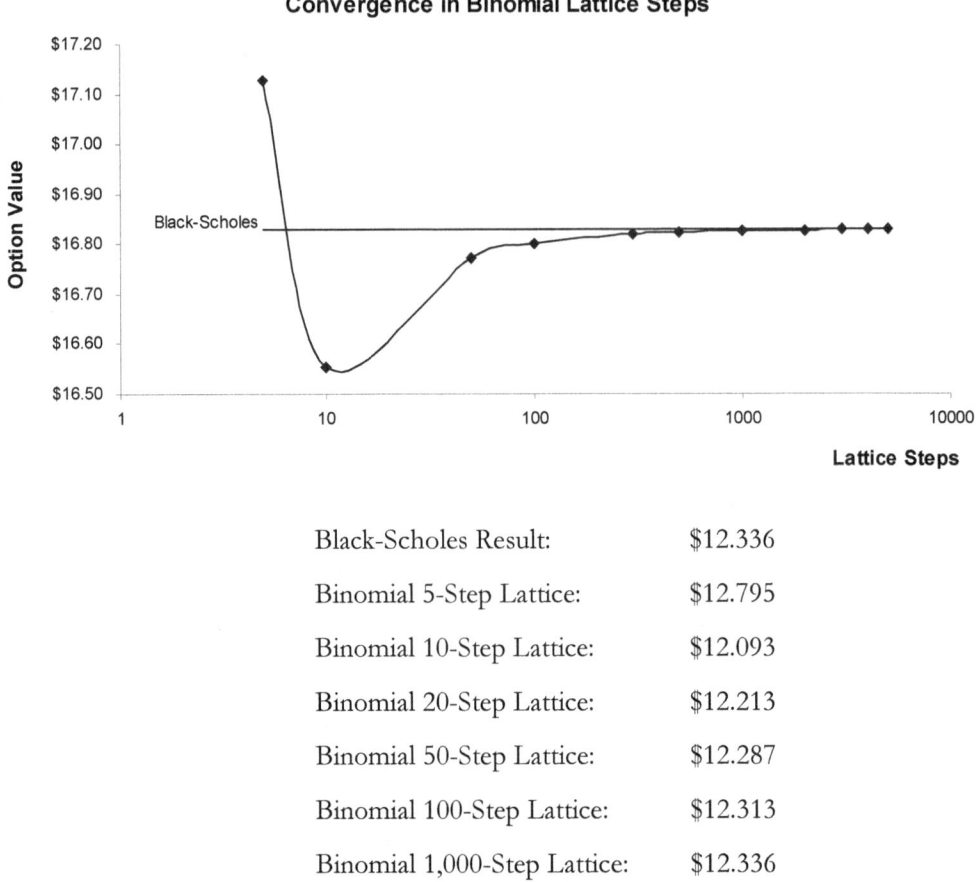

Convergence in Binomial Lattice Steps

Black-Scholes Result:	$12.336
Binomial 5-Step Lattice:	$12.795
Binomial 10-Step Lattice:	$12.093
Binomial 20-Step Lattice:	$12.213
Binomial 50-Step Lattice:	$12.287
Binomial 100-Step Lattice:	$12.313
Binomial 1,000-Step Lattice:	$12.336

Figure A1 – Convergence of the Binomial Lattice Results to Closed-Form Solutions

Appendix B: Volatility Estimates

There are several ways to estimate the volatility used in the option models:

- ***Logarithmic Cash Flow Returns Approach or Logarithmic Stock Price Returns Approach:*** Used mainly for computing the volatility on liquid and tradable assets such as stocks in financial options. Sometimes used for other traded assets such as price of oil and price of electricity. The drawback is that DCF models with only a few cash flows will generally *overstate* the volatility and this method cannot be used when negative cash flows occur. The benefits include its computational ease, transparency, and modeling flexibility of the method. In addition, no simulation is required to obtain a volatility estimate.

- ***Logarithmic Present Value Returns Approach:*** Used mainly when computing the volatility on assets with cash flows, a typical application is in real options. The drawback of this method is that simulation is required to obtain a single volatility and is not applicable for highly traded liquid assets such as stock prices. The benefit includes the ability to accommodate certain negative cash flows and applies more rigorous analysis than the logarithmic cash flow returns approach, providing a more accurate and conservative estimate of volatility when assets are analyzed.

- ***Generalized Autoregressive Moving Average (GARCH) Models:*** Used mainly for computing the volatility on liquid and tradable assets such as stocks in financial options. Sometimes used for other traded assets such as price of oil and price of electricity. The drawback is that a lot of data is required, advanced econometric modeling expertise is required, and this approach is highly susceptible to user manipulation. The benefit is that rigorous statistical analysis is performed to find the best-fitting volatility curve, providing different volatility estimates over time.

- ***Management Assumptions and Guesses:*** Used for both financial options and real options. The drawback is that the volatility estimates are very unreliable and are only subjective best-guesses. The benefit of this approach is its simplicity—this method is very easy to explain to management the concept of volatility—both in execution and interpretation.

- ***Market Proxy Comparables or Indices:*** Used mainly for comparing liquid and non-liquid assets, as long as comparable market-, sector-, or industry-specific data are available. The drawback is that it is sometimes hard to find the right comparable firms and the results may be subject to gross manipulation by subjectively including or excluding certain firms. The benefit is its ease of use.

B.1 Volatility Estimates (Logarithmic Cash Flow Returns/Stock Price Returns Approach)

The *Logarithmic Cash Flow Returns or Logarithmic Stock Price Returns Approach* calculates the volatility using the individual future cash-flow estimates, comparable cash-flow estimates, or historical prices, generating their corresponding logarithmic relative returns, as illustrated in Figure B1. Starting with a series of forecast future cash flows or historical prices, convert them into relative returns. Then take the natural logarithms of these relative returns. The standard deviation of these natural logarithm returns is the *periodic volatility* of the cash flow series. The resulting periodic volatility from the sample dataset in Figure B1 is 25.58%. This value will then have to be annualized.

No matter what the approach used, the periodic volatility estimate used in a real options or financial options analysis has to be an *annualized volatility*. Depending on the periodicity of the raw cash flow or stock price data used, the volatility calculated should be converted into annualized values using $\sigma\sqrt{P}$, where P is the number of periods in a year and σ is the periodic volatility. For instance, if the calculated volatility using monthly cash flow data is 10%, the annualized volatility is $10\%\sqrt{12} = 35\%$. Similarly, P is 365 (or about 250 if accounting for trading days and not calendar days) for daily data, 4 for quarterly data, 2 for semiannual data, and 1 for annual data.

Notice that the number of returns in Figure B1 is one less than the total number of periods. That is, for time periods 0 to 5, we have six cash flows but only five cash flow relative returns. This approach is valid and correct when estimating the volatilities of liquid and highly-traded assets—historical stock prices, historical prices of oil and electricity—and is less valid for computing volatilities in a real options world, where the underlying asset generates cash flows. This is because to obtain valid results, many data points are required, and in modeling real options, the cash flows generated using a DCF model may only be for 5 to 10 periods. In contrast, a large number of historical stock prices or oil prices can be downloaded and analyzed. With smaller data sets, this approach typically overestimates the volatility.

Time Period	Cash Flows	Cash Flow Relative Returns	Natural Logarithm of Cash Flow Returns (X)
0	$100	–	–
1	$125	$125/$100 = 1.25	ln($125/$100) = 0.2231
2	$95	$95/$125 = 0.76	ln($95/$125) = -0.2744
3	$105	$105/$95 = 1.11	ln($105/$95) = 0.1001
4	$155	$155/$105 = 1.48	ln($155/$105) = 0.3895
5	$146	$146/$155 = 0.94	ln($146/$155) = -0.0598

Figure B1 – Log Cash Flow Returns Approach

The volatility estimate is then calculated as

$$volatility = \sqrt{\frac{1}{n-1}\sum_{i=1}^{n}(x_i - \bar{x})^2} = 25.58\%$$

where n is the number of Xs, and $\bar{x}$ is the average X value.

To further illustrate the use of this approach, Figure B2 shows the stock prices for Microsoft downloaded from Yahoo! Finance, a publicly available free resource.[6] You can follow along the example by loading the example file: *Start | Programs | Real Options Valuation | Real Options Super Lattice Solver | Volatility Estimates* and select the worksheet tab *Log Cash Flow Approach*. The data in columns A to G in Figure B2 are downloaded from Yahoo. The formula in cell I3 is simply *LN(G3/G4)* to compute the natural logarithmic value of the relative returns week over week, and is copied down the entire column. The formula in cell J3 is *STDEV(I3:I54)*SQRT(52)* which computes the annualized (by multiplying the square root of the number of weeks in a year) volatility (by taking the standard deviation of the entire 52 weeks of the year 2004 data). The formula in cell J3 is then copied down the entire column to compute a moving-window of annualized volatilities. The volatility used in this example is the average of a 52-week moving window, which covers two years of data. That is, cell L8's formula is *AVERAGE(J3:J54)*, where cell J54 has the following formula: *STDEV(I54:I105)*SQRT(52)*, and of course row 105 is January 2003. This means that the 52-week moving window captures the average volatility over a 2-year period and smoothes the volatility such that infrequent but extreme spikes will not dominate the volatility computation. Of course, a median volatility should also be computed. If the median is far off from the average, the distribution of volatilities is skewed and the median should be used, otherwise, the average should be used. Finally, these 52 volatilities can be fed into Monte Carlo simulation *Risk Simulator* software and the volatilities themselves can be simulated.

---

[6] Go to http://finance.yahoo.com and enter a stock symbol (e.g., MSFT). Click on Quotes: Historical Prices and select Weekly and select the period of interest. You can then download the data to a spreadsheet for analysis.

	A	B	C	D	E	F	G	H	I	J	K	L	M
1	**Downloaded Weekly Historical Stock Prices of Microsoft**								**Volatility Computations**				
2	Date	Open	High	Low	Close	Volume	Adj. Close*		LN Relative Returns	Moving Average Volatilities			
3	27-Dec-04	27.01	27.10	26.68	26.72	52388840	26.64		-0.0108	17.87%			
4	20-Dec-04	27.01	27.17	26.78	27.01	77413174	26.93		0.0019	17.84%			
5	13-Dec-04	27.10	27.40	26.80	26.96	108628300	26.88		-0.0045	17.85%			
6	6-Dec-04	27.10	27.44	26.91	27.08	83312720	27.00		-0.0055	18.00%	*One-Year Annualized Volatility*		
7	29-Nov-04	26.64	27.44	26.61	27.23	83103200	27.15		0.0235	18.13%			
8	22-Nov-04	26.75	26.82	26.10	26.60	61834599	26.52		-0.0098	18.03%	Average	21.89%	
9	15-Nov-04	27.34	27.50	26.84	26.86	75375960	26.78		-0.0011	18.10%	Median	22.30%	
10	8-Nov-04	29.18	30.20	29.13	29.97	109385736	26.81		0.0223	18.20%			
11	1-Nov-04	28.16	29.36	27.96	29.31	85044019	26.22		0.0468	18.28%			
12	25-Oct-04	27.67	28.54	27.55	27.97	70791679	25.02		0.0084	17.71%			
13	18-Oct-04	28.07	28.89	27.58	27.74	74671318	24.81		-0.0092	17.80%			
14	11-Oct-04	28.20	28.27	27.80	27.99	48396360	25.04		0.0000	19.68%			
15	4-Oct-04	28.44	28.59	27.97	27.99	52998320	25.04		-0.0091	19.69%			
16	27-Sep-04	27.17	28.32	27.04	28.25	61783760	25.27		0.0346	19.68%			
17	20-Sep-04	27.44	27.74	27.07	27.29	59162520	24.41		-0.0082	19.62%			
18	13-Sep-04	27.53	27.57	26.74	27.51	51599880	24.61		0.0008	20.52%			
19	7-Sep-04	27.29	27.51	27.14	27.49	51935175	24.59		0.0139	21.30%			
20	30-Aug-04	27.30	27.68	26.85	27.11	45125980	24.25		-0.0127	21.25%			
21	23-Aug-04	27.27	27.67	27.09	27.46	40526880	24.56		0.0123	22.29%			
22	16-Aug-04	27.03	27.50	26.89	27.20	52571740	24.26		0.0066	22.29%			
23	9-Aug-04	27.26	27.75	26.86	27.02	51244080	24.10		-0.0041	22.42%			
24	2-Aug-04	28.27	28.55	27.06	27.14	56739100	24.20		-0.0488	22.42%			
25	26-Jul-04	28.36	28.81	28.13	28.49	65555220	25.41		0.0163	21.97%			
26	19-Jul-04	27.62	29.89	27.60	28.03	114579322	25.00		0.0198	22.11%			
27	12-Jul-04	27.67	28.36	27.25	27.48	57970740	24.51		-0.0138	22.02%			
28	6-Jul-04	28.32	28.33	27.55	27.86	61197249	24.85		-0.0250	22.04%			
29	28-Jun-04	28.60	28.84	28.17	28.57	66214339	25.48		0.0000	22.07%			
30	21-Jun-04	28.22	28.66	27.81	28.57	82202478	25.48		0.0079	22.30%			
31	14-Jun-04	26.55	28.50	26.53	28.35	97727643	25.28		0.0574	22.48%			

Figure B2 – Computing Microsoft's 1-Year Annualized Volatility

Clearly there are advantages and shortcomings to this simple approach. This method is very easy to implement, and Monte Carlo simulation is not required to obtain a single-point volatility estimate. This approach is mathematically valid and is widely used in estimating volatility of financial assets. However, for real options analysis, there are several caveats that deserve closer attention. When cash flows are negative over certain time periods, the relative returns will have negative values, and the natural logarithm of a negative value does not exist. Hence, the volatility measure does not fully capture the possible cash flow downside and may produce erroneous results. In addition, autocorrelated cash flows (estimated using time-series forecasting techniques) or cash flows following a static growth rate will yield volatility estimates that are erroneous. Great care should be taken in such instances. This flaw is neutralized in larger datasets that only carry positive values such as historical stock prices or price of oil or electricity.

This approach is valid and correct as computed in Figure B2 for liquid and traded assets with a lot of historical data. The reason why this approach is not valid for computing the volatility of cash flows in a DCF for the purposes of real options analysis is because of the lack of data. For instance, the following annualized cash flows: 100, 200, 300, 400, 500 would yield a volatility of 20.80%, as compared to the following annualized cash flows: 100, 200, 400, 800, 1600, which would yield a volatility of 0%, versus the following cash flows: 100, 200, 100, 200, 100, 200, which yields 75.93%. All these cash flow streams seem fairly deterministic and yet provided very different volatilities. In addition, the third set of negatively autocorrelated cash flows should actually be less volatile (due to its predictive cyclical nature and reversion back to a base level) but its volatility is computed to be the highest. The second cash flow stream seems more risky than the first set due to larger fluctuations but has a volatility of 0%. Therefore, be careful when applying this method to small datasets.

When applied to stock prices and historical data that are nonnegative, this approach is easy and valid. However, if used on real options assets, the DCF cash flows may very well take on negative values, returning an error in your computation (i.e., log of a negative value does not exist). However, there are certain approaches you can take to avoid this error. The first is to move up your DCF model, from free cash flows to net income, to operating income (EBITDA), and even all the way up to revenues and prices, where all the values are positive. If doing it this way, then care must be taken such that all other options and projects are modeled this way for comparability's sake. Also, this approach is justified in situations where the volatility, risk, and uncertainty stem from a certain variable above the line is used. For instance, the only critical success factor for an oil and gas company is the price of oil (price) and the production rate (quantity), where both are multiplied to obtain revenues. In addition, if all other items in the DCF are proportional ratios (e.g., operating expenses are 25% of revenues or EBITDA values are 10% of revenues, and so forth), then we are only interested in the volatility of revenues. In fact, if the proportions remain constant, the volatilities computed are identical (e.g., revenues of $100, $200, $300, $400, $500 versus a 10% proportional EBITDA of $10, $20, $30, $40, $50, yields identical 20.80% volatilities). Finally, taking the oil and gas example a step further, computing the volatility of revenues assuming no other market risks exist below this revenue line in the DCF, is justified because this firm may have global operations with different tax conditions and financial leverages (different ways of funding projects). The volatility should only apply to market risks and not private risks (how good a negotiator the CFO is on getting foreign loans, or how shrewd your CPAs are in creating offshore tax shelters).

Now that you understand the mechanics of computing volatilities this way, we need to explain why we did what we did! Merely understanding the mechanics is insufficient in justifying the approach or explaining the rationale why we analyzed it the way we did. Hence, let us look at the steps undertaken and explain the rationale behind them:

- Step 1: Collect the relevant data and determine the periodicity and time frame. You can use forecast financial data (cash flows from a DCF model), comparable data (comparable market data such as sector indexes and industry averages), or historical data (stock prices or price of oil and electricity). Consider the periodicity and time frame of the data. In using forecast and comparable data, your choices are limited to what is available or what models have been built, and are typically annual, quarterly, or monthly data, usually for a limited amount of time. When using historical data, your choices are more varied. Typically, daily data has too much random fluctuations and white noise that may erroneously impact the volatility computations. Monthly, quarterly, and annual historical data are spread too far out and all the fluctuations inherent in the time-series data may be smoothed out. The optimal periodicity is weekly data, if available. Any intraday and intraweek fluctuations are smoothed out but weekly fluctuations are still inherent in the dataset. Finally, the time frame of the historical data is also important. Periods of extreme events need to be carefully considered (e.g., dot.com bubble, global recession, depression, terrorist attacks). That is, if these are actual events that will recur and hence are not outliers but part of the undiversifiable systematic risk of doing business? In Figure B2's example above, a 2-year cycle was used. Clearly, if the option has a 3-year maturity, then a 3-year cycle should be considered, with the exception that data is not available, or if certain extreme events mitigate our using the data back that far.

- Step 2: Compute relative returns. Relative returns are used in geometric averages while absolute returns are used in arithmetic averages. To illustrate, suppose you purchase an asset or stock for $100. You hold it for one period and it doubles to $200, which means you made 100% absolute returns. You get greedy and keep it for one more period when you should have sold it and obtain the capital gains. The next period, the asset goes back down to $100, which means you lost half the value or –50% absolute returns. Your stockbroker calls you up and tells you that you made an average of 25% returns in the two periods (the arithmetic average of 100% and –50% is 25%)! You started with $100 and ended up with $100. You clearly did not make a 25% return. Thus, an arithmetic average will over inflate the average when fluctuations occur—fluctuations do occur in the stock market or for your real options project, otherwise your volatility is very low and there's no option value, and hence, no point in doing an options analysis. A geometric average is a better way to compute the return. The computation is seen below, and you can clearly see that as part of the geometric average calculation, relative returns are computed. That is, if $100 goes to $200, the relative return is 2.0 and the absolute return is 100%; or when $100 goes down to $90, the relative return is 0.9 (anything less than 1.0 is a loss) or –10% absolute returns. Thus, to avoid over inflating the computations, we use relative returns in Step 2.

$$\text{Geometric Average} = \sqrt[\text{PERIODS}]{\left(\frac{\text{Period 1 End Value}}{\text{Period 1 Start Value}}\right)\left(\frac{\text{Period 2 End Value}}{\text{Period 2 Start Value}}\right)\cdots\left(\frac{\text{Period } n \text{ End Value}}{\text{Period } n \text{ Start Value}}\right)} = \sqrt[2]{\left(\frac{200}{100}\right)\left(\frac{100}{200}\right)} = 1.0$$

- Step 3: Compute natural logarithm of the relative returns. The natural log is used for two reasons. The first is to be comparable to the exponential Brownian Motion stochastic process. That is, recall that a Brownian Motion is written as:

$$\frac{\delta S}{S} = e^{\mu(\delta t)+\sigma\varepsilon\sqrt{\delta t}}$$

To compute the volatility (σ) used in an equivalent computation (regardless of whether it is used in simulation, lattices, or closed-form models because these three approaches require the Brownian Motion as a fundamental assumption), a natural log is used. The exponential of a natural log cancels each other out in the above equation. Second, in computing the geometric average, relative returns were used, then multiplied and taken to the root of the number of periods. By taking a natural log of a root (n), we reduce the root (n) in the geometric average equation. This is why natural logs are used in Step 3.

- Step 4: Compute the sample standard deviation to obtain the periodic volatility. A sample standard deviation is used instead of a population standard deviation because your dataset might be small. For larger datasets, the sample standard deviation converges to the population standard deviation, so it is always safer to use the sample standard deviation. Of course the sample standard deviation seen below is simply the average (*sum of all and then divided by some variation of n*) of the deviations of each point of a dataset from its mean ($x - \overline{x}$), adjusted for a degree of freedom for small datasets, where a higher standard deviation implies a wider distributional width and, thus, carries a higher risk. The variation of each point around the mean is squared to capture its absolute distances (otherwise for a symmetrical distribution, the variations to the left of the mean might equal the variations to the right of the mean, creating a zero sum), and the entire result is taken to the square root, to bring the value back to its original unit. Finally, the denominator (n–1) adjusts for a degree of freedom in small sample sizes. To illustrate, suppose there are three people in a room and we ask all three of them to randomly choose a number of their choice, as long as the average is $100. The first person might choose any value, and so could the second person. However, when it comes to the third person, he or she can only choose a single unique value such that the average is exactly $100. Thus, in a room of 3 people (n), only 2 people (n–1) are truly free to choose. So, for smaller sample sizes, taking the $n-1$ correction makes the computations more conservative. This is why we use sample standard deviations in Step 4.

$$volatility = \sqrt{\frac{1}{n-1}\sum_{i=1}^{n}\left(x_i - \bar{x}\right)^2}$$

- Step 5: Compute the annualized volatility. The volatility used in options analysis is annualized for several reasons. The first reason is that all other inputs are annualized inputs (e.g., annualized risk-free rate, annualized dividends, and maturity in years). Second, if a cash flow or stock price stream of $10 to $20 to $30 that occurs in three different months versus three different days has very different volatilities. Clearly, if it takes days to double or triple your asset value, that asset is a lot more volatile. All these have to be common-sized in time and be annualized. Finally, the Brownian Motion stochastic equation has the values $\sigma\sqrt{\delta t}$. That is, suppose we have a 1-year option modeled using a 12-step lattice, then δt is 1/12. If we use monthly data, compute the monthly volatility and use this as the input, this monthly volatility will again be partitioned into 12 pieces per $\sigma\sqrt{\delta t}$. Therefore, we need to first annualize the volatility to an annual volatility (multiplied by the square root of 12), input this annual volatility into the model, and let the model partition the volatility (multiplied by the square root of 1/12) into its periodic volatility. This is why we annualize volatilities in Step 5.

B.2 Volatility Estimates (Logarithmic Present Value Returns)

The *Logarithmic Present Value Returns Approach* to estimating volatility collapses all future cash flow estimates into two present value sums, one for the first time period and another for the present time (Figure B3). The steps are shown below. The calculations assume a constant discount rate. The cash flows are discounted all the way to Time 0 and again to Time 1, with the cash flows in Time 0 ignored (sunk cost). Then the values are summed, and the following logarithmic ratio is calculated:

$$X = \ln\left(\frac{\sum\limits_{i=1}^{n} PVCF_i}{\sum\limits_{i=0}^{n} PVCF_i}\right)$$

where $PVCF_i$ is the present value of future cash flows at different time periods i.

This approach is more appropriate for use in real options where actual assets and projects' cash flows are computed and their corresponding volatility is estimated. This is applicable for project and asset cash flows, and can accommodate less data points. However, this approach requires the use of Monte Carlo simulation to obtain a volatility estimate. This approach reduces the measurement risks of autocorrelated cash flows and negative cash flows.

Time Period	Cash Flows	Present Value at Time 0	Present Value at Time 1
0	$100	$\frac{\$100}{(1+0.1)^0} = \$100.00$	—
1	$125	$\frac{\$125}{(1+0.1)^1} = \$113.64$	$\frac{\$125}{(1+0.1)^0} = \$125.00$
2	$95	$\frac{\$95}{(1+0.1)^2} = \$78.51$	$\frac{\$95}{(1+0.1)^1} = \$86.36$
3	$105	$\frac{\$105}{(1+0.1)^3} = \$78.89$	$\frac{\$105}{(1+0.1)^2} = \$86.78$
4	$155	$\frac{\$155}{(1+0.1)^4} = \$105.87$	$\frac{\$155}{(1+0.1)^3} = \$116.45$
5	$146	$\frac{\$146}{(1+0.1)^5} = \$90.65$	$\frac{\$146}{(1+0.1)^4} = \$99.72$
SUM		$567.56	$514.31

Figure B3 – Log PV Approach

In the example above, X is simply $ln(\$514.31/\$567.56) = -0.0985$. Using this intermediate X value, perform a Monte Carlo simulation on the discounted cash flow model (thereby simulating the individual cash flows) and obtain the resulting forecast distribution of X. As seen previously, the sample standard deviation of the forecast distribution of X is the volatility estimate used in the real options analysis. *It is important to note that only the numerator is simulated while the denominator remains unchanged.*

The downside to estimating volatility this way is that the approach requires Monte Carlo simulation, but the calculated volatility measure is a single-digit estimate, as compared to the *Logarithmic Cash Flow or Stock Price Approach*, which yields a distribution of volatilities, that in turn yield a distribution of calculated real options values.

The main objection to using this method is its dependence on the variability of the discount rate used. For instance, we can expand the X equation as follows:

$$X = \ln\left(\frac{\sum_{i=1}^{n} PVCF_i}{\sum_{i=0}^{n} PVCF_i}\right) = \ln\left(\frac{\dfrac{CF_1}{(1+D)^0} + \dfrac{CF_2}{(1+D)^1} + \dfrac{CF_3}{(1+D)^2} + ... + \dfrac{CF_N}{(1+D)^{N-1}}}{\dfrac{CF_0}{(1+D)^0} + \dfrac{CF_1}{(1+D)^1} + \dfrac{CF_2}{(1+D)^2} + ... + \dfrac{CF_N}{(1+D)^N}}\right)$$

where D represents the constant discount rate used. Here we see that the cash flow series CF for the numerator is offset by one period, and the discount factors are also offset by one period. Therefore, by performing a Monte Carlo simulation on the cash flows alone versus performing a Monte Carlo simulation on both cash flow variables as well as the discount rate will yield very different X values. The main critique of this approach is that in a real options analysis, the variability in the present value of cash flows is the key driver of option value and not the variability of discount rates used in the analysis. Modifications to this method include duplicating the cash flows and simulating only the numerator cash flows, thereby providing different numerator values but a static denominator value for each simulated trial, while keeping the discount rate constant. In fact, when running this approach, it might be advisable to set the discount rate as a static risk-free rate, simulate the DCF, and obtain the volatility, then reset the discount rate back to its original value.

Figure B4 illustrates an example of how this approach can be implemented easily in Excel. To follow along, open the example file: *Volatility Computations* and select the worksheet tab *Log Present Value Approach*. The example shows a sample DCF model where the cash flows (row 46) and implementation costs (row 48) are computed separately. This is done for several reasons. The first is to separate the market risks (revenues and associated operating expenses) from the private risks (cost of implementation)—of course only if it makes sense to separate them, as there might be situations where the implementation cost is subject to market risk as well. Here we assume that implementation cost is subject to only private risks and will be discounted at a risk-free, or at the cost of money close to the risk-free rate of return, to discount it for time value of money. The market-risk cash flows are discounted at a market risk-adjusted rate of return (which can also be seen as discounting at 5% risk-free rate to account for time value of money, and discounted again at the market risk premium of 10% for risk, or simply discounted one time at 15%). As discussed in Chapter 2, if you do not separate the market and private risks, you end up discounting the private risks heavily and making the DCF a lot more profitable than it actually is (i.e., if the costs that should be discounted at 5% are discounted at 15%, the NPV will be inflated). By separately discounting these cash flows, the present value of cash flows and implementation costs can be computed (cells H9 and H10). The difference will of course be the NPV. The separation here is also key because from the Black-Scholes equation below, the call option is computed as the present value of net benefits discounted at some risk-adjusted rate of return or the starting stock price (S) times the standard normal probability distribution (Φ) less the implementation cost or strike price (X) discounted at the *risk-free rate* and adjusted by another standard normal probability distribution (Φ). If volatility (σ) is zero, the uncertainty is zero, and Φ is equal to 100% (the value inside the parenthesis is infinity, meaning that the standard normal distribution value is 100%, alternatively, you can state that with zero uncertainties, you have a 100% certainty). By separating the cash flows, you can now use these as inputs into the options model, whether it's using the Black-Scholes or binomial lattices.

$$Call = S\Phi\left(\frac{\ln(S/X)+(r+\sigma^2/2)T}{\sigma\sqrt{T}}\right) - Xe^{-rT}\Phi\left(\frac{\ln(S/X)+(r-\sigma^2/2)T}{\sigma\sqrt{T}}\right)$$

Continuing with the example in Figure B4, the calculations of interest are on rows 51 to 55. Row 51 shows the present values of the cash flows to Year 0 (assume that the base year is 2002), while row 52 shows the present values of the cash flows to Year 1, ignoring the sunk cost of cash flow at Year 0. These two rows are computed in Excel and are linked formulas. You should then copy and paste the values only into row 53 (use *Excel's Edit | Paste Special | Values Only* to do this). Then, compute the intermediate variable X in cell D54 using the following Excel formula: *LN(SUM(E52:H52)/SUM(D53:H53))*. Then, simulate this DCF model using *Risk Simulator* by assigning the relevant input assumptions in the model and set this intermediate variable X as the output forecast. The standard deviation from this X is the periodic volatility. Annualizing the volatility is required, by multiplying this periodic volatility with the square root of the number of periodicities in a year.

	A	C	D	E	F	G	H	I
2			**Log Present Value Approach**					
7								
8		┌ Input Parameters ────────────			┌ Results ────────────			
9		Discount Rate (Cash Flow)	15.00%		Present Value (Cash Flow)		$328.24	
10		Discount Rate (Impl. Cost)	5.00%		Present Value (Impl. Cost)		$189.58	
11		Tax Rate	10.00%		Net Present Value		$138.67	
12								
17			**2002**	**2003**	**2004**	**2005**	**2006**	
18		Revenue	$100.00	$200.00	$300.00	$400.00	$500.00	
22		Cost of Revenue	$40.00	$80.00	$120.00	$160.00	$200.00	
26		Gross Profit	$60.00	$120.00	$180.00	$240.00	$300.00	
27		Operating Expenses	$22.00	$44.00	$66.00	$88.00	$110.00	
31		Depreciation Expense	$5.00	$5.00	$5.00	$5.00	$5.00	
35		Interest Expense	$3.00	$3.00	$3.00	$3.00	$3.00	
39		Income Before Taxes	$30.00	$68.00	$106.00	$144.00	$182.00	
40		Taxes	$3.00	$6.80	$10.60	$14.40	$18.20	
41		Income After Taxes	$27.00	$61.20	$95.40	$129.60	$163.80	
42		Non-Cash Expenses	$12.00	$12.00	$12.00	$12.00	$12.00	
46		Cash Flow	$39.00	$73.20	$107.40	$141.60	$175.80	
47								
48		Implementation Cost	$25.00	$25.00	$50.00	$50.00	$75.00	
49								
50		**Volatility Estimates (Logarithmic PV Approach)**						
51		PV (0)	$39.00	$63.65	$81.21	$93.10	$100.51	
52		PV (1)	N/A	$73.20	$93.39	$107.07	$115.59	
53		Static PV (0)	$39.00	$63.65	$81.21	$93.10	$100.51	
54		Variable X	0.0307					
55		Volatility	Simulate!					

Figure B4 – Log Present Value Approach

Now that you understand the mechanics of computing volatilities this way, we need to explain why we did what we did! Merely understanding the mechanics is insufficient in justifying the approach or explaining the rationale why we analyzed it the way we did. Hence, let us look at the steps undertaken and explain the rationale behind them:

- Step 1: Compute the present values at times 0 and 1 and sum them. The theoretical price of a stock is the sum of the present values of all future dividends (for non-dividend paying stocks, we use market-replicating portfolios and comparables), and the funds to pay these dividends are obtained from the company's net income and free cash flows. The theoretical value of a project or asset is the sum of the present value of all future free cash flows or net income. Hence, the price of a stock is equivalent to the price or value of an asset, the NPV. Thus, the sum of the present values at time 0 is equivalent to the stock price of the asset at time 0, the value today. The sum of the present value of the cash flows at time 1 is equivalent to the stock price at time 1, or a good *proxy* for the stock price in the *future*. We use this as a proxy because in most DCF models, cash flow forecasts are only a few periods. Hence, by running Monte Carlo simulation, we are changing all future possibilities and capturing the uncertainties in the DCF inputs. This future stock price is hence a good proxy of what may happen to the future stream of cash flows—remember that sum of the present value of future cash flows at time 1 included in its computations all future cash flows from the DCF, thereby capturing future fluctuations and uncertainties. This is why we perform Step 1 when we compute volatilities using the Log Present Value Returns Approach.

- Step 2: Calculate the intermediate variable X. This X variable is identical to the logarithmic relative returns in the Log Cash Flow Returns Approach. It is simply the natural logarithm of the relative returns of the future stock price (using the sum of present values at time 1 as a proxy) from the current stock price (the sum of present values at time 0). We then set the sum of present values at time 0 as static because it is the base case, and by definition of a base case, the values do not change. The base case can be seen as the NPV of the project's net benefits and is assumed to be the best estimate of the project's net benefit value. It is the future that is uncertain and fluctuates hence, we simulate the DCF model and allow the numerator of the X variable to change during the simulation while keeping the denominator static as the base case.

- Step 3: Simulate the model and obtain the standard deviation as volatility. This approach requires that the model be simulated. This makes sense because if the model is not simulated means that there is no uncertainties in the project or asset, and hence, the volatility is equal to zero. You would only simulate when there are uncertainties hence, you obtain a volatility estimate. The rationale for using the sample standard deviation as the volatility is similar to the Log Cash Flow Returns approach. If the sums of the present values of the cash flows are fluctuating between positive and negative values during the simulation, you can again move up the DCF model and use items like EBITDA and net revenues as proxy variables for computing volatility.

Another alternative volatility estimate is to combine both approaches if enough data exists. That is, from a DCF with many cash flow estimates, compute the PV Cash Flows for periods 0, 1, 2, 3, and so forth. Then, compute the natural logarithm of the relative returns of these PV Cash Flows. The standard deviation is then annualized to obtain the volatility. This is of course the preferred method and does not require the use of Monte Carlo simulation, but the drawback is that a longer cash flow forecast series is required.

B.3 GARCH Approach

Another approach is the GARCH (Generalized Autoregressive Conditional Heteroskedasticity) model, which can be utilized to estimate the volatility of any time-series data. GARCH models are used mainly in analyzing financial time-series data, in order to ascertain its conditional variances and volatilities. These volatilities are then used to value the options as usual, but the amount of historical data necessary for a good volatility estimate remains significant. Usually, several dozens—and even up to hundreds—of data points are required to obtain good GARCH estimates. In addition, GARCH models are very difficult to run and interpret and require great facility with econometric modeling techniques. GARCH is a term that incorporates a family of models can take on a variety of forms, known as GARCH(p,q), where p and q are positive integers which define the resulting GARCH model and its forecasts.

For instance, a GARCH (1,1) model takes the form of

$$y_t = x_t \gamma + \varepsilon_t$$
$$\sigma_t^2 = \omega + \alpha \varepsilon_{t-1}^2 + \beta \sigma_{t-1}^2$$

where the first equation's dependent variable (y_t) is a function of exogenous variables (x_t) with an error term (ε_t). The second equation estimates the variance (squared volatility σ_t^2) at time t, which depends on a historical mean (ω), news about volatility from the previous period, measured as a lag of the squared residual from the mean equation (ε_{t-1}^2), and volatility from the previous period (σ_{t-1}^2). The exact modeling specification of a GARCH model is beyond the scope of this book and will not be discussed. Suffice it to say that detailed knowledge of econometric modeling (model specification tests, structural breaks, and error estimation) is required to run a GARCH model, making it less accessible to the general analyst. The other problem with GARCH models is that the model usually does not provide a good statistical fit. That is, it is impossible to predict say the stock market, and of course equally if not harder, to predict a stock's volatility over time. Figure B5 shows a GARCH (1,2) on Microsoft's historical stock prices.

Dependent Variable: MSFT
Method: ML - ARCH
Date: 02/25/05   Time: 00:20
Sample(adjusted): 3 52
Included observations: 50 after adjusting endpoints
Convergence achieved after 67 iterations
Bollerslev-Wooldrige robust standard errors & covariance

	Coefficient	Std. Error	z-Statistic	Prob.
C	23.14431	1.301024	17.78930	0.0000
D(MSFT,1)	0.456040	0.062391	7.309364	0.0000
AR(1)	0.967490	0.027575	35.08601	0.0000
Variance Equation				
C	0.151406	0.028717	5.272435	0.0000
ARCH(1)	0.148308	0.053559	2.769061	0.0056
GARCH(1)	0.735869	0.097780	7.525790	0.0000
GARCH(2)	-0.867066	0.083186	-10.42325	0.0000
R-squared	0.898576	Mean dependent var		24.48620
Adjusted R-squared	0.884424	S.D. dependent var		1.290867
S.E. of regression	0.438849	Akaike info criterion		1.106641
Sum squared resid	8.281300	Schwarz criterion		1.374324
Log likelihood	-20.66602	F-statistic		63.49404
Durbin-Watson stat	1.308287	Prob(F-statistic)		0.000000
Inverted AR Roots	.97			

Figure B5 – Sample GARCH Results

B.4 Management Assumption Approach

A simpler approach is the use of Management Assumptions. This approach allows management to get a rough volatility estimate without performing more protracted analysis. This approach is also great for educating management what volatility is and how it works. Mathematically and statistically, the width or risk of a variable can be measured through several different statistics, including the range, standard deviation (σ), variance, coefficient of variation, and percentiles. Figure B6 illustrates two different stocks' historical prices. The stock depicted as a dark bold line is clearly less volatile than the stock with the dotted line. The time-series data from these two stocks can be redrawn as a probability distribution as seen in Figure B7. Although the expected value of both stocks are similar, their volatilities and hence their risks are different. The x-axis depicts the stock prices, while the y-axis depicts the frequency of a particular stock price occurring, and the area under the curve (between two values) is the probability of occurrence. The second stock (dotted line in Figure B6) has a wider spread (a higher standard deviation σ_2) than the first stock (bold line in Figure B6). The width of Figure B7's x-axis is the same width from Figure B6's y-axis. One common measure of width is the standard deviation. Hence, standard deviation is a way to measure volatility. The term volatility is used and not standard deviation because the volatility computed is not from the raw cash flows or stock prices themselves, but from the natural logarithm of the relative returns on these cash flows or stock prices. Hence, the term volatility differentiates it from a regular standard deviation.

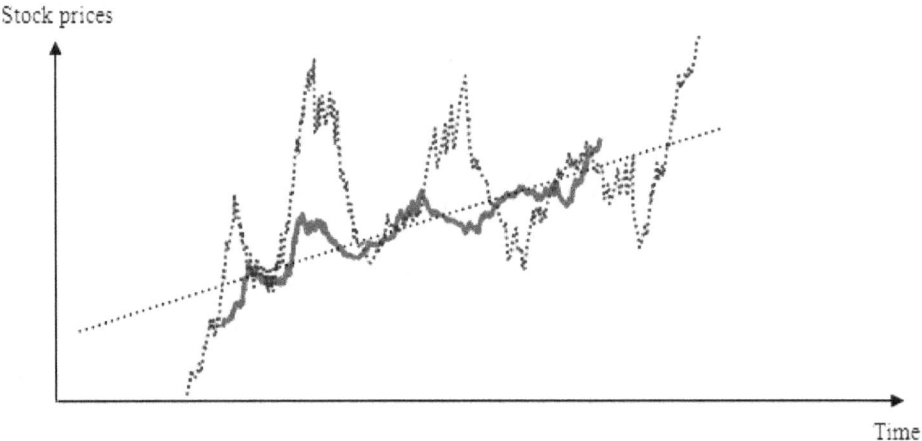

Figure B6: Volatility

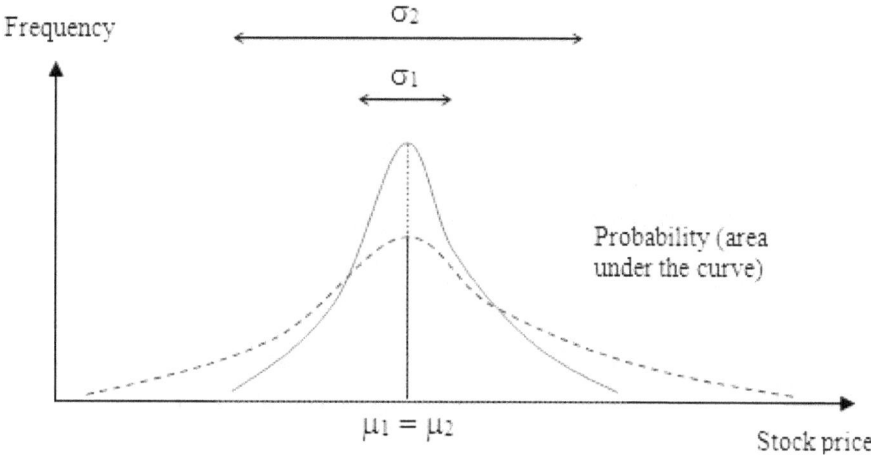

Figure B7: Standard Deviation

However, for the purposes of explaining volatility to management, we relax this terminological difference and on a very high-level, state that they are one and the same, for discussion purposes. Thus, we can make some management assumptions in estimating volatilities. For instance, starting from an expected NPV (the mean value), you can obtain an alternate NPV value with its probability, and get an approximate volatility. For instance, say that a project's NPV is expected to be $100M. Management further assumes that the best case scenario exceeds $150M if everything goes really well, and that there is only a 10% probability that this best case scenario will hit. Figure B8 illustrates this situation. If we assume for simplicity that the underlying asset value will fluctuate within a normal distribution, we can compute the implied volatility using the following equation:

$$Volatility = \frac{Percentile\ Value - Mean}{Inverse\ of\ the\ Percentile \times Mean}$$

For instance, we compute the volatility of this project as:

$$Volatility = \frac{\$150M - \$100M}{Inverse\ (0.90) \times \$100M} = \frac{\$50M}{1.2815 \times \$100M} = 39.02\%$$

Where the Inverse of the Percentile can be obtained by using Excel's *NORMSINV(0.9)* function. Similarly, if the worst case scenario occurring 10% of the time will yield an NPV of $50M, we compute the volatility as:

$$Volatility = \frac{\$50M - \$100M}{Inverse\ (0.10) \times \$100M} = \frac{-\$50M}{-1.2815 \times \$100M} = 39.02\%$$

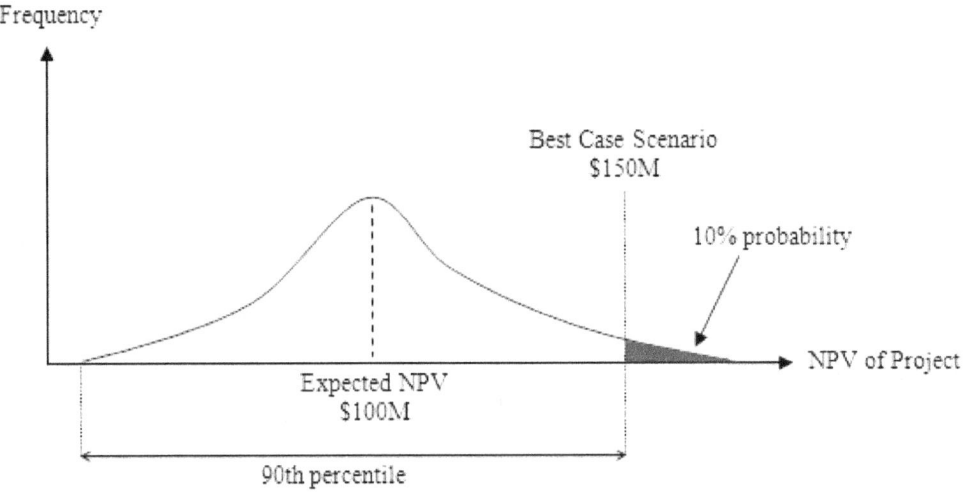

Figure B8: Going from Probability to Volatility

This implies that the volatility is a symmetrical measure. That is, at an expected NPV of $100M, a 50% increase is equivalent to $150M while a 50% decrease is equivalent to $50M. And because the normal distribution is assumed as the underlying distribution, this symmetry makes perfect sense. So now, by using this simple approach, if you obtain a volatility estimate of 39.02%, you can explain to management by stating that this volatility is equivalent to saying that there is a 10% probability the NPV will exceed $150M. Through this simple analysis, you have converted probability into volatility using the equation above, where the latter is a lot easier for management to understand. Conversely, if you model this in Excel, you can convert from volatility back into probability. Figures B9 and B10 illustrate this approach. Open the example file *Volatility Estimates* and select the worksheet tab *Volatility to Probability* to follow along.

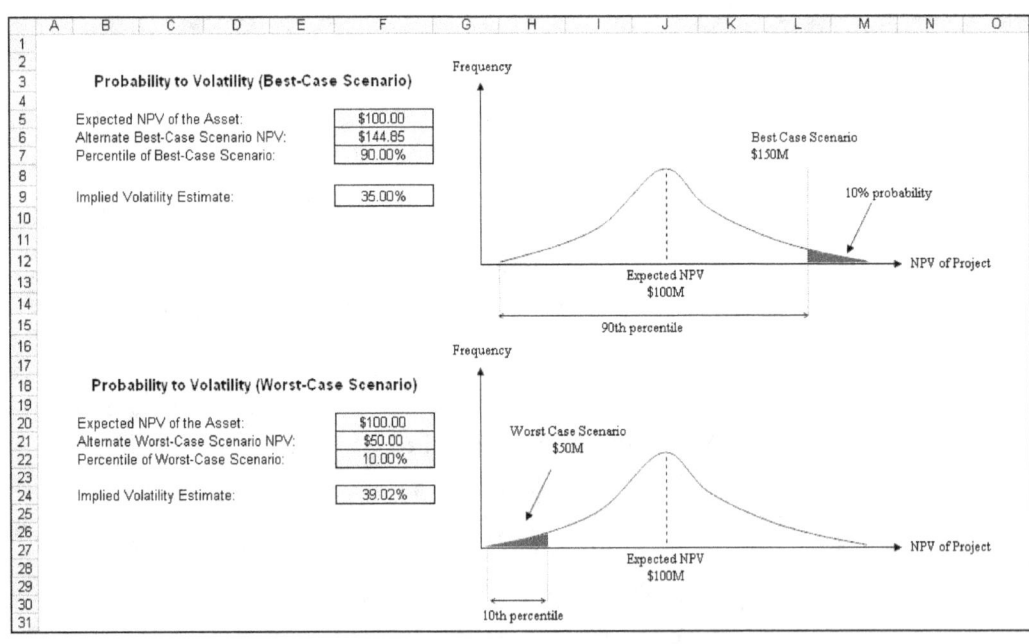

Figure B9: Excel Probability to Volatility Model

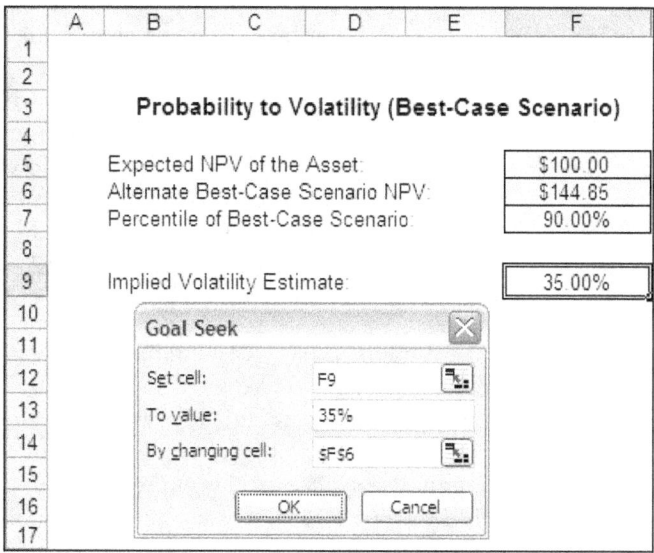

Figure B10: Excel Volatility to Probability Model

Figure B9 allows you to enter the expected NPV and the alternate values (best-case and worst-case) as well as its corresponding percentiles. That is, given some probability and its value, we can impute the volatility. Conversely, Figure B10 shows how you can use Excel's Goal Seek function (click on *Tools | Goal Seek* in Excel) to find the probability from a volatility. For instance, say the project's expected NPV is $100M a 35% volatility implies that 90% of the time, the NPV will be less than $144.85M, and that only 10% best-case scenario of the time will the true NPV exceed this value.

Now that you understand the mechanics of estimating volatilities this way, again, we need to explain why we did what we did! Merely understanding the mechanics is insufficient in justifying the approach or explaining the rationale why we analyzed it the way we did. Hence, let us look at the assumptions required and explain the rationale behind them:

- Assumption 1: We assume that the underlying distribution of the asset fluctuations is normal. We can assume normality because the distribution of the final nodes on a super lattice is normally distributed. In fact, the Brownian Motion equation shown earlier requires a random standard normal distribution (ε). In addition, a lot of distributions will converge to the normal distribution anyway (a Binomial distribution becomes normally distributed when number of trials increase; a Poisson distribution also becomes normally distributed with a high average rate; a Triangular distribution is a normal distribution with truncated upper and lower values; an so forth) and it is not possible to ascertain the shape and type of the final NPV distribution if the DCF model is simulated with many different types of distributions (e.g., revenues are Lognormally distributed and are negatively correlated to one another over time, while operating expenses are positively correlated to revenues but are assumed to be distributed following a Triangular distribution, while the effects of market competition are simulated using a Poisson distribution with a small rate times the probability of technical success simulated as a Binomial distribution). We cannot determine theoretically what a Lognormal minus a Triangular times Poisson and Binomial, after accounting for their correlations, would be. Instead, we rely on the Central Limit Theorem and assume the final result is normally distributed, especially if a large number of trials are used in the simulations. Finally, we are interested in the logarithmic relative returns' volatility, not the standard deviation of the actual cash flows or stock prices. Stock prices and cash flows are usually Lognormally distributed (stock prices cannot be below zero) but the logs of the relative returns are always normally distributed. In fact, this can be seen in Figure B11 and B12, where the historical stock prices of Microsoft from March 1986 to December 2004 are tabulated.

- Assumption 2: We assume that the standard deviation is the same as the volatility. Again, referring to Figure B12, using the expected returns chart, the average is computed at 0.58% and the 90th percentile is 8.60%, and the implied volatility is found to be 37%. Using the data downloaded, we compute the empirical volatility for this entire period to be 36%. So, the computation is close enough such that we can use this approach for management discussions. This is why the normality assumption and using a regular standard deviation as a proxy are sufficient.

- Assumption 3: We used a standard-normal calculation to impute the volatility. As we are assuming that the underlying distribution is normal, we can compute the volatility by using the standard-normal distribution. The standard normal distribution Z-score is such that:

$$Z = \frac{x - \mu}{\sigma} \text{ this means that } \sigma = \frac{x - \mu}{Z}$$

and because we normalize the volatility as a percentage (σ^*), we divide this by the mean to obtain:

$$\sigma^* = \frac{x - \mu}{Z\mu}$$

In layman's terms, we have:

$$Volatility = \frac{Percentile\ Value - Mean}{Inverse\ of\ the\ Percentile \times Mean}$$

Again, the inverse of the percentile is obtained using Excel's function: *NORMSINV*.

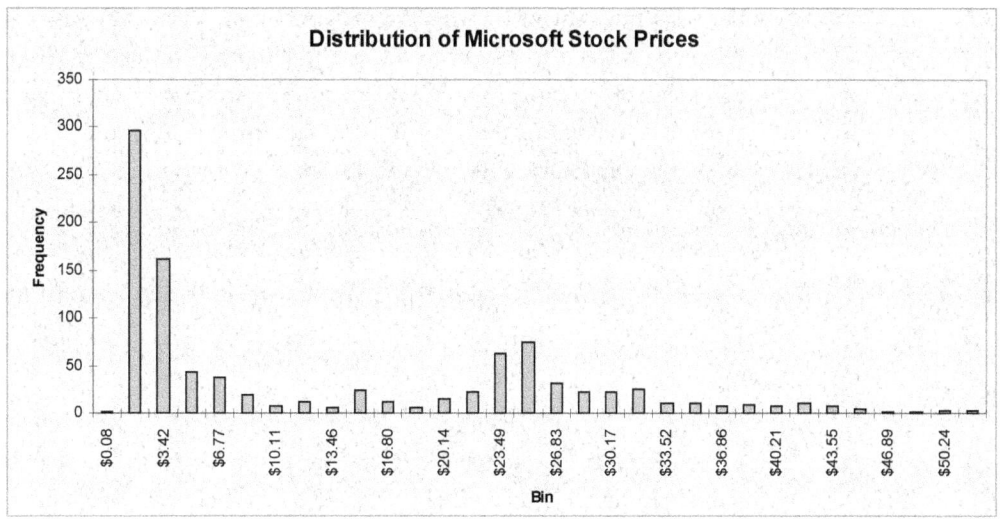

Figure B11: Probability Distribution of Microsoft's Stock Price (Since 1986)

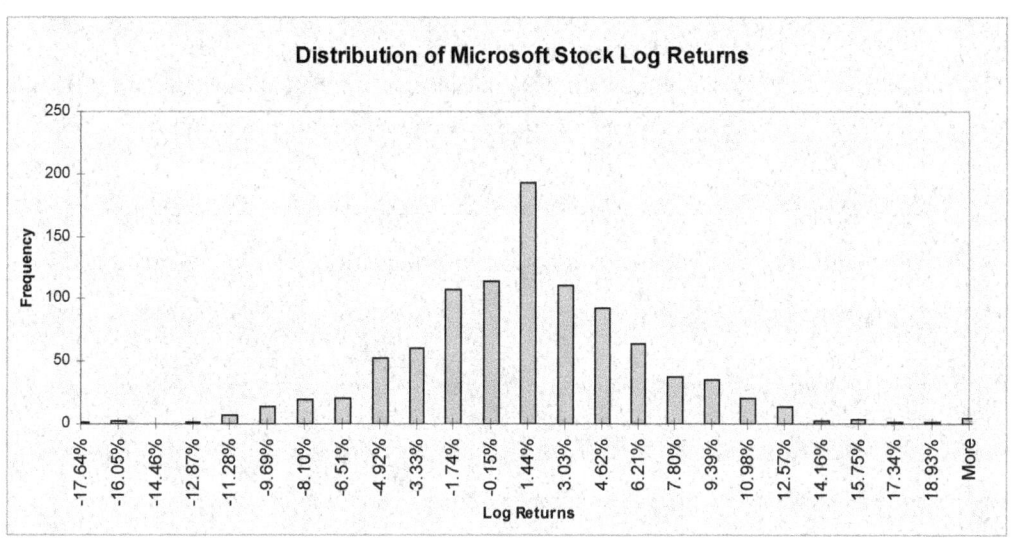

Figure B12: Probability Distribution of Microsoft's Log Relative Returns

B.5 Market Proxy Approach

An often used (not to mention abused and misused) method in estimating volatility applies to publicly available market data. That is, for a particular project under review, a set of market comparable firms' publicly traded stock prices are used. These firms should have *functions*, *markets*, *risks*, and *geographical locations* similar to those of the project under review. Then, using closing stock prices, the standard deviation of natural logarithms of relative returns is calculated. The methodology is identical to that used in the logarithm of cash flow returns approach previously alluded to. The problem with this method is the assumption that the risks inherent in comparable firms are identical to the risks inherent in the specific project under review. The issue is that a firm's equity prices are subject to investor overreaction and psychology in the stock market, as well as countless other exogenous variables that are irrelevant when estimating the risks of the project. In addition, the market valuation of a large public firm depends on multiple interacting and diversified projects. Finally, firms are levered, but specific projects are usually unlevered. Hence, the volatility used in a real options analysis (σ_{RO}) should be adjusted to discount this leverage effect by dividing the volatility in equity prices (σ_{EQUITY}) by $(1+D/E)$, where D/E is the debt-to-equity ratio of the public firm. That is,

we have $\sigma_{RO} = \dfrac{\sigma_{EQUITY}}{1+\dfrac{D}{E}}$.

This approach can be used if there are market comparables such as sector indexes or industry indexes. It is incorrect to state that a project's risk as measured by the volatility estimate is identical to the entire industry, sector, or the market. There are a lot of interactions in the market such as diversification, overreaction, and marketability issues that a single project inside a firm is not exposed to. Great care must be taken in choosing the right comparables as the major drawback of this approach is that it is sometimes hard to find the right comparable firms and the results may be subject to gross manipulation by subjectively including or excluding certain firms. The benefit is its ease of use—industry averages are used and requires little to no computation.

Appendix C: Technical Formulae – Exotic Options Formulas

Black and Scholes Option Model – European Version

This is the famous Nobel Prize-winning Black-Scholes model without any dividend payments. It is the European version, where an option can only be executed at expiration and not before. Although it is simple enough to use, care should be taken in estimating its input variable assumptions, especially that of volatility, which is usually difficult to estimate. However, the Black-Scholes model is useful in generating ballpark estimates of the true real options value, especially for more generic-type calls and puts. For more complex real options analysis, different types of exotic options are required.

Definitions of Variables

S present value of future cash flows ($)

X implementation cost ($)

r risk-free rate (%)

T time to expiration (years)

σ volatility (%)

Φ cumulative standard-normal distribution

Computation

$$Call = S\Phi\left(\frac{\ln(S/X)+(r+\sigma^2/2)T}{\sigma\sqrt{T}}\right) - Xe^{-rT}\Phi\left(\frac{\ln(S/X)+(r-\sigma^2/2)T}{\sigma\sqrt{T}}\right)$$

$$Put - Xe^{-rT}\Phi\left(-\left[\frac{\ln(S/X)+(r-\sigma^2/2)T}{\sigma\sqrt{T}}\right]\right) - S\Psi\left(-\left[\frac{\ln(S/X)+(r+\sigma^2/2)T}{\sigma\sqrt{T}}\right]\right)$$

Black and Scholes with Drift (Dividend) – European Version

This is a modification of the Black-Scholes model and assumes a fixed dividend payment rate of q in percent. This can be construed as the opportunity cost of holding the option rather than holding the underlying asset.

Definitions of Variables

S — present value of future cash flows ($)

X — implementation cost ($)

r — risk-free rate (%)

T — time to expiration (years)

σ — volatility (%)

Φ — cumulative standard-normal distribution

q — continuous dividend payout or opportunity cost (%)

Computation

$$Call = Se^{-qT}\Phi\left(\frac{\ln(S/X)+(r-q+\sigma^2/2)T}{\sigma\sqrt{T}}\right) - Xe^{-rT}\Phi\left(\frac{\ln(S/X)+(r-q-\sigma^2/2)T}{\sigma\sqrt{T}}\right)$$

$$Put = Xe^{-rT}\Phi\left(-\left[\frac{\ln(S/X)+(r-q-\sigma^2/2)T}{\sigma\sqrt{T}}\right]\right) - Se^{-qT}\Phi\left(-\left[\frac{\ln(S/X)+(r-q+\sigma^2/2)T}{\sigma\sqrt{T}}\right]\right)$$

Black and Scholes with Future Payments – European Version

Here, cash flow streams may be uneven over time, and we should allow for different discount rates (risk-free rate should be used) for all future times, perhaps allowing for the flexibility of the forward risk-free yield curve.

Definitions of Variables

S	present value of future cash flows ($)
X	implementation cost ($)
r	risk-free rate (%)
T	time to expiration (years)
σ	volatility (%)
Φ	cumulative standard-normal distribution
q	continuous dividend payout or opportunity cost (%)
CF_i	cash flow at time i

Computation

$$S^* = S - CF_1 e^{-rt_1} - CF_2 e^{-rt_2} - \ldots - CF_n e^{-rt_n} = S - \sum_{i=1}^{n} CF_i e^{-rt_i}$$

$$Call = S^* e^{-qT} \Phi\left(\frac{\ln(S^*/X) + (r - q + \sigma^2/2)T}{\sigma\sqrt{T}} \right) - X e^{-rT} \Phi\left(\frac{\ln(S^*/X) + (r - q - \sigma^2/2)T}{\sigma\sqrt{T}} \right)$$

$$Put = X e^{-rT} \Phi\left(-\left[\frac{\ln(S^*/X) + (r - q - \sigma^2/2)T}{\sigma\sqrt{T}} \right] \right) - S^* e^{-qT} \Phi\left(-\left[\frac{\ln(S^*/X) + (r - q + \sigma^2/2)T}{\sigma\sqrt{T}} \right] \right)$$

Chooser Options (Basic Chooser)

This is the payoff for a simple chooser option when $t_1 < T_2$, or it doesn't work! In addition, it is assumed that the holder has the right to choose either a call or a put with the same strike price at time t_1 and with the same expiration date T_2. For different values of strike prices at different times, we need a complex variable chooser option.

Definitions of Variables

S present value of future cash flows ($)

X implementation cost ($)

r risk-free rate (%)

t_1 time to choose between a call or put (years)

T_2 time to expiration (years)

σ volatility (%)

Φ cumulative standard-normal distribution

q continuous dividend payments (%)

Computation

$$Option\ Value = Se^{-qT_2}\Phi\left[\frac{\ln(S/X)+(r-q+\sigma^2/2)T_2}{\sigma\sqrt{T_2}}\right] - Se^{-qT_2}\Phi\left[\frac{-\ln(S/X)+(q-r)T_2-t_1\sigma^2/2}{\sigma\sqrt{t_1}}\right]$$

$$- Xe^{-rT_2}\Phi\left[\frac{\ln(S/X)+(r-q+\sigma^2/2)T_2}{\sigma\sqrt{T_2}}-\sigma\sqrt{T_2}\right] + Xe^{-rT_2}\Phi\left[\frac{-\ln(S/X)+(q-r)T_2-t_1\sigma^2/2}{\sigma\sqrt{t_1}}+\sigma\sqrt{t_1}\right]$$

Complex Chooser

The holder of the option has the right to choose between a call and a put at different times *(T_C* and *T_P)* with different strike levels *(X_C* and *X_P)* of calls and puts. Note that some of these equations cannot be readily solved using Excel spreadsheets. Instead, due to the recursive methods used to solve certain bivariate distributions and critical values, the use of programming scripts is required.

Additional Definitions of Variables

Ω cumulative bivariate-normal distribution

q continuous dividend payout (%)

I critical value solved recursively

Z intermediate variables *(Z_1* and *Z_2)*

Computation: First, solve recursively for the critical *I* value as below:

$$0 = Ie^{-q(T_C-t)}\Phi\left[\frac{\ln(I/X_C)+(r-q+\sigma^2/2)(T_C-t)}{\sigma\sqrt{T_C-t}}\right]$$

$$-X_Ce^{-r(T_C-t)}\Phi\left[\frac{\ln(I/X_C)+(r-q+\sigma^2/2)(T_C-t)}{\sigma\sqrt{T_C-t}}-\sigma\sqrt{T_C-t}\right]$$

$$+Ie^{-q(T_P-t)}\Phi\left[\frac{-\ln(I/X_P)+(q-r-\sigma^2/2)(T_P-t)}{\sigma\sqrt{T_P-t}}\right]$$

$$-X_Pe^{-r(T_P-t)}\Phi\left[\frac{-\ln(I/X_P)+(q-r-\sigma^2/2)(T_P-t)}{\sigma\sqrt{T_P-t}}+\sigma\sqrt{T_P-t}\right]$$

Then using the *I* value, calculate

$$d_1 = \frac{\ln(S/I)+(r-q+\sigma^2/2)t}{\sigma\sqrt{t}} \text{ and } d_2 = d_1-\sigma\sqrt{t}$$

$$y_1 = \frac{\ln(S/X_C)+(r-q+\sigma^2/2)T_C}{\sigma\sqrt{T_C}} \text{ and } y_2 = \frac{\ln(S/X_P)+(r-q+\sigma^2/2)T_P}{\sigma\sqrt{T_P}}$$

$$\rho_1 = \sqrt{t/T_C} \text{ and } \rho_2 = \sqrt{t/T_P}$$

$$Option\ Value = Se^{-qT_C}\Omega(d_1;y_1;\rho_1) - X_Ce^{-rT_C}\Omega(d_2;y_1-\sigma\sqrt{T_C};\rho_1)$$

$$-Se^{-qT_P}\Omega(-d_1;-y_2;\rho_2) + X_Pe^{-rT_P}\Omega(-d_2;-y_2+\sigma\sqrt{T_P};\rho_2)$$

Compound Options on Options

The value of a compound option is based on the value of another option. That is, the underlying variable for the compound option is another option. Again, solving this model requires programming capabilities.

Definitions of Variables

S	present value of future cash flows ($)
r	risk-free rate (%)
σ	volatility (%)
Φ	cumulative standard-normal distribution
q	continuous dividend payout (%)
I	critical value solved recursively
Ω	cumulative bivariate-normal distribution
X_1	strike for the underlying ($)
X_2	strike for the option on the option ($)
t_1	expiration date for the option on the option (years)
T_2	expiration for the underlying option (years)

Computation

First, solve for the critical value of I using

$$X_2 = Ie^{-q(T_2-t_1)}\Phi\left(\frac{\ln(I/X_1)+(r-q+\sigma^2/2)(T_2-t_1)}{\sigma\sqrt{(T_2-t_1)}}\right)$$
$$-X_1e^{-r(T_2-t_1)}\Phi\left(\frac{\ln(I/X_1)+(r-q-\sigma^2/2)(T_2-t_1)}{\sigma\sqrt{(T_2-t_1)}}\right)$$

Solve recursively for the value I above and then input it into

$$Call\ on\ call = Se^{-qT_2}\Omega\left[\frac{\ln(S/X_1)+(r-q+\sigma^2/2)T_2}{\sigma\sqrt{T_2}};\frac{\ln(S/I)+(r-q+\sigma^2/2)t_1}{\sigma\sqrt{t_1}};\sqrt{t_1/T_2}\right]$$
$$-X_1e^{-rT_2}\Omega\left[\frac{\ln(S/X_1)+(r-q+\sigma^2/2)T_2}{\sigma\sqrt{T_2}}-\sigma\sqrt{T_2};\frac{\ln(S/I)+(r-q+\sigma^2/2)t_1}{\sigma\sqrt{t_1}}-\sigma\sqrt{t_1};\sqrt{t_1/T_2}\right]$$
$$-X_2e^{-rt_1}\Phi\left[\frac{\ln(S/I)+(r-q+\sigma^2/2)t_1}{\sigma\sqrt{t_1}}-\sigma\sqrt{t_1}\right]$$

Forward Start Options

Definitions of Variables

S	present value of future cash flows (\$)
X	implementation cost (\$)
r	risk-free rate (%)
t_1	time when the forward start option begins (years)
T_2	time to expiration of the forward start option (years)
σ	volatility (%)
Φ	cumulative standard-normal distribution
q	continuous dividend payout (%)

Computation

$$Call = Se^{-qt_1}e^{-q(T_2-t_1)}\Phi\left[\frac{\ln(1/\alpha)+(r-q+\sigma^2/2)(T_2-t_1)}{\sigma\sqrt{T_2-t_1}}\right]$$

$$-Se^{-qt_1}\alpha\,e^{(-r)(T_2-t_1)}\Phi\left[\frac{\ln(1/\alpha)+(r-q+\sigma^2/2)(T_2-t_1)}{\sigma\sqrt{T_2-t_1}}-\sigma\sqrt{T_2-t_1}\right]$$

$$Put = Se^{-qt_1}\alpha\,e^{(-r)(T_2-t_1)}\Phi\left[\frac{-\ln(1/\alpha)-(r-q+\sigma^2/2)(T_2-t_1)}{\sigma\sqrt{T_2-t_1}}+\sigma\sqrt{T_2-t_1}\right]$$

$$-Se^{-qt_1}e^{-q(T_2-t_1)}\Phi\left[\frac{-\ln(1/\alpha)-(r-q+\sigma^2/2)(T_2-t_1)}{\sigma\sqrt{T_2-t_1}}\right]$$

where α is the multiplier constant.

Note: If the option starts at X percent out-of-the-money, that is, α will be *(1 + X)*. If it starts at-the-money, α will be 1.0 and *(1 – X)* if in-the-money.

Generalized Black-Scholes Model

Definitions of Variables

S	present value of future cash flows ($)
X	implementation cost ($)
r	risk-free rate (%)
T	time to expiration (years)
σ	volatility (%)
Φ	cumulative standard-normal distribution
b	carrying cost (%)
q	continuous dividend payout (%)

Computation

$$Call = Se^{(b-r)T}\Phi\left(\frac{\ln(S/X)+(b+\sigma^2/2)T}{\sigma\sqrt{T}}\right) - Xe^{-rT}\Phi\left(\frac{\ln(S/X)+(b-\sigma^2/2)T}{\sigma\sqrt{T}}\right)$$

$$Put = Xe^{-rT}\Phi\left(-\left[\frac{\ln(S/X)+(b-\sigma^2/2)T}{\sigma\sqrt{T}}\right]\right) - Se^{(b-r)T}\Phi\left(-\left[\frac{\ln(S/X)+(b+\sigma^2/2)T}{\sigma\sqrt{T}}\right]\right)$$

Notes:

$b = 0$:   Futures options model

$b = r - q$:   Black-Scholes with dividend payment

$b = r$:   Simple Black-Scholes formula

$b = r - r^*$:   Foreign currency options model

Options on Futures

The underlying security is a forward or futures contract with initial price F. Here, the value of F is the forward or futures contract's initial price, replacing S with F as well as calculating its present value.

Definitions of Variables

X	implementation cost (\$)
F	futures single point cash flows (\$)
r	risk-free rate (%)
T	time to expiration (years)
σ	volatility (%)
Φ	cumulative standard-normal distribution
q	continuous dividend payout (%)

Computation

$$Call = Fe^{-rT} \Phi\left(\frac{\ln(F/X)+(\sigma^2/2)T}{\sigma\sqrt{T}}\right) - Xe^{-rT} \Phi\left(\frac{\ln(F/X)-(\sigma^2/2)T}{\sigma\sqrt{T}}\right)$$

$$Put = Xe^{-rT} \Phi\left(-\left[\frac{\ln(F/X)-(\sigma^2/2)T}{\sigma\sqrt{T}}\right]\right) - Fe^{-rT} \Phi\left(-\left[\frac{\ln(F/X)+(\sigma^2/2)T}{\sigma\sqrt{T}}\right]\right)$$

Two-Correlated-Assets Option

The payoff on an option depends on whether the other correlated option is in-the-money. This is the continuous counterpart to a correlated quadranomial model.

Definitions of Variables

S present value of future cash flows (\$)

X implementation cost (\$)

r risk-free rate (%)

T time to expiration (years)

σ volatility (%)

Ω cumulative bivariate-normal distribution function

ρ correlation (%) between the two assets

q_1 continuous dividend payout for the first asset (%)

q_2 continuous dividend payout for the second asset (%)

Computation

$$Call = S_2 e^{-q_2 T}\Omega\left[\frac{\ln(S_2/X_2)+(r-q_2-\sigma_2^2/2)T}{\sigma_2\sqrt{T}}+\sigma_2\sqrt{T}; \frac{\ln(S_1/X_1)+(r-q_1-\sigma_1^2/2)T}{\sigma_1\sqrt{T}}+\rho\sigma_2\sqrt{T}; \rho\right]$$

$$-X_2 e^{-rT}\Omega\left[\frac{\ln(S_2/X_2)+(r-q_2-\sigma_2^2/2)T}{\sigma_2\sqrt{T}}; \frac{\ln(S_1/X_1)+(r-q_1-\sigma_1^2/2)T}{\sigma_1\sqrt{T}}; \rho\right]$$

$$Put = X_2 e^{-rT}\Omega\left[\frac{-\ln(S_2/X_2)-(r-q_2-\sigma_2^2/2)T}{\sigma_2\sqrt{T}}; \frac{-\ln(S_1/X_1)-(r-q_1-\sigma_1^2/2)T}{\sigma_1\sqrt{T}}; \rho\right]$$

$$-S_2 e^{-q_2 T}\Omega\left[\frac{-\ln(S_2/X_2)-(r-q_2-\sigma_2^2/2)T}{\sigma_2\sqrt{T}}-\sigma_2\sqrt{T}; \frac{-\ln(S_1/X_1)-(r-q_1-\sigma_1^2/2)T}{\sigma_1\sqrt{T}}-\rho\sigma_2\sqrt{T}; \rho\right]$$

Appendix D – Quick Install and Licensing Guide

This section is the quick install guide, for more advanced users. For a more detailed installation guide, please refer to the next section. The SLS software requires the following minimum requirements:

- Windows 7, Windows 8, or Windows 10 and beyond
- Excel 2007, Excel 2010, or Excel 2013 and beyond
- .NET Framework 2.0 or higher
- Administrative rights (during installation only)
- 2GB of RAM or more (4GB recommended)
- 200MB of free hard drive space

To install the software, make sure that your system has all the prerequisites: (Windows 7, Windows 8, Windows 10, and beyond; Excel 2007, Excel 2010, Excel 2013, and beyond; .NET Framework 2.0, and beyond; administrative rights; 2GB of RAM or more; and 200MB of free hard drive space). Install the Real Options SLS software by either using the installation CD or going to the following web location: www.realoptionsvaluation.com, clicking on *Downloads*, and selecting Real Options SLS. You can either select to download the FULL version (assuming you have already purchased the software and have received the permanent license keys and the instructions to permanently license the software) or a TRIAL version. The trial version is exactly the same as the full version except that it expires after 14 days, during which you would need to obtain the full license to extend the use of the software. Install the software by following the onscreen prompts. If you have the trial version and wish to obtain the permanent license, visit www.realoptionsvaluation.com and click on the *Purchase* link (left panel of the web site) and complete the purchase order. If you are purchasing or have already purchased the software, simply download and install the software.

There are two licenses required to run Real Options SLS. The first is a license for the Real Options SLS software (single asset lattice models, multiple assets and multiple phased models, multinomial lattices, and the lattice maker). The second is a license for the Exotic Financial Valuator and the SLS Functions accessible inside Excel. To license your software, follow the simple steps below:

Preparation:

1. Start Real Options SLS (click on Start, Programs, Real Options Valuation, Real Options SLS, Real Options SLS).

2. Click on the "1. License Real Options SLS" link and you will be provided with your HARDWARE ID (this starts with the prefix *SLS* and should be between 12 and 20 digits). Write this information down or copy it by selecting the identification number, right-click your mouse and select Copy, and then Paste it in an e-mail to us.

3. Click on the "2. License Functions & Options Valuator" link and write down or copy the HARDWARE FINGERPRINT (it should be an 8 digit alphanumeric code).

4. Purchase a license at www.realoptionsvaluation.com by clicking on the Purchase link.

5. E-mail admin@realoptionsvaluation.com these two identification numbers and we will send you your license file and license key. Once you receive these, please install the license using the steps below.

Installing Licenses:

1. Save the SLS license file to your hard drive (the license file we sent you after you purchased the software) and then start Real Options SLS (click on Start, Programs, Real Options Valuation, Real Options SLS, Real Options SLS).

2. Click on the "1. License Real Options SLS" and select ACTIVATE, then browse to the SLS license file that we sent you.

3. Click on the "2. License Functions & Options Valuator" and enter in the NAME and KEY combination we sent you.

ADDITIONAL ROV REFERENCE BOOKS

Modeling Risk: Applying Monte Carlo Risk Simulation, Strategic Real Options, Stochastic Forecasting, Portfolio Optimization, Data Analytics, Business Intelligence, and Decision Modeling, 3rd Edition
1112 Pages (2015)
ISBN: 9781943290000
Thomson-Shore & ROV Press

Modeling Risk: Applying Monte Carlo Simulation, Real Options Analysis, Stochastic Forecasting, and Optimization
610 Pages (2006)
ISBN: 0471789003
Wiley Finance

Modeling Risk: Applying Monte Carlo Risk Simulation, Strategic Real Options Analysis, Stochastic Forecasting, and Portfolio Optimization, 2nd Edition
986 Pages (2010)
ISBN: 9780470592212
Wiley Finance

Valuing Employee Stock Options: Under 2004 FAS 123
320 Pages (2004)
ISBN: 0471705128
Wiley Finance

Real Options Analysis: Tools and Techniques for Valuing Strategic Investments & Decisions, 2nd Edition
670 Pages (2005)
ISBN: 0471747483
Wiley Finance

Applied Risk Analysis: Moving Beyond Uncertainty
460 Pages (2003)
ISBN: 0-471-47885-7
Wiley Finance

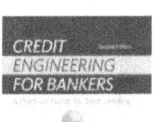

Credit Engineering for Bankers
(With Morton Glantz)
1000 Pages (2010)
ISBN: 9780123785855
Elsevier Academic Press

Real Options Analysis Course: Business Cases and Software Applications
360 Pages (2003)
ISBN: 0471430013
Wiley Finance

Advanced Analytical Models: Over 800 Models and 300 Applications from Basel II Accords to Wall Street and Beyond
1000 Pages (2008)
ISBN: 9780470179215
Wiley Finance

Real Options Analysis: Tools and Techniques for Valuing Strategic Investments & Decisions
416 Pages (2002)
ISBN: 0-471-25696-X
Wiley Finance

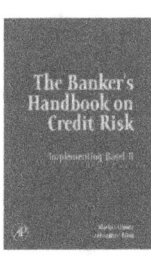

The Banker's Handbook on Credit Risk: Implementing Basel II
(With Morton Glantz)
420 Pages (2008)
ISBN: 9780123736666
Elsevier Science

See Dr. Mun's other books, articles, whitepapers, technical papers, and academic journal publications on his company's website at www.rovusa.com and www.realoptionsvaluation.com.